PRIVATE SCHOOLS AND PUBLIC ISSUES

PRIVATE SCHOOLS AND PUBLIC ISSUES

The Parents' View

Irene Fox

MACMILLAN

First published 1985 by
THE MACMILLAN PRESS LTD
London and Basingstoke
Companies and representatives
throughout the world

Printed in Hong Kong

British Library Cataloguing in Publication Data
Fox, Irene
Private schools and public issues.
1. Public schools, Endowed (Great Britain)
2. Parents—Great Britain—Attitudes
I. Title
373.2′22′0941   LA635
ISBN 0–333–36328–0

To the memory of my father

Contents

Contents

Preface

Private education in general and the public schools in particular have been the subject of public and political debates which extend well beyond educational arguments to include a consideration of the very nature of the society in which the schools are to be found.

On the one hand, the private sector is attacked both for creating a class-divided society and for reproducing such a society by serving as a mechanism for allocating individuals to top positions within it, binding them into a unified class able to exercise hegemonic control. On the other hand, these selfsame schools are staunchly defended for preserving the freedom of choice which is central to the workings of a market economy, for furnishing this economy with a highly educated élite, and for both providing educational standards against which the maintained sector can be measured and upholding the cultural and moral standards of our society.

With the battle-lines clearly drawn between the opposing factions, there is one interest group whose members have used the market as a means of expressing their own views, the parents who have turned their backs on the educational provision of the maintained sector and have chosen to buy their children's education. They have largely remained silent about their reasons for doing so and few attempts have been made to elicit their motives. This silence has not precluded claims being made on their behalf and their motives for using the private sector are generally assumed to be concerned with purchasing privilege for their children. The few who have written about the public schools from the inside are not the parents' representatives but are mainly headmasters and ex-headmasters who bring a professional interest to bear upon the subject. The bulk of this book is an attempt to go some way towards remedying this gap in the literature. It seeks to examine, through the eyes of those who use the public schools, the nature of the relationship between education and its wider social context. Can the public schools be said to be perpetuating a class-divided society by recruiting exclusively from a monied upper class or from the élites, binding them into a ruling class, or do they merely reflect a society which is already divided on other grounds? The book is based upon interviews with 190 sets of parents drawn at random from those using a stratified sample of the 122 traditionally independent public schools in which to educate their sons in the academic year 1979–80 and is a unique attempt to present in detail the views of a section of the population which has been much discussed but rarely researched. No apology is made for confining this research to the parents of boys; this is a reflection of the sexist nature of our society and the distinctiveness of the education of boys and girls, each requiring a separate analysis; only an enhancement of the available resources would have made this possible.

Chapter 2 provides a detailed examination of where the parents of today's public schoolboys are located within the British class structure. This is linked to their social origins in order to explore the senses in which today's pupils can be said to be recruited from the existing ruling class, upper class or élite or merely from a motley of discrete classes which fail to form a unified whole. The educational background of these parents is used to assess the part that a public school education has played in producing the class formations from which the pupils are drawn – does such an education coincide with or cut across any class cleavages that exist amongst the parents of today's public schoolboys?

Whilst classes emerge from their occupational and economic bases, they are consolidated through the normative integration of their members; this in turn is reflected in shared values and beliefs and results in social cohesion, aspects of which are explored in detail throughout the book. Chapter 3 examines the parents' social and kin networks in order to establish the extent to which the networks of the parents who have themselves been to the public schools are separate and indeed distinct from those without this form of education: the part that a public school education plays in the process of social closure, excluding those who lack it from membership of the 'old-boy' network and finally the advantages that inclusion brings in terms of gaining access to financial and other forms of aid.

The reasons for choosing a public school education are many and varied but parents who buy education for their children are buying a mixture of the advantages, intrinsic as well as instrumental, that they believe it can bring to their sons. These beliefs, in turn, devolve from a perception of the wider social order in which their sons are going to have to live and work; a view as to whether or not there are significant cleavages in Britain, the nature of the crucial differences upon which these are based and the opportunities for individual movement up as well as down the class hierarchy. As such perceptions are so closely linked to the belief system they can be used to provide a measure of the degree of normative integration of the members of the sample. This measure can be extended to include an assessment of the parents' values as they touch upon issues of class. Chapter 4 thus seeks to ascertain the degree of homogeneity characterising the parents' perceptions of the social order as well as their value judgements about the legitimacy of the perceived divisions in Britain. Perceptions and evaluations of this order give rise to parents' hopes and aspirations for their sons and give meaning to their stated reasons for choosing a public school education. Chapter 5 examines this relationship and looks in greater detail at how the parents' values and beliefs are linked to their statements about the advantages that accrue from a public school education.

The variation in the choice of a particular school could be an index of the existence of several separate groups or classes using the public schools such that the members of each group seek to maintain its distinctive identity by educating their sons in separate establishments, each perceived as having its own subculture, but which collectively have come to be known as the 'public schools'. Chapter 6 considers how, based upon evidence of the match between the parents' stated preferences for a particular school and the one which is actually being used, the schools define their own role in the process of perpetuating distinctive social groups – do they still select on 'social' grounds or increasingly on academic ones?

Finally through an examination of the factors influencing the parents' choice of a particular school it is possible to discern whether the public school sector does enjoy the homogeneity with which the public and political debates treat it, varying only with respect to the schools' technical efficiency in bringing about their stated aims, or whether the choice of a particular type of school (day or boarding, large or small, near or far) is indeed a sign of the heterogeneity of those who are using the schools today.

IRENE FOX

Acknowledgements

It is only in preparing this list of acknowledgements that I have come fully to appreciate the wealth of effort and goodwill that has contributed to the publication of this book. Inevitably there is the difficulty of acknowledging all those who have contributed as well as a danger of including those whose advice I have welcomed but not always heeded.

The research upon which this book is based was made possible by the encouragement and the sabbatical leave given to me by the Polytechnic of Central London. It became a reality as a result of the support and the invaluable advice that I received from the Headmasters' Conference, its Political and Public Relations Sub-Committee and in particular from Frank Fisher, David Jewell, Bruce McGowan, Canon Peter Pilkington and John Rae. As a consequence I received the full co-operation of the headmasters whose schools were selected to represent the traditionally independent HMC schools and through their efforts I was able to interview the parents selected for the research.

My thanks are also due to many of my colleagues at the Polytechnic of Central London, in particular to: Chris Maslin, Margaret Menari and indeed all of the members of the computer unit for their advice, assistance and patience; to Barbara Roweth and Dick Wiggins for their help with the statistical analysis and presentation; and to my immediate colleagues Professor Ray Lees and Frank Warner for their continued advice and comments.

Tessa Bridgeman and Professor John Westergaard gave me invaluable assistance at the very outset of the research; Ted Tapper and the original members of the research team studying the Assisted Places Scheme – Professor Tony Edwards, Mary Fulbrook and Geoff Whitty – all provided detailed comments on Chapter 1. The Independent Schools Information Service (ISIS) generously financed the expenses incurred in collecting the data and proved to be the perfect sponsor of research, giving me complete freedom to collect and publish my findings. Its press officer, Jane Capon, has proved to be a mine of information and willingly provided me with all the background details that I requested. The director of ISIS, Tim Devlin, has been a constant source of advice and encouragement from the very outset until the final word of the conclusion of this book.

I am particularly grateful to Helen Bocarro, who almost succeeded in typing the manuscript before I had written it; it is difficult to envisage a more willing and unselfish typist. Similarly, Tina Crotty managed to unscramble the statistical tables and to render them legible. My husband and children, Clive, Robin and Kate, have had to live with the total disruption of their family life and I have taken them very much for granted; to them, to all the above mentioned and to those whom space precludes inclusion I say a very sincere thank you. Last but certainly not least I thank 'the parents' who gave so very generously of their time, their hospitality and above all of themselves – I hope I have done them justice.

IRENE FOX

List of Tables

1 The Social Context

SOCIOLOGICAL PERSPECTIVES

Education does not take place in a vacuum but rather it is located within social space – a society which has a history, structures, institutions, people, classes and values. As such, the meaning that any particular form of education has, both for those who use it and those who do not, needs to be understood within the context of the society within which it is occurring.

In Britain, the private schools in general and the public schools in particular consistently attract a level of public debate which is out of all proportion to their numerical importance. The content of this debate provides a clear reflection of the nature of the society in which we live today.

The private sector of education has been attacked on a large number of wide-ranging fronts. Whilst these attacks have been directed generally at the whole sector, they are focused upon its oldest and most prestigious members – the public schools. The attempt to define precisely what constitutes a public school is bedevilled by a lack of consensus as to where the boundary which separates them from the remainder of the private secondary sector is to be drawn. The precise number of public schools ranges from the six which were exempted in 1818 from investigation by the Charity Commissioners by virtue of the fact that they were endowed schools of some historical significance, taught the classics and were patronised by the aristocracy and the gentry, to the 217 schools whose headmasters are currently members of the Headmasters' Conference. In essence, these attacks fall into four main, if somewhat overlapping, categories. The schools allegedly preserve a class-divided society; allocate individuals to roles within society in such a manner as to monopolise the top positions, allowing a small and controlled amount of upward mobility of new blood; facilitate the social closure of those in the top positions in order to produce a unified social class and

1

finally, as a consequence, they effectively diminish the maintained sector both materially and educationally. Let us examine each of these criticisms in turn.

Preserving a class-divided society

Today's public schools are located within a capitalist society, characterised by the private ownership of the means of production orientated towards the maximisation of market profits. The division of society into strata is not unique to capitalism but an historical truism for the process of social stratification is in fact a dual process: initially that of differentiation whereby differences between people, or more accurately social roles, are merely noted and subsequently that of the evaluation that any society attaches to these differentiated roles in order that they can be hierarchically ordered into strata. What is unique to capitalism in general is the criteria used in the formation of strata and to British capitalism in particular, the early and slow transition from agrarian and mercantile capitalism to that of industrial capitalism. New ruling groups came to replace old ones gradually through the repeated interpenetration of old and new strata, old and new values. Thus the old landed order merged itself with new industrial power but sought to maintain its distinctive identity and system of values. The public schools are a product of this interpenetration of landed, commercial and industrial interests and the manner in which they allegedly play a major role in keeping alive and indeed legitimating the ideology underpinning the stratification of capitalist Britain is discussed by a variety of authors at varying levels of abstraction.

Whilst Bottomore[1] does not specifically mention the public schools, he discusses the way in which Western societies maintain and nurture the whole ideology of élite rule in so far as they emphasise the selection of exceptional individuals for élite positions and the rewards of income and status of scholastic achievement, rather than raising the general level of education throughout the community. It is the process of legitimating and consolidating the divisions between the élite and the non-élite which is central to Bottomore's argument. Both Rubenstein and Hoare forge the link specifically between the public schools and the sustainment of social class. Rubenstein[2] claims that 'to take a small group of the wealthy and to educate them separately from the remainder of society is to assure the continuation of a class-ridden society such as Britain'. Whilst Hoare[3] highlights the manner in which the schools 'are the key element in both the forma-tion and the continued pre-eminence of the existing hegemonic class' and 'infect the maintained sector with their values'.

Evidence that the schools exempted from the investigations of the Charity Commissioners, with the addition of a seventh, had secured their position in the second half of the nineteenth century such that they could proceed to maintain control over the dominant ideology and produce the leaders of society is provided by the report of the Taunton Commission in 1867. In a consideration of the number of social classes in Britain at the time and the differing purpose of education for each of these classes, each requiring a different form of education, the Taunton commissioners identified the top class as the aristocracy and the gentry of independent means whose sons required a cultural education based upon a classical curriculum and they named the top seven public boarding schools as those which were providing this form of education. It is debatable whether at this date it was the schools which were producing the leaders of society or the leaders of society who were furnishing the top public schools with their status through their patronage. The fact that over one hundred years later these same seven schools, namely Eton, Harrow, Win-chester, Westminster, Charterhouse, Rugby and Shrewsbury along with the later additions to the still loosely defined public schools, continue to attract such a high level of public interest reinforces Hoare's view that they form a point of reference for the whole British education system, defining the norms and values from which all other strata flow. Without them the fulcrum upon which our stratified society rests would begin to crumble. It is when one turns to examine the precise manner in which the schools are able to achieve this that one becomes clearer as to the exact way in which the public schools can be said to form the basis of a class divided society; it is not merely that they provide a clearly identifiable mechanism for recruiting members of the upper strata but that their very existence symbolises the principle of hierarchy as opposed to egality.

The detailed method by which the principle of hierarchy is fostered within the public schools themselves is well documented. It is widely asserted that traditionally the schools have paid more attention to providing their pupils with leadership qualities than with academic qualifications. Macdonald[4] refers to the way in which the public schools are characterised by rigid hierarchies of authority, rank, prestige and privilege, at the heart of which lies the house system. In each house, pupils are listed in order of precedence and are given clearly and explicitly stated privileges and privations. As the boys progress up the school, so their privileges are increased accordingly, as exemplified by the system of 'fagging'. The exclusion of the family through the system of boarding serves to reinforce this process. McConnell,[5] in his study of Eton, discusses how the particularism of family life is ill-suited to a process of socialisation which is based upon universalistic principles and evidence in a similar vein is presented by Royston Lambert when he quotes one headmaster who defines the parent as 'a nuisance created by the motor car'.[6]

A somewhat different perspective on the same phenomenon of hierarchy is provided by Correlli Barnett who lays the responsibility for Britain's decline at the door of her public schools.[7] It is, argues Barnett, this very principle of hierarchy with its call for obedience to authority that has crushed the competitive spirit which was the driving force of Britain's success as a colonial and industrial power. The emphasis on the team versus individual spirit and literally 'playing the game' rather than seeking to win, gentlemanly values of an earlier era, is used by Barnett in support of his argument. Notwithstanding the fact that Barnett's primary purpose is to show the different ways in which the public schools' outdated culture can be seen to be held responsible for the fact that Britain had moved from being the richest country in the world in the closing decades of the nineteenth century to the brink of bankruptcy in 1942, he serves to emphasise the point that the schools have succeeded in producing a degree of conformity to the principle of hierarchy not only amongst their own pupils but throughout society at large. This principle was most clearly reflected in the 'tripartite structure of British secondary education which reached its pinnacle between 1945 and 1964, with the grammar schools seeking to ape the customs and traditions of the public schools, leaving the secondary modern schools to socialise their pupils into the routine manual tasks at the bottom of the hierarchy.[8] The transition to the comprehensive system owes more to the meritocratic principles of many Tories and Socialists alike than to the more egalitarian ones of certain sections of the Labour party, and shows few signs of moving away from this position. Changing the location of secondary education without seeking to change the values which underpin it serves to ensure the continued supply of new recruits to manual labour and thereby helps to maintain capitalism without posing any challenge to the system itself.

The accuracy of Macdonald's[9] stereotype of the principle of hierarchy in the schools, based upon seniority and authority, is difficult to assess but it has been challenged both from within and outside the public school sector. Rae[10] traces the demise of this process since the 1960s when the teenage revolution reached the public schools. Such a system could not co-exist for long with the new wave of permissiveness in personal behaviour and increasing emphasis on nonconformity and individuality. Tapper and Salter,[11] discussing changes within the public schools, identify how the structures of the schools underpinning hierarchy are functioning in a different way. Referring to the prefect system they say that 'the old hierarchical model, dependent upon the possession of age-related, formal roles has been replaced by numerous, at least partially differentiated arenas within which status and power is more closely bound up with individual skill and initiative'. The declining importance of the house system, documented by Tapper and Salter, is part of this process of change.

However, evidence such as that furnished by Rae and by Tapper and Salter of the decline of the traditional methods of producing hierarchy within the schools does not deny the notion of hierarchy *per se* but merely suggests that its basis is shifting and the grounds for arguing that the schools play an important part in preserving a class divided society remain.

Monopolising the top positions in society

Turning our attention to the second front upon which the public schools have been attacked, namely that they succeed in monopolising the top positions in society, Giddens speaks for many when he writes that 'the public schools . . . continue to play a dominant role in the self-perpetuation of recruitment to élite positions in Britain'.[12] It is this concern in the liberal tradition with the political arithmetic of the incumbency of élite positions rather than with the actual existence of a class-divided society, that has dominated the literature linking the public schools to social stratification. Long before the nineteenth century it was argued that the schools which were originally funded for poor scholars had effectively been taken over by the upper classes. Today the literature overflows with terms such as 'élite', 'ruling class', 'governing class' and 'upper class', a proliferation of terminology which serves to confuse rather than to clarify. It is not my intention to add to this proliferation but merely to try and establish some sign-posts to guide the reader through the maze, for surely what matters in an advanced industrial society such as Britain is the nature and source of the distribution of power and not the titles which are given to its holders. Thus one needs to consider the methods by which people come to exert power over others and control over their own life chances.

In its crudest form Marxist theory states that in every society two categories of people may be distinguished – a ruling class and one or more subject classes. The dominant position of the ruling class is to be explained by its possession of the major means of economic production but its decisive political dominance is consolidated by its control over the machinery of the state and the hold which it establishes over the production of ideas. The paradox of capitalism is the way in which it is able to survive the contradiction between the idea of competition and equality of opportunity, such that membership of the ruling class is technically open, and the widespread acceptance of the inequality of condition that is the result of the use which the victors in this competition have made of their power – limiting further competition in order that they may keep and pass on their accumulated wealth. From this perspective, concern with the public schools is, as has already been discussed, a concern both with the way in which they produce and disseminate the ideas which are used to legitimate hierarchy and their facilitation of access to favourable positions within it. The ruling class needs to be clearly distinguished from the upper class which, according to Bottomore,[13] has a disproportionate share of wealth and income and has developed a distinctive life-style but does not enjoy undisputed political power. Its significance lies in its ability, generated by its wealth, to secure access to those educational processes which are believed to be vital in maximising life chances.[14]

It is in the writings of Pareto and Mosca that the political theory of élites finds its roots. They used the theory in support of a critique of the Marxist theory of class which attributes political power to economic power. Crucial to élite theory is the belief that power in society is so diffuse, competitive and fragmented that it is constantly subject to countervailing checks which render improbable hegemonic control by a single group. Pareto defined élites in two distinct ways: first as excellence in any particular area, thus the élite is a group of people who share the fact that they have the highest indices in their branch of activity. In theory, the incumbents of all such positions could be examined through the use of inflow analysis to discover whether they are drawn predominantly from the public schools but in practice the empirical data available relies more heavily upon Pareto's second use of the term élite: here he makes the distinction between the governing élite and the non-governing élite, bringing us close to a consideration of power based upon factors other than property. He observed that the upper strata of society, the governing élite, contain certain groups of people, not always sharply defined, that he called 'aristocracies' and he went on to refer to 'military, religious and commercial aristocracies and plutocracies'.[15] Pareto was primarily concerned with the division between the governing élite and the non-élite and paid scant attention to the detail of who actually composed the governing élite. The important point for us at this stage is that the composition of the élite changes over time as a result of both the recruitment of new members and of the incorporation of new social groups. It is thus that the studies of élites in Britain have come to focus upon the education of those who have reached élite positions within élite occupations, positions which are not necessarily dependent upon the ownership or even the direct control of the means of production. Estimates vary, but the traditional élite occupations such as the church, the army and the judiciary all have in excess of 75 per cent of their senior members drawn from the public schools.[16] Amongst the newer élites: the civil service, parliament and industry, one finds the proportions of senior members with a public school education are, on average, lower ranging from 80 per cent of the directors of financial firms to 48 per cent of MPs.[17]

When considering how the public schools are allegedly securing access to these élite positions one needs to examine the way in which they have participated in the transition initially from birth to property and more recently from property to academic skills as the criterion for social selection. The method of buying social advantage by being seen to have a monopoly of the right credentials, however loosely these are defined, began with the entry of the sons of the nineteenth century industrialists into the public schools. The gradual acceptance of the newly emerging industrial élite into the established élite was brought about by the fusion of two processes of social change: on the one hand the belated move into industry of the second sons of the established élite, occasioned by the system of primogeniture (such that the second sons of the landed gentry entered commerce and their second sons went into industry) and on the other hand the 'gentrification' of the descendants of the members of the newly emerging élite occupations in industry. It is to their readiness to play their part in this process of gentrification that the public schools owe their buoyancy and growth and the process of buying social advantage continues today. In evidence to the Public Schools Commission in 1968 the CBI reports 'the public school tends to bring out at an early age the qualities of leadership, self-reliance, self-confidence and self-discipline', qualities which lie at the heart of the public school ethos. In an article describing the relationship between the 'gentlemen', members of the established élite, and 'players', members of the middle stratum of practical men, Coleman,[18] like Barnett, considers the possible effects of the gentrification of the players on Britain's industrial development. He questions rather than concludes the possible relationship between the taming of the driving thrust of the players and the fortunes of British industry. But the debate as to whether or not the qualities traditionally fostered by the public schools did in fact affect Britain's progress either positively or negatively is rapidly becoming a matter of historical interest and is serving to obscure an accelerating change that is occuring both within British industry and the public schools. At the very end of his article Coleman introduces a theme which is developed by Tapper and Salter,[19] namely that the changeover to modern professional management is more crucial to the development of the contemporary firm than either the style of the gentlemen or the thrust of the players. The change that they identify can be seen most clearly in the way that the schools are modifying their selection procedures. These do vary but where there is competition for entry, ability rather than money or connections would appear to be the overriding criterion for selection. In a world of growing certification the schools can only survive if they can be seen to be delivering the goods. To this end, the willingness of the traditionally independent schools, as well as of those which lost their direct grant status under the 1976 Education Act, to participate in the Assisted Places scheme must be seen, alongside the rush on the part of the ex-direct grant schools to establish bursaries, as evidence of the schools' shift towards selection on the basis of ability. It is in this sense that the schools can be viewed in their role as sponsors of controlled upward mobility.

Nevertheless, the facts remain and studies of existing élites show that not only are their numbers drawn disproportionately from the public schools, but that their members who have been so educated reach their positions more quickly than their state educated counterparts. Clements[20] notes that the public school and Oxbridge recruits to managerial positions in industry advance more speedily in their promotion and Coleman cites records from the archives of Courtaulds to show that in 1938 the average age of its directors who had been to public school was fifty, some six years lower than the age of those who had not been so educated. In a manner similar to the evidence already discussed, the close relationship between an Ox-bridge education and incumbency of élite positions has also been documented[21] and the fact that the public schools in turn also have a disproportionate share of the Oxbridge places, has served to further reinforce the public school/élite connection.

Examining the relationship between the public schools and social stratification simply in terms of access to élite positions has a number of deficiencies. There are rarely any details which link family back-ground, form of education and élite membership which can be used to show whether the schools serve to promote upward social mobility or to preserve élite positions for the sons of existing members. Kalton's[22] analysis in 1964 of the records of the 1962–3 entrants to and leavers from the public schools is the only study to date which looks at the schools in terms of their social class intake, and there has been no attempt to apply outflow analysis to the schools in order to dis-cover the destinations of all their pupils or to relate these to social origins.

More seriously, the discussion up to this point has reflected the overriding interest of the literature in the relationship between the public schools and the élite, at the expense of a consideration of the schools and the lower echelons of the 'top' positions. Mosca is not as stark as Pareto in his differentiation between élites and non-élites. He states that in 'modern times the élite is not simply raised high above society: it is ultimately concerned with society through a sub-élite, a much larger group which comprises to all intents and purposes the whole new middle-class of civil servants, managers and white collar workers, scientists, engineers and scholars and intellectuals. This group does not only supply recruits to the élite, it is itself a vital element in the government of society'.[23] Thus it too can be consid-ered to be part of the élite, in the broadest sense of the term.

By comparison with the attention lavished by social scientists upon the education of the élite in Pareto's sense of the word, that of the sub-élite or the top class has been sorely neglected. There are many reasons for this, but not least amongst them is the diversity of the occupations that compose it and the difficulty of focusing research upon a population which is so widely dispersed occupationally. The elaboration and identification by Goldthorpe and the Oxford Social Mobility Group[24] of the notion of the service class (first introduced by the Austro-Marxist Renner[25]) has gone some considerable way towards mitigating this neglect. Lying at the apex of the occupational

hierarchy, the service class is the class of the intermediate strata –
intermediate between the élite (economic or other) and the masses.
Its members differ from the mass of wage labour in as much as they
do not create surplus value and their occupations afford them with
incomes which are 'high, generally secure and likely to rise over their
lifetime'. Possibly of even greater importance for us, they are positions which 'typically involve the exercise of authority . . .'. The
intermediate and higher echelons of the service class of modern
society, labelled Class I by the Oxford Social Mobility Group is 'the
class of those exercising power and expertise on behalf of the corporate bodies plus elements of the classic bourgeoisie who have not yet
been incorporated into this new formation'.[26] The most systematic
attempt to link education with incumbency of these top positions is
provided by Heath. Whereas Halsey[27] and his colleagues show that
6.6 per cent of the male population included in the Oxford Social
Mobility Survey attended a private or direct grant secondary school,
Heath's more detailed analysis of the data reveals that this proportion
is nearly trebled for the members of Class I, standing at nearly 18 per
cent, but there is a considerable variation between the constituent
occupations of this top class, ranging from 32 per cent of all self-
employed professionals to 14.6 per cent of the industrial managers.[28]
It is difficult to disentangle the focal concern of our interest, the
public schools, from the myriad of statistics but whereas Halsey *et al.*
show 5 per cent of the sample attended a public school or a private
secondary school, Heath's unpublished data[29] suggests that 8 per cent
of Class I males had been to a public school and 5½ per cent had been
to other private schools. Sixty-five per cent of the public school
educated Class I males had been born into that class but only 7 per
cent had been recruited from the manual classes, making it difficult to
disentangle the respective roles of the type of school, the family and
the individual when trying to assess the significance of the public
schools in securing access to Class I positions.

Facilitating the social closure of those in top positions

The élite by its very nature is composed of diverse elements, the
magnitude of the diversity depending upon the definition of élite
which is used. Pareto's governing élite, as we have seen, embraces
both new and traditional elements whilst Mosca extends the definition to include the sub-élite which both governs and supplies recruits

to the governing élite; in its expanded sense the term 'élite' can loosely be equated with the service class. Even in its narrower sense, the élite includes men from a wide range of occupations and a variety of educational and social backgrounds. How can such a motley of people be said to function as a unified class, maintaining the class nature of our society and sharing the common goal of ensuring the recruitment of their sons to these selfsame positions? The problem is magnified when one broadens the definition to include all the members of Class I. Do the public schools indeed function to bind together the disparate elements of the élite such that they come to form a unified ruling class, monopolising not only property and political power but also the control of ideas? What of those members of the élite who have not been to a public school?

The normative integration required to bind the members of the élite is brought about through the content of the education itself, through the mechanism of political socialisation. Whereas political socialisation remains covert and goes largely unrecognised in the maintained sector of education, the public schools are charged by Miliband[30] with embracing this function and acting overtly as agents of conservatism.

> Today, as in the past, [these] élite schools consciously seek to instil into their charges a conservative philosophy whose themes remain tradition, religion, nationalism, authority, hierarchy and an exceedingly narrow view of the meaning of democracy, not to speak of a marked hostility to socialist ideals and purposes.

Lambert[31] reveals how this is achieved when he states that the public school sets out to educate the 'whole man'. It is the concern with the 'whole man' which produces the normative integration upon which a unified ruling class rests, for its rules through the common experiences and values as well as background of its members.

Moving beyond the process of normative integration, we need to consider how the public schools promote the qualities in their pupils which favour the interests of the social groups to which they belong and from which others are excluded. This is secured through the phenomenon of the 'old boy network' which finds expression in three main areas; first in interlocking directorships such that the segments of the financial and industrial élite have a shared rather than competing economic interest. In 1970 73 out of the 85 organisations studied by the Cambridge Élite Studies[32] were linked to each other by at least one shared directorship. Secondly, in the connection between the political élite and the economic élite, largely the result of the holding of directorships in industrial and financial organisations by Tory MPs. Finally and less tangibly, through the personal ties and connections which are established at school but are difficult to document in the fluidity of later life. Such informal contacts do not lend themselves readily to being measured taking place as they do in the privacy of the home or, to a declining extent, in the gentlemen's London clubs. Such informal contacts provide the participants with information and with help in kind if not in cash. Included in this old boy network are not only the current holders of positions of power in parliament and on boards of directors but also the members of Mosca's more broadly defined élite – the managers, the civil servants, the intellectuals, the media men, etc. These are the men who, it is generally alleged, combine to preserve the essential character and structure of Britain.

The effects on the maintained system of education

Leaving the arena of political arithmetic, we return to one particular aspect of our earlier assessment of the effect of the existence of the public schools upon the rest of British society, namely upon the maintained sector of education. It is concern with the damage that the public schools inflict, in terms of resources and through their effect on the curriculum, on this sector that gives renewed vigour to the Labour party's long standing commitment to secure the demise of the private sector. All schools are composed of a number of resources which are essentially material and human and they combine in varying proportions to produce the school as it appears to the outside world. The current cuts in educational expenditure, whether real or consistent with the falling school rolls, have been contrasted with the cost of all the private schools to both central and local government. These costs arise from the cumulation of the boarding fees paid on behalf of children of diplomats and armed forces as well as the fees paid by some local education authorities for their bright pupils; tax and rate relief enjoyed by the schools by virtue of their charitable status; tax relief on appropriate endowment policies; the assisted places scheme and the training of the teachers at the state's expense. Estimates of the total of such costs vary according to who is doing the estimating but were totalled to be in excess of £450 million by Neil Kinnock[33] in July 1981.

Over and above the strictly material loss to the maintained sector we need to consider the effects of the loss of human capital. Halsey[34] *et al* when commenting upon the skewed class composition of the private schools, point to the loss to the maintained schools of political pressure exerted by the more articulate and experienced parents who have defected to the private sector, to say nothing of the material resources and organising skills that they can bring to the parent-teacher associations. In 1980 the maintained secondary school sector had a teacher–pupil ratio of 1:16.6, whereas the ratio within the public schools (as defined by the membership of their headmasters of the Headmasters' Conference) was 1:12. The reduced quantity of teachers in the maintained sector is more to do with government policies than poaching by the public schools but can the same be said of quality? The public schools pay their teachers on a scale that is normally higher than the Burnham rates and they are able, in general, to offer their staff more attractive working conditions with pupils who are comparatively highly motivated, even if only as a result of the mediating influence of the parents. Whilst difficult to quantify, it is not unreasonable to assume that the public schools are well placed to select the cream of the teaching profession. Whether the pupils themselves are more intelligent is another area of uncertainty. The schools use academic entrance examinations to control the selection of pupils and in general display an eagerness to raise the academic level of their intake, but it is the ability of the parents to pay the fees that, in the main, determines who will go to them. Nevertheless the maintained sector, by having to compete with the public schools, is losing pupils who are capable of achieving examination successes well beyond those in the maintained schools, and who could therefore provide the academic leadership in the schools.

A somewhat different interpretation of the effect of the academic ethos of the public schools and their pupils on the maintained sector is provided by the exponents of the 'new sociology of education',[35] who focus their attention upon the way in which curricula are constructed and developed. To quote from the Labour party[36]

perhaps the most damaging consequence of the existence of the private sector is the way in which parts of the maintained sector have been influenced by the élitist value of the private school system so that the success of its schools is judged in relation to these values. Thus schools have been judged on the narrow ground of GCE examinations, university entrants and the professions of "old boys".

This has since been exacerbated by the 1981 Regulations governing Education (School Information) which compel the maintained schools to publish their external examination results in order to facilitate the freedom of choice of parents when they come to choose a maintained school, a freedom which was enhanced by Section 6 of the 1980 Education Act. Rhodes Boyson[37] has recently launched his call to establish certain schools as 'centres of excellence where talented staff and pupils could be brought together', as a response to his fear of Britain becoming a Third World country. In order to be able to compete in these terms the maintained schools continue to organise knowledge and the way in which it is taught into tight packages which correspond to the GCE syllabuses but which have little practical value. Thus in the battle for control over what is to be defined as knowledge the public schools have the commanding position with the result that innovation in the maintained sector is severely hampered.

POLITICAL AND EDUCATIONAL CHANGES

The private sector has not remained unscathed by these and the other forces which have assailed it and some would argue that it has emerged fitter and leaner from its turbulences of the 1960s and 1970s.

In seeking to identify the main crises facing this sector of education it is necessary to be more precise than hitherto about its structure and composition for not all parts of the sector have had to face the same experiences. With the exception of the workhouse schools, educational provision in Britain remained exclusively in the hands of the voluntary and private sectors until 1870.

It was not until 1833 that the state first sought to assist the voluntary effort through the introduction of a parliamentary grant for education, £20 000 to be used in the towns where the rapidly expanding population had outgrown the resources available to make even the most rudimentary provision for the children of the poorer classes. Secondary provision, the focal concern of this book, remained outside the state until the passing of the 1902 Education Act and was initially composed of three main types of school: the public, the endowed grammar and the private. Whilst the private schools could be distinguished by their total dependence upon the market for the supply of their pupils, and the endowed grammar schools by the fact that they had been endowed at various points in history to provide an education for the poor, originally to train them as choristers or to teach them Latin grammar (hence the name), the public schools were in their turn less easily identifiable.

Deterred by the limited curriculum offered by the grammar schools, the aristocratic and landed families favoured the use of private tutors and although a few of the grammar schools, notably Westminster, Eton and Winchester, received aristocratic patronage as early as the eighteenth century, it was not until the reforms inspired by Arnold of Rugby in the first half of the nineteenth century that the demand for institutional schooling grew such that an increasing number of the grammar schools came to find favour with the aristocracy, giving rise to the term 'the great schools' – the forerunners of the public schools. In addition to these older foundations, new schools came into being in the middle of the nineteenth century as existing demand was inflated both by the middle classes seeking gentrification and by the growth of competitive entry into the civil service and even Sandhurst. Some of these schools were strictly proprietary, restricting their entry to the sons of 'gentlemen' whilst others were the product of the establishment of new charitable foundations. The term 'public', used to describe the most prestigious of the endowed and the proprietary schools is of uncertain origin. Lawson and Silver[38] identify it as a term which strictly belongs to all endowed schools in order to distinguish them from their private counterparts and Rae[39] sees these very endowments, as well as the schools' boarding facilities, as its basis for both meant that the schools were open to the public in general and were not restricted to any social or geographical group. A second sense in which, according to Rae, the schools merit the name 'public' is the contrast that they provided to the private tutoring originally favoured by the aristocracy and gentry. It was not until 1869 that the establishment of the Headmasters' Conference by Edward Thring, the headmaster of Uppingham school, provided the public schools with their first opportunity to establish a collective identity. In 1868 the Endowed Schools Bill was published in response to the findings of the Taunton Commission, in turn established to investigate amongst other things the misuse of the endowments of the grammar schools. The great schools had already been the subject of investigation by the Clarendon

Commission and had been dealt with by the 1868 Public Schools Act and the Endowed Schools Bill of that same year proposed to reform the charities on which the remaining endowed schools were based. The headmasters of these schools were so incensed by the proposals that they met at a London tavern to discuss their collective response. It was the success of this meeting that prompted Thring to invite seventy headmasters to Uppingham to continue their discussions on a regular basis and although only fourteen responded to his original invitation gradually an increasing number of them were attracted to the idea of a committee that was formed specifically to look after the interests of their schools. The criteria for representation had not been fully formalised but the important point is that membership of the conference was by invitation and technically this remains the position today, with the proportion of pupils engaged in sixth form work being an important criterion.

A further division within the private secondary sector came with the introduction of the direct grant schools. These were brought into being by the 1902 Education Act (and became operative in 1907), enabling all grammar schools which charged fees to attract a higher rate of grant from the Board of Education if they offered not less than 25 per cent of their places to local education authorities and central government, whilst maintaining control over entry by the administration of a selective test. In return, central government had control over the fees that were charged and the erection of new buildings, with representation on the governing bodies shared between the schools and the appropriate education authority. These schools aimed to provide a ladder of upward mobility for the bright children from poor homes and remained hybrids of the state and the private sectors of education until their final demise in 1976. Over the years the headmasters of the boys' direct grant schools were invited to join conference and therefore these could be considered to be public schools.

Today there are more than two thousand private schools ranging in size from five to in excess of seventeen hundred pupils and, although there are no precise statistics, about a half of them are believed to provide secondary school places for an estimated 200 000 pupils.[40] In addition to the 217 public schools whose headmasters currently belong to the HMC, there are those of lower academic standing whose headmasters are members of the Society of Headmasters of Independent Schools (40 in all); the 22 schools whose governing bodies are members of the Governing Bodies Association but whose headmasters do not belong to either of the relevant bodies; the 234 girls' schools whose governing bodies are represented on their own associations; an amorphous organisation of 214 junior, secondary and all age schools belonging to the Independent Schools' Association Incorporated and finally those schools which are registered with the DES but do not belong to any known body. The only unifying feature of all these schools is the fact that they are not maintained by the state and are therefore largely dependent upon the market to supply them with their pupils and it is for this reason that many choose to call themselves 'independent schools'. The heterogeneity that marks this sector of education with its divergent facilities, academic standards and problems is parallelled by the differences to be found between the most prestigious of these schools, the 217 schools represented in the HMC. Educating some 120 000 secondary age pupils this is the single largest grouping of schools and divisions between them are inevitable. The most obvious division is between the member schools which have always been independent of state grants and the 74 former direct grant schools – a division which was formalised by the practice of the ex-direct grant heads meeting in their own sub-committee until the schools ceased to function as direct grant schools. These schools were mainly day schools which admitted their pupils at the age of eleven and this they still do. This continues to distinguish them from the traditionally independent day schools which, like their boarding counterparts, select the majority of their pupils at the age of thirteen, using the Common Entrance examination but an increasing number are introducing an additional selection at the age of eleven in order to attract pupils from the maintained primary schools. All the day schools, ex-direct grant and traditionally independent alike, need to be distinguished from the boarding schools which have a different ethos and organisational structure. Rae refers to the lingering tension between the so-called 'great schools' and the less well known, smaller and newer schools but the divisions run even deeper than this for the headmaster of one well known boarding school was, for the purposes of this research, able to divide both the traditionally independent and the ex-direct grant schools into three leagues. Allocation to these leagues was determined by academic standing and the reputation of the schools both within the HMC and the wider community and reflects their size and required standards in the common entrance examination.

The public schools as a body have never been free of their critics. The initial criticism, focused upon the abuse of their endowments which finally resulted in the formation of the HMC as a defensive body (the first political act of the public schools), has given way to more recent concern with the schools' social divisiveness. Ever since its infancy there has been a strand within the Labour party which has called for the schools' abolition and in 1931 Tawney summarised the argument against them when he wrote:

> The idea that differences of educational opportunity among children should depend upon differences of wealth amongst parents is barbarity. . . [41]

But, until recently, the party as a body has remained ambiguous about its precise attitude towards the private sector. Even Aneurin Bevan, interviewed in *Tribune* in 1955 said, 'I do not favour private education but would not prohibit it. Different levels of income will always find expression in different levels of education'.

Earlier proposals to bring the two sectors of education closer together or possibly to integrate them have since yielded to a polarisation of the programmes of the two main political parties. In 1942, Butler asked Lord Fleming to head a committee to consider how the public schools specifically could be brought into closer association with the general system of education. The reasons for establishing this committee were as much to do with the anxiety over the schools' future as with the search for greater equality. The pre-war slump and the falling birth-rate gave rise to a fear, shared by the schools and the government alike, that they would become citadels of privilege with relatively few people able to afford their fees. In its report two years later,[42] the Fleming Committee recommended that the schools should be opened to all children who would be able to benefit from the education that they provided, irrespective of the income of their parents. Local education authorities would be able to take a minimum of a quarter of the places in those schools wishing to enter the scheme. The terms offered to the schools were favourable for they would not be required to change their character but the suggested mode of selection was cumbersome and the costs high with the result that the local authorities made only occasional small-scale arrangements along the lines suggested by the report.

The final attempt at integration was made by the Wilson government soon after the Labour party was returned to power in 1964. Fulfilling his party's pledge in the 1964 election manifesto that 'labour will set up an educational trust to advise on the best way of integrating the public schools into the state system of education', the Secretary of State for Education, Anthony Crosland, constituted the

Public Schools Commission and charged it with 'examining the ways of integrating the public schools with the state system of education'. The definition of the term 'public school' was stretched to include not only the schools represented in the HMC, but also those girls and boys schools whose governors belonged to the Governing Bodies Association. Asking the commission to focus upon the possibilities of integrating the schools with the state system was seen as a compromise between leaving them alone and the demands of the left wing of the party to take them over completely. In the event, the commission under the chairmanship of Sir John Newsom turned its attention initially to the boarding schools for these were both seen as the most socially divisive and as capable of providing boarding places which were much needed by the state sector. When it was published in 1968, the Newsom Report[43] recommended that those schools suitable and willing to enter an integrated sector should be given every encouragement to do so, the remaining boarding schools should make at least 50 per cent of their places available to meet boarding need amongst local education authority pupils, with boarding need and not academic ability to be the criterion for selection. The schools would need to make some considerable adjustments in their internal arrangements in order to cater for the local authority pupils whose background was not one of familiarity with boarding. The adjustments envisaged by the commission included more free time as opposed to organised leisure activities; increased opportunities to maintain home contact through the introduction of weekly boarding and a modification of the prefectorial system so as to eliminate excessive authority and hierarchical organisation. The report recognised that the system would take time to implement and that progress towards integration would be gradual. It also recommended the termination of fiscal and similar reliefs to schools which were registered as charities but which had long since ceased to perform any truly charitable acts. The fate of the first report was to fall victim to the compromising nature of its terms of reference for the schools and the Conservative party opposed its recommendation to sacrifice academic standards to boarding need, whilst those in the Labour party who wished to see the schools abolished altogether did not seek to promote a report which at best would dilute the schools' potency but which effectively would enable them to serve as ladders of opportunity out of the maintained system, just as the direct grant schools had done before. It was to the direct grant and the independent day schools that the commission, now under the chairmanship of

David Donnison, turned its attention next. In the introduction to its 1970 report,[44] the Donnison committee confirmed its belief in the values associated with a grammar school education – academic achievement, rigorous intellectual demands and so on, but it denied that early selection was conducive to achieving these goals. In supporting the already accelerating move towards comprehensive secondary schooling, the commission envisaged that the schools which had come under its scrutiny would have to take a greater part in this move towards comprehensivisation. To this end, the report recommended that the direct grant schools, which were heavily dependent upon state funding but operating a highly selective system of intake such that less than one in eight of their pupils came from manual homes, should participate in the move towards comprehensive reorganisation, but the commission members were divided as to how this should be achieved. It was agreed that the independent schools should retain their legal right to provide education but all means should be used to encourage them to join the comprehensive scheme and this included the recommendation that the local education authorities should cease their practice of purchasing places for their very intelligent children, except in 'exceptional circumstances'. The commission could find no justification for integrating the independent day schools into the state system for, unlike their boarding counterparts, they did not meet the need for boarding places and relatively little emphasis was placed upon their social divisiveness. Thus there was no great urgency to find quick ways of undermining these schools and the agreed policy was to allow them to slowly wither away and die.

Unlike the first report, the second report with its decisive proposals to bring the direct grant schools to an immediate end was accepted by the Labour party as a whole but its implementation was delayed by the surprise victory of the Heath government in the 1970 general election and it was not until the Labour party was returned to office in 1974 that it was able to deliver its first blow to the private sector in the form of the Direct Grant Grammar Schools (Cessation Grant) Regulations in 1975. These withdrew the direct grant status of the endowed grammar schools and offered them the choice between becoming totally independent and entering the maintained system as comprehensive schools. In the event, 119 of the 173 schools chose the first option and joined the private sector. In 1976 Labour passed its Education Act which restricted the local authority practice of buying places in the independent schools, making it a requirement that the

Secretary of State's approval should be sought beforehand with the effect that within a year the number of new places purchased had fallen by over 60 per cent from 7000 in 1976/7 to under 3000 in 1978/9.[45] The return to office in 1974 of the Labour government followed an election campaign that was more openly aggressive to the private sector than that of any of its predecessors; in its first election manifesto of that year it committed itself to the withdrawal of tax relief and charitable status which had been amongst the recommendations of the Newsom report and in the second manifesto it made reference to its intention to phase out the public schools. It is the benefits which derive from their charitable status which is the nub of the confusion over the terminology used to describe these schools, such that the labels 'private' and 'independent' have distinct political overtones. Whilst 'independent' accurately reflects the fact that the schools are indeed independent of any specific government grants, the term 'private' is used by the Labour party to deny their total independence from the state in view of the considerable financial benefit that is derived from their charitable status as well as their ability to draw upon the services of teachers whose training has been paid for by the private purse. The precise value of this transfer of public assets to the private schools (private by virtue of the fact that notwithstanding their charitable status they have to look to the market for the majority of their pupils) was the subject of a protracted correspondence in the *Guardian* in July 1981 but the principle stands, the costs of the withdrawal of the schools' charitable status would put private education beyond the reach of many parents. It was the Labour government's inability to extract the schools from the intricate laws governing charities that prevented them from fulfilling their 1974 election pledge to deprive the schools of this status and a separate committee was established in 1976 under the chairmanship of Lord Goodman to look into the means of achieving this.

The Labour party, once again in opposition but now shorn of part of its right wing by the formation of the Social Democratic Party, is more firmly resolved than ever to finally rid this country of the private schools and, in conjunction with the TUC, it has worked out a detailed plan to do so within ten years of its return to office.[46] If all measures to undermine the financial viability of the schools should fail, the plan proposes to make it illegal for the schools to charge fees for education, although it has been suggested that such action may well contravene the European Convention of Human Rights.[47]

In assessing the total impact of the Labour party upon the private sector of education it is tempting to conclude that the scales do in fact come down in its favour. It is paradoxical that it was not the strictly private schools but the direct grant schools which fell victim to the Labour party's first attempt to put its long standing antipathy towards the private sector into action. The result of the decision of the 119 ex-direct grant schools to join the private sector after the withdrawal of their grant aid was to increase the size of that very sector which the Labour party sought to destroy. However, it is not Labour's indecisive policy towards the private sector but its equally indecisive attempts to introduce fully comprehensive schooling that has probably had the greater impact upon the fortunes of the private sector. The increase in the proportion of children in comprehensive secondary schools which began under the Tories in the mid-1950s accelerated after Crosland had issued Circular 10/65 requiring local education authorities to produce plans for reorganisation into comprehensive schools. Szamuely writing in the second set of Black Papers to be published in 1969[48] predicted that 'with the abolition of the grammar schools all well-to-do parents would send their children to the private schools'. Richard Crossman had similar fears believing that his party's commitment to eliminate the grammar schools ran counter to its wish to undermine private education.[49]

The rate at which the proportion of pupils in comprehensive schools increased as a result of Circular 10/65 continued unbated even during the interregnum of the 1970–74 Heath government when Mrs Thatcher was Secretary of State for Education. The proportion, and frequently the number, of pupils in private secondary schooling was beginning to fall at the time that Circular 10/65 was issued and continued to do so until the early 1970s when the numbers began to rise, with increasing acceleration until they reached a new peak in 1981. In the absence of any direct evidence it is difficult to conclude that this growth in both the number and proportion of pupils who are being privately educated is directly attributable to the programme of comprehensivisation but it would be equally difficult to dismiss such a suggestion out of hand.

The re-election in 1983, with an increased majority, of the Thatcher government removed the immediate threats of the Labour party and secured the short term future of the private sector. The Tories have remained steadfast in their support for this sector and within a year of their return to office in 1979 they had passed an Education Act which confirmed their belief in parental freedom of choice and, with the introduction in 1981 of the Assisted Places

Scheme they enlarged the number of parents able to exercise a genuine choice between the two alternative forms of provision. As a result of the establishment of 5500 assisted places annually the private secondary schools, mainly the public schools, have witnessed an increase in the size of their market without having to yield any of their control over selection procedures, curriculum content or organisational detail. Tempting as participation in the assisted places scheme has been, for not only does it broaden the market but it also assists the schools in raising the academic standards upon which their reputation is increasingly coming to rest, the Labour party's pledge to withdraw all assisted place pupils immediately on their return to office has made the schools wary of becoming over-dependent on government funded pupils.

Despite the temporary becalming of the political waters and the removal of abolition from the immediate political agenda, the private sector has had to remain vigilant. The trials and tribulations that it has faced have not been confined to the Labour party's ever heightening antipathy towards it. In addition to the political challenge the schools faced a number of other crises in the 1960s and 1970s. Not least amongst these was the challenge posed by the increasing cost of their education, the result of the effects of inflation. Whilst the cost of living index rose by 148 per cent between January 1966 and January 1976, the schools were particularly affected by the rocketing price of heating oil and the escalation in staff salaries. The rapid increase in staff salaries is directly attributable to the Labour government's fulfillment of its 1974 election pledge to implement the Houghton Report on Teachers Pay which had recommended average increases of 30 per cent and which the private schools had to match. As staff costs account for about 70 per cent of the boarding schools' expenditure it is no surprise that the rise in boarding fees outstripped inflation, increasing by 200 per cent over the decade. It is this astronomical rise in their fees that brought the growing anxiety amongst the headmasters and governors of the boarding schools to a head. Warnings that public boarding schools would not be able to weather the economic storm had come fairly frequently and can be traced back at least as far as the mid-1950s. George Lyttleton, a housemaster at Eton and the governor of many schools wrote to a publisher friend in 1956:

My days are disagreeably full of school governors' meetings . . .
The knell of the independent schools seems to have struck –

literally – six times as many parents are talking of last straws and camels' backs than ever before. . . .[50]

The outcome of anxieties of this nature was that the boarding schools began to seek new markets and in the process succeeded in setting themselves in competition both with each other and the remainder of private sector in general. The most important of these new markets was sought amongst those parents who would never have considered boarding their children but who were not within the reach of the day schools, which in any case were not as prey to the effects of inflation and were agreeably full. As the boarding schools succeeded in attracting more and more day pupils they came increasingly under the scrutiny of their parents for in addition to allowing some of their pupils to return home nightly, the schools introduced a more flexible system of exeats such that in many of them once or twice termly exeats yielded to fortnightly or even weekly boarding. In order to facilitate the search for new pupils amongst those who would not have boarded, the schools modified their selection procedures and began to admit pupils at the age of eleven, opening junior departments or expanding their preparatory departments. Although most of the new pupils attracted by this method came, as intended, from the maintained primary schools some were attracted from the preparatory schools causing friction between the schools concerned. But the biggest rift between the secondary schools in the private sector was caused by the poaching of the market which had hitherto been the preserve of the girls' schools, the result of the decision by many public schools to either go fully co-educational or, even worse as far as the girls' schools are concerned, to admit girls into their sixth forms. By 1979, ten years after Marlborough admitted its first female pupil, there were 8732 girls in HMC schools and this had virtually doubled to 15500 by 1983. Not only were the public schools seeking an increase in the quantity of its pupils, but in a period of growing competition they were also seeking quality, for membership of the HMC is heavily dependent upon the proportion of pupils engaged in sixth form work and the admission of girls into the sixth form is a useful addition to these numbers.

The introduction of girls and the expansion of the number of day pupils has to some extent consigned the charge of the masculine monasticism of the schools to past history, but this was also due to the changes necessitated by the social unrest that existed in the schools in the 1960s.[51] The generation of pupils that came to the schools at this time had not escaped the effects of the 'permissive society' where pre-war restrictions had been relaxed and the era of the governess and to a large extent the nanny had disappeared. They came to adolescence in the swinging sixties and were not immune from the influence of the new fashions, the pop culture and the drug scene as well as the general cult of individualism that pervaded the air. The social unrest which reached its climax in the student unrest of 1968 extended downwards to the cloistered public schools where pupils had already found common cause for demonstration in marches organised by the CND and where there was growing resistance to the hierarchic structure and beating and fagging. This social unrest was manifested in the boarding schools in a diluted form and rarely amounted to more than trivial defiance of authority by the wearing of long hair; the refusal to sing in the chapel or to attend on parade in the combined cadet force or to play in the team games which were so much a part of the public school tradition. The schools were caught unawares by this rebellion but gradually they reformed many of their long standing traditions: power was taken away from the house prefects and was given to the housemasters; chapel attendance at some schools was made voluntary as was the combined cadet force; and the individual sports such as squash and swimming were increasingly catered for.

Ever conscious of its public image and political foes, the HMC appointed a public relations consultant in 1962, and in 1963 it revamped its publicity committee into the Political and Public Relations Committee and launched a trade magazine – *Conference*. As a hundred years earlier, it was the headmasters of the public schools who initiated action to defend the private sector from external hostilities but, as the Labour party increased its offensive, in the 1970s the various factions of the private sector sought to bury their differences and combined to fight on the principle of independence, making it difficult for the Labour party to concentrate on a single target such as the public schools. Despite the formidable economic problems and political rivalries, the main factions were able to unite sufficiently to launch the Independent Schools Information Service (ISIS) in 1972 to act as both an information and a public relations body. Soon after, as the need for political retaliation heightened, and encouraged by the initial success of ISIS, the leading associations of the private schools sharpened their political teeth and formed a representative negotiating body known eventually as the Independent Schools Joint Council (ISJC). Its first major task was to negotiate with the 1974–9 Labour government over its decision to withdraw the system of Her Majesty's Inspectors recognising certain independent schools as efficient. The ISJC, having failed in this, is now setting up its own accreditation system. It was this body that negotiated the introduction of the Assisted Places scheme and in the run up to the 1983 election it set up a sub-committee, an action committee, to promote the interests of the private schools nationwide through a network of local groups. The HMC, the pioneer of political action, maintained a back seat but kept a watchful eye on both ISIS and the ISJC and without its support neither would have functioned.

Whilst the private schools have responded collectively to the political challenge and stand together to face the future, the reform that each has undergone over the last two decades has resulted from the initiatives of their individual headmasters and boards of governors. The need to respond to the social and economic pressures experienced by the private sector, and the boarding schools in particular, has produced more changes than all the commissions, reports and half-hearted attempts at abolition.

2 Who are the Parents?

In Chapter 1 the arguments which have been used to link the possession of a public school education with the notion of privilege were rehearsed. In particular, the voluminous amount of data on élites and their education[1] leaves no doubt that a strong and positive correlation exists between the two phenomena. It is the precise nature and extent of the privilege which is still open to debate and this will be discussed at points throughout the book. Whilst the schools as a social institution are symbolic of the values embedded in a class divided society, an obsession with privilege *per se* must not be allowed to preclude a more careful and detailed examination of the background of those currently 'enjoying' a public school education than has hitherto been undertaken. It is only through such an examination that one can begin to move towards a clearer delineation of the pattern and boundaries of the privilege which is conventionally associated with the public schools.

Data about the social background of the public schools' pupils has been and largely remains conspicuous by its absence. Certainly the original public schools such as Eton, Winchester and Westminster were founded with the intention of providing an education for poor scholars, but as the growth in these schools' reputation came to match the failure of their original endowments to meet their current costs, a ready market was found amongst the gentry which assisted in meeting this deficit. Gathorne-Hardy[2] cites the register at Eton as a vivid illustration of this process, showing how the early domination of the school by the sons of the local tradesmen gradually yielded to that of the sons of noblemen. Bamford[3] in his analysis of the four Clarendon schools whose records in the first half of the nineteenth century were adequate for the purpose, namely Eton, Harrow, Rugby and St Paul's, found that by this time the boarding schools were being used predominantly by the gentry whilst the day school, St Paul's, drew increasingly from the professional classes as the century progressed. As newer foundations, for example Cheltenham College, emerged to meet the demand engendered by the changing occupational, economic and social conditions of the nineteenth century, so they took care to exclude the sons of other than gentlemen and Bamford[4] cites examples of a similar attitude amongst the headmasters of the older foundations. It was not until 1964 that Graham Kalton was invited by the Headmasters' Conference to conduct a factual survey of its member schools. As a part of this survey, facts were collected about every boy entering the schools in the academic year 1962–3, providing a unique analysis of the social composition of the public schoolboys of the time. This showed that fewer than 5 per cent of the entrants to the traditionally independent schools had fathers in manual occupations; the bulk (90 per cent) were drawn from the Registrar-General's top two social classes, the professional and intermediate occupations.[5] Kalton's information about the fathers' occupations is taken from the headmasters' own records and does not contain the further detail necessary to obtain a finer gauge of their social standing. Similarly Halsey *et al.'s* most recently published data (although relating mainly to an earlier period of time than Kalton's, using information about those males born in England and Wales in the period 1913 to 1952) found that 67 per cent of those who had been educated at an HMC school originated in Classes I and II.[6]

Thus the information available to date on the social background of public schoolboys is scarce and any detail is virtually non-existent. The 190 sets of parents used in this research as a sample of those who are educating their sons in the traditionally independent public schools display the same notable degree of homogeneity in class terms as found by Kalton and Halsey in their studies.[7] The use of virtually the same class classification as that employed by Halsey[8] and his colleagues reveals that 75 per cent of the fathers are (or were in the case of the two who are deceased) members of the two top classes which comprise the service class, although this contained fewer than 25 per cent of the employed male population aged 20–64 at the time of the 1971 census. This over-representation is particularly pronounced at the apex of the class structure, Class I, which contains 69 per cent of the total sample but only 14 per cent of the 1971 population. Thus leaving to one side for the moment the question of whether this form of education does in fact constitute a privilege or indeed confer any advantage, at first sight it is obvious that in class terms the class composition of today's public school pupils is remarkably skewed, even after allowing for the difference in the age composition of their fathers.

THE SEARCH FOR AN ÉLITE

A closer examination of the occupational titles which are used to compose the seven classes employed by this research begins to show some of the diversity which does in fact characterise the boys and their parents. A comparison of the titles found in the sample with those of the male working population, as revealed by the 1971 census, shows that 17 out of the 36 major categories are represented within the public schools. However, Table 2.1 shows that certain occupations are very heavily over-represented and in particular those which are characterised by self-employed status: the proprietors of large businesses, the self-employed and the farmers, whilst the manual workers are virtually absent. Today's public schoolboys are indeed drawn from a narrower and higher range of occupational backgrounds than is typical of the population nationally, but what evidence is there to support the belief, encouraged by the findings of the inflow analysis used in the studies of British élites, that a public school education is largely confined to the sons of the existing élites?

The service class is relatively large and hides within it those who by virtue of their position in the sphere of production or in specific social organisations can be deemed to be members of the economic élite or other élites and who therefore form a superior class. The very small size of this superior class is such as to render its members invisible in any large scale study such as that carried out by the Oxford Social Mobility Group. Many of the writers who have sought to operationalise the concept of 'élites' have done so in terms of occupations which enable those in positions at their apices to wield considerable amounts of influence and power. Following the work of Boyd[9] the search for the élite members of this sample begins with the combination of occupational *situs* and high positions within these occupations.* This yielded only one élite member out of the total of 188 fathers who are still living, a senior civil servant. This virtual failure to identify an occupational élite amongst the fathers may be the result of a number of factors. By focusing the research on the parents who are normally resident in mainland Britain, some élite members of the armed forces or of the foreign office (to say nothing of tax exiles) may well have been excluded. Additionally, it may be the

---

* Legal profession (High court judges and above), Armed Services (Lieut.-General, Air Vice-Marshal and Rear-Admiral and above), Civil Service (under-secretary and above), Church (assistant bishop and above), Foreign Service (ambassador and heads of embassies and legations), Directors of Clearing Banks.

TABLE 2.1   *Main occupations of fathers*

	Per cent in the sample (1)	Per cent in the general population (2)	(1)/(2)
CLASS I	69.1	9.9	7.0
Administrators and officials	25.9	2.9	8.9
Managers in commerce and public utilities	11.6	1.1	10.5
Senior civil servants	3.2	0.28	11.4
Managers in mass communications	1.1	0.03	36.7
Senior local authority administration	2.1	0.36	11.4
Sales managers	3.2	0.8	4.0
Headmasters, senior police	2.6	0.29	9.0
Officers in the armed services	2.1	0.14*	15.0
Self-employed professionals	18.4	0.79	23.3
Doctors, lawyers and accountants	6.8	0.35	19.4
Dentists and architects	3.7	0.17	21.8
Engineers, surveyors and pharmacists	4.2	0.16	26.3
Chiropodists, physiotherapists	1.1	0.02	105
Stock and insurance brokers	2.6	0.01	260
Industrial managers	8.9	1.4	6.4
Large proprietors	5.9	0.02	295
Employed professionals	10.0	4.78	2.1
ALL CLASS II	8.9	13.16	0.68
CLASS IV	20	9.4	2.1
Small proprietors	10.5	6.4	1.6
Farmers	10.0	0.79	12.6
CLASS VII Lorry driver	0.5	—	—

*Estimated by Oxford Occupational Mobility Sample (N = 9457) 1972.

relative youthfulness of the fathers which accounts for their failure to have reached élite positions at the particular point in the family life-cycle when they were studied. Age was not one of the questions included in the interview schedule but 20 per cent of the fathers for whom such information is available have been in their present occupational positions for less than five years and a total of 44 per cent for less than ten. Limited circumstantial evidence such as this does suggest that many of the fathers are still young enough to expect further occupational mobility and some may well constitute tomorrow's élite if not today's. However, analysis of their occupational *situs* rather than status does not lend much weight to the possibility of the size of the élite amongst the users of the public schools being substantially increased in this way. There are no barristers, from whom the judiciary are normally recruited, only two members of the clergy, four civil servants and five bankers. When these are added to the four members of the armed forces there is a total of fifteen, or 8 per cent of the fathers who are even possible candidates for membership of the élite as defined by Boyd. For the third possible explanation of the dearth of élite members to be found within the sample one needs to look at the way in which Boyd has operationalised the term. While he explains at length his criteria for the selection of the highest indices within the élite occupations used, his reasons for confining his analysis to the eight *situs* chosen and in particular for omitting the industrial and commercial élite remain obscure. Ingham[10] considers the relationship between industrial and financial capital in Britain and the way in which the latter is believed to dominate the economy despite Marx's view that the repeal of the Corn Laws marked the beginning of the rule of industrial capital. Consequent upon this domination by financial capital is the belief that the industrial bourgeoisie occupies a subordinate position within the ruling class and in relation to the state – the alliance that exists between land and financial capital such that landowners wishing to diversify their economic portfolios invest in the city without tarnishing themselves in industry confirms this belief. Scott,[11] on the other hand, in discussing the rise of the business class sees it as emerging out of the propertied class which itself was formed from the unison of agrarian, commercial and industrial capital. He defines the business class in terms of participation in the control of the thousand largest firms in the economy which, by virtue of their size, dominate the various markets in which they operate.

There is inevitably an element of subjectivity when any categorisation has to be made, but in adhering to the discussion about the nature of élites in the opening chapter and in particular to the importance of locating the source of power over others and control over one's own life chances, Boyd's use of the term has been both broadened and stretched. By including a brigadier, eighteen managing directors or chairmen of 'large' companies (defined as having more than twenty-five employees) and two chief executives of local authorities it was ultimately possible to locate 22 members of an 'occupational' élite or nearly 12 per cent of the fathers in the study. This definition of the occupational élite does not match that of Scott's business class for it extends far beyond participation in the control of the top thousand firms that he used and includes those with far less economic power. A notable omission from the definition is the ownership of land. The relationship between land and other forms of capital is complex due to the transformation of the pattern of land ownership during the twentieth century. On the one hand, the agricultural depression encouraged many large landowners to sell some of their land to the tenants and to invest their money in industry, commerce and the city, thereby creating a new class of small landowners. On the other hand, those possessed of other forms of capital continued with the search for gentrification through the acquisition of land which had begun in the previous century and more recently fiscal policies have encouraged the purchase of land by large companies seeking to reduce their tax liability. None of those classified as members of the occupational élite gave any indication of substantial land ownership but 8 per cent of the fathers do own land in excess of 240 acres (the average size of full-time farms), two-thirds strictly as working farmers. Any possible implications of this omission of land ownership from the definition of the occupational élite is largely compensated for by the decision to invoke a second, more thorough measure of élite status. Allocation to the occupational élite is on the basis of self-report, another index of élite position involves ascription, that is a third party decides the criteria for allocation to the élite. Thus by the use of various directories which are selective in terms of who they include* it is possible to identify twenty members of the male sample who have received public acknowledgement of their social position and who thus are termed the 'social' élite. Contained within this 'social' élite are four large landowners (owning in excess of 600 acres) with no obvious connection to other forms of capital but who may well be shareholders of some significance; one member of the landed gentry who is also a member of parliament as well as a member of a well known family of industrialists; two fathers who would appear to have 'moved' or 'bought' into land in a large way using capital from other sources and finally one father who has similarly bought land, albeit totalling less than 240 acres. Those without land include a member of the clergy,

---

* Directory of Directors, Burke's Landed Gentry, Business Who's Who, Top Directors, Who's Who.

two company directors and a manager in industry. A cross-reference of the membership of the occupational and the social élites reveals eight fathers common to both, thus 34 fathers or 18 per cent of the male sample can be labelled 'élite'. Conversely, however, with only one manual worker nearly 82 per cent of the fathers remain within what is conventionally known as the 'middle class'.

Not included amongst either the occupational or the social élite are those who nevertheless are linked to them by their service relations. Either by providing specialised skills as professionals or by engaging in operational management to implement strategy, up to half of the fathers using the schools could be said to form a sub-élite in the sense used by Mosca as discussed in the opening chapter. These are men who whilst not actually part of the élite serve its needs either directly as employees or indirectly as self-employed professionals and as a consequence enjoy similar privileges and benefits, arguably taking on many of the norms and values of the élite members. Mosca has suggested that it is from their midst that members of the élite are recruited and whilst this may not necessarily occur within the lifetime of one generation, the sons of the members of the sub-élite may well form the élite of tomorrow and a public school education might well be seen by their parents as an important part of this process.

WHAT ABOUT THE WOMEN?

The sociological literature on class is hallmarked by its failure to incorporate women into its analysis, leaving them as an adjunct to their husbands and fathers. Sociology has been referred to as the discipline which studies less than 50 per cent of its subject matter (a situation somewhat altered by the growth of women's studies). Perhaps this can be explained by the limited role that some empirical sociologists have defined for the discipline as the purveyor of social facts and in this sense empirical findings do no more or less than reflect society's definition of women's role in the economy. Certainly the difficulties of constructing an index of women's class position are even greater than those associated with constructing such an index for men. Whilst young single women have an overall employment rate which is very similar to that of men, the picture alters dramatically and indeed becomes more complex on their marriage. The employment rate of married women is around half of that for men and varies according to age, their own and their husband's occupation as well as the number and ages of their children. Even allowing for the currently high rate of unemployment, the expectation is that men will be in virtually continuous employment from the termination of full time education until retirement; for women the expectation is very different, it is a minority who will preserve such an uninterrupted work pattern, some give up work permanently on the birth of the first child whilst others do not resume until all the children are of school age. Partly as a consequence of this broken work pattern women are rarely to be found at the apex of the occupational hierarchy and even in those fields where there is a relatively high concentration of women, for example school teaching and medicine, the top positions are overwhelmingly filled by men. None of the women in this research are members of the occupational élite identified nor indeed are mentioned in their own right in any of the directories used to construct the social élite. Findings of this nature have led Giddens[12] to conclude that women's role in the class system is peripheral. The mothers in this sample are no exception for although only 3 per cent of them have children who are still under school age, 43 per cent are not working and 27 per cent have either never worked or not done so since marriage. Of those who are in employment, about one-third are working full time and their main occupations are listed in Table 2.2. From this it can be seen that there is a heavy concentration in the typically female occupations: the minor professions and the white collar clerical and secretarial jobs.

The failure of sociology to include women in much of its work on class can be more easily appreciated when confronted by statistics such as these. Parkin[13] has argued that women's claim over resources are more usually determined by their fathers' and/or husbands' than their own position within the labour market. He goes on to say that '. . . only if the disabilities attaching to female status were felt to be so great as to over-ride differences of a class kind would it be realistic to regard sex as an important dimension of stratification'. The same point of view, expressed differently, is made succinctly by one of the respondents, the wife of an accountant:

> I don't work and therefore must go at the bottom end . . . if you earn money you can put yourself into a class – I have no money of my own – the money is given to me to care for the family.

In Britain there is a low correspondence between the occupational distribution of men and that of their working wives, as can be seen

TABLE 2.2 *Mothers' employment*

Type of occupation	Occupational status							As a proportion of total
	None	*Temporary*	*Part-time*	*With husband*	*Self-employed*	*Full time*	*Total*	
No job (%) (75)	100	0	0	0	0	0	100%	0.4
Major professions (%) (2)	0	0	0	0	0	100	100%	0.01
Executive (%) (2)	0	0	0	0	0	100	100%	0.01
Lower professions (%) (39)	0	8	46	3	3	41	100%	0.21
Administrative (%) (12)	0	0	17	8	0	75	100%	0.06
Musician/artist (%) (4)	0	25	25	0	0	50	100%	0.02
Own business (%) (15)	0	0	0	27	73	0	100%	0.08
Secretarial/clerical (%) (26)	0	15	40	19	4	23	100%	0.14
Shop assistant (%) (5)	0	20	80	0	0	0	100%	0.03
Student (%) (2)	100	0	0	0	0	0	100%	0.01
Farming/horses (%) (6)	17	0	0	50	33	0	100%	0.03

TABLE 2.3   *Social class position of married women (economically active and retired with classified occupations)*

Registrar General's class	Husbands (%)	Wives (%)
I	5.3	0.9
II	19.8	16.2
III (Non-manual)	11.3	35.4
III (Manual)	39.0	10.0
IV	17.5	28.2
V	7.1	9.4
Total	100%	100%

SOURCE   *Social Trends,* HMSO, 1975.

from Table 2.3, yet there has been a wholesale failure to consider the impact of such a divergence upon the class position of families where both partners do work or the possible influence that the woman's occupational position may have upon life-styles and attitudes.

Although the occupations of the working mothers in this sample have not been classified into the classes used for their husbands, a cursory glance at Table 2.2 is sufficient to suggest that a maximum of 2 per cent of the working mothers are in Class I by virtue of their own occupations, the bulk falling into Classes II and III, confirming the view expressed by Parkin that these women's claim over resources is primarily determined by their husbands' occupations rather than their own. At best they have been able to maintain their careers at the level reached on first entering the labour market whilst watching the growth of their husbands' careers. Twelve per cent of the men had their first jobs in the manual sector, Classes V – VII, but only an eighth of them remained there ten years later and all have since been upwardly mobile into the non-manual sector, 54 per cent having reached Class I.

There are growing doubts about the usefulness of occupation as an indicator of class position[14] and the data on women's occupations highlights the need to query in general the value of current occupation as an indicator of class and in particular how much it alone can tell us about attitudes towards a subject such as education. Certainly such attitudes can only be understood fully in terms of the transmission of cultural as well as material capital to both of the parents. One of the most notable illustrations of this point is Jackson and

Marsden's[15] documentation of the over-achievement of working class (as defined by the fathers' occupations) entrants to grammar school and how this is associated with a mother who has been downwardly mobile through marriage. At first sight the comparison of the social origins of the mothers in this research (measured by their own fathers' occupational class) with the current class position of their husbands suggests that these mothers have in fact achieved upward mobility through marriage but a closer inspection of Table 2.4 which shows the social origins of both partners in the marriage reveals that the picture is somewhat more complex for the mothers had a noticeable tendency to marry men with lower social origins than their own but who have achieved their upward mobility. Thus some of the mothers may well have brought both cultural and material capital into their marriages.

TABLE 2.4   *Mothers' social origins and (a) husbands' origin, (b) husbands class*

(a) Husbands' fathers' class	Mothers' fathers' class position				
(b) (Husbands' class)	*I-II (%)*	*III (%)*	*IV (%)*	*V-VII (%)*	*Total (%)*
I-II	62	36	30	29	47
	(81)	(100)	(64)	(83)	(78)
III	7	0	14	10	8
	(0)	(0)	(0)	(0)	(0)
IV	22	21	45	38	29
	(18)	(0)	(36)	(17)	(21)
V-VII	9	43	11	33	15
	(1)	(0)	(0)	(0)	(1)
Total	100%	100%	100%	100%	100%

A more detailed study of the social origins of the boys in the public schools unmasks still further the diversity that is contained within the term 'middle class'. The Oxford Social Mobility Group, comparing the class position of its respondents with that of their fathers, shows how the expansion of the service class has resulted in a very considerable amount of upward mobility. The high degree of openness in the recruitment to the service class is particularly marked at its apex for only 24 per cent of the members of Class I were found to have fathers in the same class.[16] Although both the rate and range of the upward mobility enjoyed by the fathers using the public schools falls short of that found by the Oxford Social Mobility Group, the increased opportunities for such mobility are clearly reflected in their origins.

Over a half of all the Class I fathers are first generation members of their class, 13 per cent coming from manual backgrounds. The origins of those in the occupational and social élites can be seen by extracting these fathers from Class I and comparing them with the remaining members. The experience of mobility into Class I characterising the non-élite and the occupational élite is remarkably similar, it is the social élite which exhibits a high degree of closure, excluding those who at the very least do not originate in Class I. Boyd[17] in his analysis of the origins of the élites that he studies shows that between 55 per cent and 89 per cent of their members, depending upon the particular élite being considered, are first generation members of an élite. Whilst the information about the origins of the fathers in this sample is not quite as detailed as that of Boyd's, evidence that is available does show that at least 40 per cent of the members of the social élite have inherited their position, mainly through land, and only 20 per cent are definitely not the sons of élite fathers.

Table 2.5 also contains information about those fathers belonging to Class IV, the *petit bourgeoisie*. The members of this class are remarkably stable, especially when compared to the findings of the Oxford Mobility Study and this is probably the result of the over-representation of farmers in the sample, a community renowned for its occupational continuity. It is also of interest to note the comparatively high amount of downward mobility from Class I experienced by the fathers in this sample, indicating the presence of a group of men whose norms and values possibly reflect those acquired during an earlier and possibly more prosperous period in their lives, of which private education may be an example.

Whilst the Oxford Mobility Study gathered information about two generations only, in over 80 per cent of the cases in this research it has been possible to compare class position of three generations of males, enabling a more profound analysis of the extent of class stability or mobility. The evidence shows that it is indeed the social élite which is the most stable in terms of membership of its class, confirming the social closure exhibited over two generations. Fifty-five per cent of the members of this élite are third generation members of Class I,[18] as compared to only 29 per cent of the occupational élite and 20 per cent of the remaining Class I males (both of whom are drawn from a variety of occupational backgrounds such that their class position is not strictly hereditary).

TABLE 2.5 *(a) Social origins of men using the public schools*

Male respondents:	Male respondents' fathers' class					
	I	*II*	*III*	*IV*	*V–VII*	
All Class I males (129)	46	9	11	21	13	= 100%
(All Class I males in Oxford Mobility Study)	24	13	10	13	40	= 100%
Occupational élite only (14)	57	<	43		>	= 100%
Social élite (20)	90	0	5	5	0	= 100%
Class I males excluding members of both élites (95)	36	<	64		>	= 100%
All Class IV males (40)	23	3	0	68	8	= 100%
(All Class IV males in Oxford Mobility Study)	6	4	6	37	47	= 100%

NOTE Each respondent was asked to name his father's present or last main occupation. The Oxford Mobility Study used the father's occupation at the time that the respondent was aged 14 and by this token the present study probably under-estimates the amount of social mobility.

(b) Social stability of Class I males*

	1st generation	2nd generation	3rd generation
Occupational élite	43	28	29 = 100%
Social élite	10	35	55 = 100%
Other Class I males	64	16	20 = 100%

*Where the information for three generations is available

Another form of mobility is through marriage. In general the parents are remarkably endogamous, particularly at the upper fringes. Seventy-two per cent of the men born into Classes I and II married women from the same background but 30 per cent of those with manual origins did succeed in marrying women from Class I and II, indicating the possibility of early upward mobility through marriage. Conversely, Table 2.4 does indicate the extent of downward mobility that some women have experienced through marriage. Okley,[19] writing about girls' boarding education, stresses the common class backgrounds that these girls share with their future husbands, yet only 62 per cent of the women in this research with origins in Classes I and II did in fact marry men from these classes and 9 per cent married those with manual origins. Once again the social élite displays the practice of closure, 75 per cent are married to women who originate in Class I.

Whilst it has been possible to identify amongst the sample of fathers who use today's public schools a small élite, amounting to no more than 7 per cent of the total, who exhibit a high degree of social closure in terms of both recruitment and marriage, the remaining members are heterogeneous with respect to their current occupations and the degree of success within them as well as their own social origins and those of their wives. Though in these same terms the parents cannot be said to be a microcosm of society, neither can they be described as homogeneous and therefore they bring with them the potential for a wide range of attitudes, beliefs and styles of living.

A FINANCIAL ÉLITE

Bamford[20] has discussed how, historically, the top public schools showed a reluctance to widen their intake; the picture today has been shown to be somewhat different for many of these selfsame schools ruthlessly pursue both the academic excellence upon which their reputation rests and the pupils upon which their very future depends. Frequently academic excellence is achieved at the expense of the shattered hopes of those of their old boys who have failed to secure the place for their sons which they feel to be rightfully theirs. However, with average day fees standing at £1200 p.a. and those for boarders in excess of £2500 p.a. in 1980, with few schools able to make more than token provision for bursaries, a limited government financed Assisted Places scheme and more than 50 per cent of the parents educating at least two children simultaneously in the private sector, the financial wherewithal of the parents is the ultimate determinant of who, in the main, will receive this form of education. It is therefore possible that parents are using their sometimes considerable financial resources to transform their wealth into power by promoting their sons into the élite via a public school education.

Any evaluation of the financial status of the parents is fraught with difficulties. The relationship between the three main components: capital, earnings and unearned income is complex whilst the quality of the information made available is very variable. On the one hand, a discussion of personal financial position is still considered taboo by many and 16 per cent of the respondents declined to answer any or some of the questions relating to this part of the interview. On the other hand, some fathers went to great lengths to explain just how they arrange their financial affairs. Such explanations included descriptions of the way in which income and expenses are shared out between wives and other family members in order to minimise tax burdens; an explanation by a senior partner in a renowned firm of stockbrokers, reporting no unearned income, of how the current rates of taxation on investment income make it imperative for finances to be arranged to produce capital growth rather than income and an insight into the tax inducements to farmers which are designed to encourage them to re-invest in land with the consequent drawing as income the minimum amount necessary to meet daily living expenses. The very nature of this sample, at the apex of the occupational hierarchy and with 50 per cent self-employed, means that its members are exceedingly well placed financially and occupationally to gain access to the professional advice necessary to ensure the optimum distribution of financial resources between income and capital and between family members. As a consequence, any conclusions about the financial status of the parents must be treated with the caution that is due (Table 2.6).

An upper class was defined in Chapter 1 in terms of the financial resources that its members have at their disposal to maximise life chances. In income terms alone these parents are undoubtedly wealthy; whilst the median income of the 150 men who are both earning and answered the relevant question is £14 024, over two and a half times that of the median non-manual male income in 1979, the modal income lies in the range £15–20 000. Fifty-eight per cent of the fathers did have an income below this amount but more than a fifth earned in excess of £20 000. There is an obvious association between type of occupation and earned income such that those in Class II are the lowest earners and those in Class I the highest, but there are also differences in the earning power of occupations within classes. The Class I men who are self-employed are clearly well rewarded, 57 per cent of the proprietors of large businesses and 40 per cent of the self-employed professionals earn in excess of £20 000 per annum and stand in marked contrast to the professionals who are employees, 61 per cent of whom earn less than £12 000 annually. Membership of both the occupational and the social élite is similarly associated with this high level of earned income but few of those in Class IV, also composed of the self-employed: farmers and the proprietors of small businesses, reported earned incomes in excess of £12 000 per annum.

TABLE 2.6 *Distribution of parents' annual gross earned income (156)*

Fathers		None	U.£3	£3-4	Mothers ('000s) £4-5	£5-6	£6-8	£8+	As a proportion Total of total	
None	%	0	0	0	40	40	20	0	100%	0.032
Under £6000	%	40	40	0	10	10	0	0	100%	0.064
£6–8000	%	30	30	20	10	0	10	0	100%	0.064
£8–10 000	%	33	27	13	13	7	0	7	100%	0.096
£10–12 000	%	53	21	5	0	11	5	5	100%	0.122
£12–15 000	%	42	39	3	7	3	3	3	100%	0.20
£15–20 000	%	52	36	6	3	0	0	3	100%	0.21
£20–50 000	%	68	16	0	0	0	10	6	100%	0.20
£50–000+	%	100	0	0	0	0	0	0	100%	0.013
As a proportion of the total		0.481	0.282	0.051	0.058	0.045	0.045	0.038		

(Median non-manual income 1979 men: £5283.00 p.a. Women: £3161.80 p.a.
SOURCE *Social Trends*, HMSO).

It is difficult to assess the full impact of the mother's income upon the decision to educate children privately for whilst the fathers' incomes are undoubtedly well above the norm, the fees to be paid are high and there are many fathers whose earned income is well below the amount required to meet them. The majority of mothers who do earn have an income which is below the non-manual average for women, £3432, but whilst there is no overall relationship between fathers' and mothers' incomes the rate of employment amongst women who are married to Class II men is well in excess of the average for the whole sample, only 11 per cent being without work of some sort. More generally, fewer of the low income fathers, those with less than £12 000 p.a., have wives who do not work or whose earnings fall below the female norm of less than £3000 and the reverse is true for high earners. It therefore appears that the mother's income is an important factor in the decision of some parents to educate their children privately and despite the relatively low level of such incomes a significant number of parents mentioned its importance.

But for writers adopting a Marxist perspective it is the ownership of capital rather than the level of earned income which is the cornerstone of an individual's financial position, for capital is associated not only with high income and the variety of fringe benefits which such an income normally brings, but also with accumulation, investment income and with power. The nature and extent of power conferred by the ownership of capital depends upon both the amount and the form in which it is held: if capital is held as company stocks and shares in sufficiently large amounts it is able to confer considerable power. The whole question of the form of possession is complex for there is the distinction between voting and non-voting shares and even within voting shares there are majority and minority shareholders, the amount of power depending upon the manner in which the shares are distributed. Potentially at least, in addition to those who are linked to the business class by their service relations, Mosca's sub-élite, there are those of property who follow careers outside the world of business but who are nevertheless people of considerable wealth with families who have preserved their links with business, links which can be used to help their children to enter the world of business. If the parents who use the public schools include people such as these amongst their number it is likely that their reasons for wanting a public school education will differ from those who are not linked with the business class in this way. Accurate estimates of the ownership and distribution of wealth are exceedingly difficult to obtain, in the absence to date of a wealth tax personal wealth holders are not obliged to disclose the magnitude of their wealth. These difficulties are discussed in the Reports of the Royal Commission on the Distribution of Income and Wealth (the Diamond Report) which provides the most comprehensive summary to date of the way in which personal wealth is distributed between wealth holders; the asset composition of personal wealth and how different assets vary in their distribution between wealth holders. Detailed statistics such as these enable the distinction to be made between what Halsey has termed 'property for power' (financial assets, land holding of some magnitude and property other than that used as a family home) and 'property for use'.[21] For example, the Diamond Report shows that in 1976 less than 1 per cent of all wealth holders (estimated as 50 per cent of the adult population) held more than £100 000 as personal wealth but approximately 50 per cent of listed company shares and other company securities were concentrated within this wealth range.[22] Whilst the evidence of the Diamond Committee clearly shows the maldistribution of personal wealth in Britain, by excluding any consideration of institutional wealth it underestimates the power that is concentrated in the hands of the few who control this form of wealth. The information about the wealth holding of the parents in this sample is restricted to details of personal wealth that can be loosely equated with property for power for it concentrates upon but does not distinguish between the possession of land, property other than the principal residence, company shareholdings and other financial assets and excludes any consideration of wealth held as personal goods and chattels or the value of the principal residence. Table 2.7 shows the proportions of both the fathers and the mothers holding different amounts of wealth.

The reports of the Diamond Committee do not combine all forms of financial and agrarian wealth in a manner which can be used in direct comparison with these findings but the distribution of total wealth amongst wealth holders in 1974 is included in Table 2.7 for the purpose of comparison.[23] Although barely comparable[24] this does highlight the enormous concentration of wealth that is to be found amongst some of the men in the sample, over a fifth of the fathers have financial and/or agrarian capital valued at more than £100 000. Although 10 per cent of the men declared themselves to be void of all forms of financial wealth, they are virtually all home owners and therefore unlikely to own less than £5000. This concentration of

TABLE 2.7   *The distribution of wealth of (a) all parents in the sample and (b) all wealth holders in 1974 as estimated by the Diamond Report*

Range of wealth in £000s	(a)		(b)	
	Fathers (155)	Mothers (155)	Male wealth holders	Female wealth holders
None	9.7	43.9	(Estimated to be 50 per cent)	
Under 5	23.2	25.2	51.2	60.8
5–10	11.6	8.4	23.9	19.2
10–20	9.7	2.6	17.2	13.1
20–50	11.6	7.7	5.8	5.4
50–100	12.3	5.2	1.3	1.1
100–200	7.1	2.6	0.3	0.4
200+	14.8	4.5	0.1	0.1
Total	100%	100%	100%	100%

wealth is not quite as marked amongst the women and whilst no consideration is made of the fact that it may be the wife and not the husband who is the owner of the family home, Table 2.7 does show the disproportionately high number of women who possess capital that exceeds £20 000 in value. Research such as this which is seeking to distinguish a financial upper class from an essentially bourgeois population is primarily interested in the distribution of wealth at the higher end of the scale. It is inevitable that there should be an element of subjectivity when any attempt is made to define 'the higher end of the scale'. The decision to define those who possess wealth in excess of £100 000 as wealthy is primarily the result of the desire to maintain consistency with the category of 'top wealth-leavers' in the work of Harbury and Hitchens (discussed below). In view of the effects of inflation this may be too generous an estimate of the wealthy members of this sample but against this is the fact that the last Labour government had announced its intention of introducing a tax on the *total* wealth of tax units in excess of £150 000 and this makes the estimate rather conservative.

This research, and others,[25] has failed to locate any women who might be considered as potential members of the financial upper class by virtue of their occupational roles, but this does not exclude the possibility of membership through marriage or descent. Scott[26] in defining the members of the 'business class' includes not only the directors, top executives and principal shareholders of the thousand largest companies in Britain but also the members of their families. In this sense the women in this sample may be members of the financial upper class either through their ownership of wealth or through the familial ties described by Scott. It is difficult to disentangle the source of the wealth owned by the 7 per cent of the women who have assets valued in excess of £100 000 and who can therefore be termed 'wealthy'. Eighty per cent of them are married to men who are similarly wealthy and who may well have rearranged their own capital within the marriage and there are only two women who have clearly acquired their wealth by descent.

In the absence of any specific discussion with the parents of the precise form in which their assets are held it is equally difficult to disentangle the source and form of the fathers' wealth, but the relationship between their occupation and ownership of capital does throw some considerable light on this subject. Table 2.1 indicates the extent of the over-representation of farmers amongst the parents using the public schools and two-thirds of them own at least part of the land that they farm. With the currently high price of farmland it would be exceedingly difficult for these farmers not to fall within the top wealth bracket and thus it is that the single largest proportion of the wealthy who use the public schools are not the owners of the means of production in the Marxist sense of the term but those who ostensibly derive their living from farming the land that they own, either as working farmers or with the assistance of a farm manager. Sixty-six per cent of all farmers but only 50 per cent of the proprietors of large businesses own capital in excess of £100 000, the latter presumably holding it as share capital. There is no direct evidence that the farmers hold any other forms of capital apart from land for none of them are listed in the *Directory of Directors* or *Business Who's Who,* but this does not preclude the possibility that some are substantial shareholders either through family inheritance or as a result of the earlier divestment of part of their land.

Newby *et al.*[27] have made the location of farmers in the British class structure the focal point of their research. They discuss Weber's identification of the need to differentiate the factions within the propertied class, each faction possessing a different justification theory of property, and how this is part of the difficulty of discussing farmers in terms of a class structure which is essentially urban based.

Those in farming see a natural inequality which is believed to be legitimate in view of the stewardship of land, preserving it and passing it from one generation to the next. The wife of a substantial landowner and working farmer, listed in *Burke's Landed Gentry,* explains the meaning of stewardship:

> People who inherit estates feel deeply for them and put their whole life into maintaining them for the benefit of a whole lot of people, providing employment, enjoyment and preserving Britain.

The over-representation of farmers in the public schools does appear to distort many of the findings but in turn their presence, or the presence of so many connected with land, does serve to highlight many of the characteristics of a traditional public school education.

The diverse forms in which those who are wealthy but do not own land or large businesses hold their wealth can only be gleaned from a detailed analysis of the interviews with these parents. There is little evidence of widespread shareholding of any substance but several of these fathers have judiciously moved into land ownership in the manner already discussed but do not necessarily hold the associated values. The divorce between the ownership and the control of the large joint stock companies has focused attention upon managers who have what is termed 'possession' of capital, the power to put the means of production into operation, without necessarily having legal ownership. Studies have concluded[28] that many managers are shareholders of some significance and that even more are drawn from the same social background as the core of the business class, operating within the same normative and relational framework. Whilst only 20 per cent of the fathers who have been classed as managers in industry do have capital assets that exceed £100 000 only a slightly lower proportion of them than of those who own large enterprises have fathers who were also members of Class I. Only one out of the four wealthy managers has obviously acquired the wealth for himself and he has clearly built up his capital through the gradual purchase of land. A greater disparity exists between the social origins and the wealth holding of those who hold senior positions in commercial and public enterprises. Drawn from Class I origins in proportions equal to those who own large businesses, far fewer of them, only 8 per cent, own capital of £100 000 or more and they clearly hold it as financial assets in the enterprises with which they are associated. In addition to two wealthy proprietors of businesses classed as small because of the low number of employees, there are four professionals in the top wealth bracket. One is the proprietor of a large school of accountancy and can more accurately be described as an entrepreneur and the other three are more obviously linked to the financial upper class by their service relations. Two are accountants who in addition to owning considerable tracts of land are listed in the *Directory of Directors* as the directors of several companies and therefore do not appear to have a consolidated shareholding in any single company, whilst the third is the stockbroker who is likely but not inevitably to have a dispersed rather than consolidated portfolio.

Information about the unearned income of the parents adds little to the knowledge about the form in which wealth is held but it does throw some further light upon the extent to which members of the sample are linked to the financial upper class as the beneficiaries of family wealth without participating in the ownership or even the control of the means of production. Forty-one per cent of the fathers and 67 per cent of the mothers have no unearned income and included amongst these are many of the members of the occupational elite who clearly, in the cases of those who possess it, are using their wealth as working capital. Few of the remaining parents have unearned income of any substance, only 16 per cent of the men and 10 per cent of the women have such an income which exceeds £3000 annually. A closer examination of the capital assets of these parents provides little evidence to suggest that many have a financial stake in wealth without owning it directly. Three of the men do have an unearned income without the capital necessary to yield it and three of the landowners are the declared beneficiaries of family trusts, thus six men do appear to be receiving income from capital which they do not own. Similarly, there are seven women, 5 per cent in all, who are linked to the financial upper class in this way. In the absence of any knowledge about the financial assets of the kin of the respondents it is impossible to extend the estimation of the true size of the financial upper class amongst parents of public schoolboys to include those who are linked to it through family membership in the way that Scott suggests.

The true size of the membership of the financial upper class is under-estimated by virtue of the fact that 70 per cent of both the fathers and the mothers still have at least one parent alive and several of them discussed how legal ownership, even if not the actual control, of the family assets remains with the living parent. Although many of those interviewed are undoubtedly members of the financial upper class in the sense that they stand to inherit considerable wealth, many of them felt that such an inheritance would come too late to be of much practical use.

Harbury and Hitchens[29] have studied the practice and significance of inheritance more generally and they discuss its importance in the process of capital accumulation. They show that in the period 1956–73, 49 per cent of those who died leaving estates valued in excess of £100 000 had fathers who had left similar sized estates. It is the farmers in this sample who appear to be the most likely to have acquired their wealth with the advantage of inheritance. Newby *et al.*[30] discuss the impact of the inflation in land prices upon the institution and practice of family farming. To farmers the real value of land lies in the value of the products which it yields and it is only to those who invest in land that the anticipated capital growth is of any immediate value. The farmers interviewed by Newby felt that it is the intervention of the financial institutions and other private investors which has caused the inflation in land prices and it is this which is making it increasingly difficult to keep farm holdings intact for taxation is succeeding in breaking up the large estates. How true this is discussed in detail elsewhere[31] but three-quarters of the fathers interviewed have inherited farms from relatives and wish to preserve them for their own sons. The owners of the large businesses divide exactly into two categories: the inheritors (family businessmen) and the entrepreneurs (self-made businessmen) whilst the professionals who are holders of wealth have accumulated capital as a result of their own efforts. As a rough estimate and in the absence of sufficiently detailed information it would appear that, with the exception of the farmers, two-thirds of the wealthy fathers who use the public schools today have created rather than acquired their wealth.

Drawing together the information received from the 155 men and women who answered the relevant questions, there is no doubt that the majority of men are affluent in terms of income alone, but this does not necessarily make them members of the financial upper class. In all there are 39 men (21 per cent) who can be considered to be part of this upper class by virtue of the fact that they either own capital in excess of £100 000 and/or are in receipt of an unearned income of some considerable amount, at least £5000 annually. Included in this number are the thirteen owners of land, mainly working farmers, who have no obvious stake in financial capital but who do own valuable land which can be sold and converted into financial assets.

Fourteen of the men in this financial upper class are also members of
the occupational or social élite, leaving twenty-five, 13 per cent of
the living fathers, to be added to the total of 18 per cent who are
members of these élites thus making a total of nearly one-third of the
fathers who enjoy power or wealth in varying forms. If one adds to
these the two women who clearly have capital and unearned income
in their own right and the four who are beneficiaries of trust funds, 34
per cent of the boys in today's public schools are united by the fact
that they come from an immediate family background which although
part of a unified class hierarchy extends well into its upper reaches.
They share in common parents who by virtue of economic position,
occupational role or social standing are members of the élite.
Whether they are sufficiently integrated ideologically or relationally
for the son of an earl to feel that he shares a common class position
with that of the son of a manufacturer of pots and pans is open to
debate.

Just as it is important to distinguish between the impact of the
public schools as a social institution and the manner in which they
serve to advantage certain sections of society, so it is necessary to
consider the impact of capitalism as a mode of production separately
from the specific benefits that accrue to the owners of the means of
production. It can be argued that all of the many parents who are
members of the service class are linked to capitalism and clearly
benefit from the institutional arrangements that it generates. Thus
one would expect to find that these parents share with those who are
more obviously the owners of capital a commitment to the values of
capitalism which as a system has served them well.

EDUCATION — THE BASIS OF A RULING CLASS?

A ruling class is distinguished from a financial upper class by its
ability to exercise control over the uses to which wealth is put. In
addition to the control ensuing from legal ownership, Marx himself
wrote of the importance of the control of ideas, termed by Gramsci as
'hegemonic control'. There is, however, a failure by Marxists to
specify in a systematic fashion the method by which the economic
hegemony of the capitalist class becomes translated into the political
domination of the ruling class. As a precondition of the exercise of
hegemonic control as a ruling class, members of the financial upper
class and their lieutenants, the service class, need to be cohesive and

integrated into the appropriate ideology. A public school education has been identified by Hoare as a key element in the formation of this hegemonic class, whilst Miliband and Lambert have provided some of the detail of how this is achieved.[32]

Lambert[33] in describing the ethos of a public school education was essentially concerned with the boarding schools. The categorisations used for the purpose of this research have been discussed in Chapter 1 and Table 2.8 shows the extent to which the boys public schools are still self-recruiting for one-third of today's fathers have themselves

TABLE 2.8 *Parents' education*

		Fathers (%)		Mothers (%)
(a)	*Primary*			
	State	45.7		43.7
	Mixed	6.5		4.2
	Abroad	6.5		6.3
	Private day	15.6		36.3
	Private board	26.0		9.5
	Total	100%		100%
(b)	*Secondary*			
	Non-selective	11.2		18.0
	Abroad	7.5		2.6
	Grammar	30.0		30.0
	Mixed	1.0	Mixed/Convent	10.5
	Direct grant	7.0		5.8
	Non-HMC private	10.2	Day private	9.5
	Day HMC	9.0	Boarding private	18.4
	Boarding HMC	24.6	Boarding Public	5.3
		(Major 17.6)		
	Total	100%		100%
(c)	*Further*			
	None	37.8		29.5
	Part-time	11.4	Finishing school	6.3
	Agriculture	2.2		2.1
	Sandhurst, etc.	2.7	Nursing/physiotherapy	19.0
	Professional articles	9.2	Teaching training	12.6
	Polytechnic/HE	6.0	Secretarial/commercial	18.0
	University	15.7		9.0
	Oxbridge	15.1		3.7
	Total	100%		100%

been public school educated, the majority at boarding school and over a half at Britain's top boarding schools. To this figure some may wish to add the 10 per cent of fathers who have been educated in the non-HMC fee paying schools. Conversely, nearly a half of the fathers received their secondary education outside the private sector, albeit predominantly as grammar school pupils, and 7 per cent in the hybrid direct grant schools whose ethos at that time was probably closer to that of the grammar than the public schools.

Writing as recently as 1959, Snow[34] has argued that an absorption rate of 25 per cent of new blood is the maximum amount tolerable if the public schools are not to lose their essential character. Whilst the level and type of further education received by the women in this sample differs markedly from that of the men, the primary and secondary experiences of the two sexes is closely matched, as can be seen from Table 2.8. This suggests that Snow's figure of 25 per cent as the acceptable level of new blood is being grossly violated. A comparison of the secondary education experiences of husbands and their wives, Table 2.9, shows that nearly a quarter of the men who have been educated outside the strictly private sector of education, that is excluding the direct grant schools, are married to women who come from within.

Comparatively little has been written about the nature and purpose of girls' private education and this has not been a topic of concern to those writing about the relationship between education and privilege. Whilst Okley's reference[35] to the practice of sending girls to boarding school in preparation for marriage to boys from a similar background suggests that the content of their education is unconcerned with preparing them to take an active part in the activities of the ruling class, no doubt part of their socialisation is an anticipation of their role as the wives and mothers of such men. As such the education of these women could be considered an entitlement to cultural inclusion within the ruling class, enabling them to bring its values into their own marriages. However, even if one takes into consideration those parents where the wife but not the husband has had a private secondary education, the fact remains that the public schools today are having to incorporate into their midst something of the order of a minimum of 43 per cent of boys whose parents were not themselves strictly schooled into their subculture.

Like the public schools, the universities provide a particular form of socialisation and nowhere is this more marked than at Oxbridge

TABLE 2.9   *A comparison of the secondary education of husbands and wives*

| | Husbands | | | |
| | | Private | HMC | |
Wives	*DG, state or abroad* *(104)* *(%)*	*Non-HMC* *(19)* *(%)*	*Day* *(15)* *(%)*	*Boarding* *(46)* *(%)*
DG, state or abroad	69.2	53.0	60.0	24.0
Convent	8.7	11.0	7.0	8.6
Day private	8.7	16.0	13.0	15.2
Boarding private	11.5	16.0	20.0	37.0
Boarding public	1.9	5.0	0	15.2
Total	100%	100%	100%	100%

where the ethos of the 'gentleman' and the values of the ruling class survive to this very day. Whilst fewer than one in 115 boys leaving school today can expect to obtain a place at one of the Oxbridge colleges, no less than 15 per cent of the fathers in this sample are Oxbridge graduates. An analysis of the relationship between type of secondary schooling and the nature of further education received highlights the 'public school–Oxbridge connection' in action for a quarter of those men who have been to a public school but only 12 per cent of the grammar school educated men are Oxbridge graduates. Thus 9 per cent of the fathers have had both a public school and an Oxbridge education, whilst a further 42 per cent have had one or another but not both, making a total of over 50 per cent of the fathers who have been exposed directly to the values of the ruling class during at least a part of their education.

It was argued in the opening chapter that some writers see the full significance of the public schools as extending beyond the manner in which they prepare selected individuals for privileged and powerful social roles to include their impact upon the maintained sector of education. It is in this sector that the majority of the population is socialised into accepting the educational norms laid down by the ruling class and in which the existing division of labour is reproduced. Smith[35] discusses the way in which those who were sponsored into the grammar schools were set apart from the multitude and were offered a sense of cultural inclusion with the ruling élite whilst segregated from them relationally through the latter's use of the public schools. It is in this sense that the majority of the parents using the public schools today could be said to be at least potentially a part of the ruling class, having been socialised into the exercise of hegemonic control.

THE PUBLIC SCHOOL – A LADDER TO PRIVILEGE?

Do the experiences of these fathers confirm the assertion that a public school education does in fact confer extra advantages upon those who have been educated in this manner, or is it merely a *rite de passage* – a stage through which children from already privileged social backgrounds pass *en route* to similar positions in society? More specifically, but for consideration in later chapters, how does the actual experience of such an education affect attitudes towards the education of their own sons?

At first sight it might appear that the experiences of the fathers in this sample do confirm the claims that have been made that a public school education is indeed a ladder of opportunity, the opportunity to not only reach the higher echelons of the service class but also to belong to the high status group. Table 2.10 shows the association that does exist between a public school education and membership of both of these groups.

Whilst the figures confirm that there is indeed a strong relationship between an education in one of Britain's top public schools and membership of the social élite, they do not show any difference between these schools and their more minor counterparts when it comes to access to positions within Class I more generally. A more detailed analysis of the way in which the different types of secondary schools are linked to the specific occupations within Class I does suggest that the specific form of schooling received might determine the type of occupation ultimately achieved. Those who are employed either as managers in industry or as senior administrators in commerce or government, that is positions as the agents of capital or of the state, are the most likely of all the fathers to have been to one of the major boarding schools. Those who own the means of production, the proprietors of the large businesses, are equally as likely to have achieved their success through the non-selective part of the state system as to have inherited it, passing through the major public

TABLE 2.10 *Main forms of fathers' secondary education and (a) current class position, (b) membership of the social élite*

(a) Class	I	II	IV
School			
Major boarding	21.2	7.1	16.3
Other HMC	20.3	14.3	10.3
Total 'Public'	**41.5**	**21.4**	**27.1**
Other private	8.5	14.3	13.5
Grammar	40.7	50.0	37.8
Other state	9.3	14.3	21.6
Total	100%	100%	100%

(b) Membership of social élite		
School	Yes (%)	No (%)
Major boarding	50.0	15.0
Other HMC	25.0	17.0
Total 'Public'	**75.0**	**32.0**
Other private	5.0	12.0
Grammar	20.0	43.0
Other state	0	14.0
Total	100%	100%

schools on their way. The self-employed professionals, on whose specialised skills the business class is increasingly dependent, are drawn disproportionately from the grammar and the minor public schools. These professionals have been able to market their skills at a high price for it is this occupational group which has the highest median income of the whole sample and this probably accounts for the fact that it is the grammar school and not the public school educated fathers who have the highest median income. This pattern is not reproduced in the ownership of capital, for again it is those who have been educated at the polar ends of the secondary education spectrum, the major boarding and the non-selective state schools, who are the most likely to own capital in excess of £100 000. Thus whilst it is possible to show that those who have had the experience of an education at a top public school are advantaged in some respects relative to their peers from the other schools, it is difficult to conclude that it is this particular form of schooling which is the source of their advantage.

The relationship between occupational class, élite membership, financial position and type of education is complicated by class of origin. Table 2.5 reminds us of the extent to which both the social élite and Class I are self-recruiting, 90 per cent of the members of the social élite are at least second generation members of Class I as are 46 per cent of all the Class I men.

From Table 2.11 it can be seen that there is a direct relationship between class of origin and type of secondary schooling such that a public school education is largely, but not exclusively, dependent upon Class I origins and therefore it is crucially important to attempt to disentangle the effects of schooling and of class of origin upon ultimate success. Once class of origin has been controlled for the advantages that appear to be associated with a public school education largely disappear. It has already been estimated that between 40 and 80 per cent of the members of the social élite have actually inherited their élite status and though type of schooling may help to consolidate this status it plays no part in initiating what is essentially a process of ascription on the basis of birth. A member of the landed gentry will remain so irrespective of the type of school that he attends and the inheritance of a substantial business enterprise is similarly independent of schooling. At best a public school education might assist in maintaining membership of the upper class. The four members of the social élite who have clearly achieved this position through their own efforts have done so without the advantage of a public school education but have been upwardly with the help of a grammar school education.

TABLE 2.11 *Relationship between fathers' class of origin and main forms of secondary education*

Type of school	Class of origin						
	I (71) (%)	II (10) (%)	III (14) (%)	IV (50) (%)	V (2) (%)	VI (12) (%)	VII (11) (%)
HMC boarding	42.0	30.0	20.0	16.0	0	0	0
HMC day	21.0	10.0	0	2.0	0	8.0	0
Other private	10.0	20.0	0	20.0	0	0	0
State grammar	26.0	40.0	67.0	48.0	100.0	75.0	18.0
Other state	1.0	0	13.0	14.0	0	17.0	82.0
Total	100%	100%	100%	100%	100%	100%	100%

TABLE 2.12 *Relationship between secondary education and class position of those fathers originating in Class I (n=70)*

	School			
Class	*Major boarding (%)*	*Other HMC (%)*	*Other private (%)*	*Grammar (%)*
I	81.0	91.3	57.1	83.3
II	4.8	4.3	28.6	5.6
IV	14.3	4.3	14.3	11.1
Total	100%	100%	100%	100%

A more general comparison of the results of the different forms of secondary schooling experienced by those fathers originating in Class I shows that those who have been grammar school educated are as likely to have remained in this class as are their public school educated peers.

The numbers are small but the variation between the grammar and the public schools is statistically insignificant. What Table 2.12 does clearly demonstrate is the relative failure of the non-HMC private schools to secure the class position of their Class I pupils, for it is those fathers who have been educated at these private schools who are significantly the least likely to have remained in Class I.

Not only are the public schools demonstrably no better than the grammar schools in assisting the men in this sample to remain in their original class, but they also fail to exhibit any distinctive qualities as the promoters of upward mobility – virtually all of those who originate in Classes II and III have succeeded in arriving in Class I, irrespective of the type of secondary schooling received. The financial status of those originating in the manual Classes V–VII has virtually denied them access to a public school education, but this has not prevented these fathers from achieving Class I positions, for the same proportions of grammar school educated fathers from the manual classes and public school educated fathers from Class I are to be found in Class I positions today. It is findings such as these which have enabled Heath[37] to describe the public schools as 'Fulfilling a role of perpetuation and transmission of privilege from one generation to another . . . leaving the grammar, technical and direct grant schools to act as the escalators of upward mobility'.

The fathers of today's public schoolboys who are themselves members of Class I have entered this class and the different occupations of which it is composed through a variety of different routes. The dominant mode of entry is through the inheritance of privilege, origins in Class I and education at a public school, and it is this which accounts for the preponderance of ex-public school pupils in the Class I occupations. The subsidiary modes of entry into Class I, each associated with approximately 17 per cent of the men in this class are: the inheritance of cultural capital in the form of origins in Classes I or II allied with a grammar school education and entrance from the remainder of the non-manual sector also via a grammar school education. Minority modes of entry are those of buying in from Classes II to IV, 8 per cent entered from a public school and 6 per cent from other private schools; winning a scholarship from the shopfloor, a method associated with only 9 per cent of the fathers who nevertheless account for 36 per cent of the employed professionals and finally mobility from the shopfloor without any obvious assistance – merely 5 per cent of the Class I fathers entered this way but they account for just over a fifth of the owners of large businesses.

The only sign that an education at one of Britain's top boarding schools might be an advantage in securing occupational position comes from the significantly high proportion of industrial managers who are recruited from these schools. It would appear from the limited evidence in this research that the opportunity to join the captains of industry is enhanced by an education at a top public school, supporting the findings of the Clements study that public school educated managers move into senior positions with greater speed. An alternative interpretation, supported by these findings, is that many of today's industrial managers are in fact yesterday's owners of industry. Unable to withstand the changing face of British capitalism they have been forced to sell their own companies to larger organisations and in the process have been able to secure their own position by remaining with the parent company in a managerial capacity. The fact that they have been public school educated is purely incidental to this process. What they are unable to secure is the position of their own sons.

Together with the small number of professionals in Class II and the Class IV farmers and proprietors of small businesses, these are the parents of today's public schoolboys. Superficially, these pupils appear to have been recruited from a homogeneous background characterised by its location at the higher end of the occupational, financial and educational hierarchies. The parents' positions within the social division of labour orientates them towards the capitalist rather than the proletarian class. Nevertheless, the origins, experiences and even current material position of these parents are sufficiently diverse to suggest that their common position within the social division of labour has not been consolidated to form a unified social class but that factions can be identified, each with its own social network and distinctive normative framework.

The significance of these findings is limited both by the social context within which they have taken place and the design of the research itself. This research has concentrated upon a self-selected group of people, those who are able to pay for the education of their sons; hence it under-estimates the extent of downward mobility amongst public school educated fathers who can no longer afford to pay the school fees and it focuses attention upon the successful as opposed to the unsuccessful grammar school educated fathers. Halsey's[38] findings show a considerable exodus from the private sector in the sense that 52 per cent of the sample members who had at least one parent privately educated at secondary level had not received a similar education themselves, 31 per cent had been to a grammar school and 21 per cent to a totally non-selective school. Further unpublished details of the findings of the Oxford Mobility Studies,[39] which cover the whole male population between the ages of twenty and sixty, do however lend support to this research's conclusions about the relationship between education and class position. Confining the analysis to class position without providing the detail of occupational and financial status these unpublished details confirm that once class of origin has been controlled for the grammar schools are seen to be as effective as the public schools both in securing the class position of those originating in Class I and in promoting mobility into this class. It is the other private schools, used by a larger proportion of those in Class IV than of those in any other class, which are less successful in assisting their pupils to achieve such mobility. Finally, the figures show how the non-selective state schools largely fail to locate their pupils (irrespective of their social origins) in Class I occupations.

The fathers interviewed in this research and, in the case of the later cohorts at least, in the Oxford Mobility Studies, were building their careers during a period of economic expansion which fostered the growth of 'room at the top', hence the opportunities for the upward mobility of the grammar school educated fathers. Their sons are currently being educated in a totally different economic climate, one which may herald long term contraction of employment opportunities such that downward mobility will be the order of the day. This, in conjunction with the virtual demise of the grammar schools, may mean that a public school education is all that remains to confer occupational advantage.

3 The Parents' Social Networks

In the previous chapter it was seen that a third of the families using the public schools today are to be found in 'top positions' in the variety of senses in which the term is used. The remainder are embedded in sections or factions of the middle class and whilst they share economic and occupational positions which can be defined as privileged they are in turn, like some of the top people, drawn from a wide range of social and educational backgrounds. The parents are involved in a series of networks and as such participate in the formation of the occupational and economic networks as discussed in Chapter 2 as well as in those which are based upon kin, friendships and community. The social relationships engendered by these informal networks vary in terms of depth, range and content. Mitchell[1] distinguishes between the morphological and the interactional links of networks: the former relates to the patterning of the links of which the networks are constituted, describing their structure and composition; the interactional characteristics define the nature of these links (which vary in intensity, frequency and durability), and show how different networks serve many functions, both instrumental and expressive. Although individuals are constrained in the choice of the members of their kin network they are relatively free to choose the form and amount of interaction in which they engage with kin whilst membership of friendship and community based networks is largely a matter of choice. Blau[2] has stressed the importance of the norm of reciprocity in human behaviour such that where relationships are free from the sort of external constraints that are to be found in occupational and kin networks, people will typically seek interaction with those who are approximately their social equals with the result that situations of subordination and superordination are less likely to arise. It is in this sense that membership of friendship and community networks is largely a matter of choice and the composition of these networks reveals with whom people actually choose to spend their leisure time. Whilst the purpose of these networks is largely expressive they nevertheless do perform a range of instrumental functions.

Our concern with the social networks of the parents is manifestly threefold: initially they provide an example of the strategy of social closure whereby individuals seek to exclude those who are in different (usually inferior) positions within the social hierarchy. Such exclusion may be symptomatic of mere status differences with different life-styles and few shared interests, or it might be the product of the desire of those long-established in their class to limit access to social and economic opportunities whilst those who have been upwardly mobile seek to purge themselves of the reminders of their more humble past. More specifically, the research affords the opportunity to examine the role that a public school education plays in the formation of friendship networks which serve to supplement or possibly replace kin as a source of mutual aid, both financial and in kind, providing the means of entry into the 'old-boy' network and forming the basis of direct personal ties. Finally, interest turns upon the issue of community involvement and whether there is any evidence that those who have been educated in the public schools are both more involved and more active in community associations, evidence which could be used to support the idea that one of the primary purposes of such an education is to integrate its pupils around the norm of service to the community.

Various studies have documented the morphological and interactional characteristics of the kin networks of the different social classes and in particular have focused upon the effects of social mobility on the relationships between kin members. Titmuss[3] has provided a careful analysis of the manner in which the members of (financial) upper class families are locked into a web of complex financial arrangements which are used to minimise the effects of taxation. The laws governing the transfer of wealth during and after one's lifetime have become increasingly complex since Titmuss produced his account but the effect of this has been to produce a corresponding increase in the sophistication of the responses from the wealth holders and their financial advisers such that the web is drawn more tightly and (notwithstanding their separation by geographical and social mobility), family members are bound together more closely. Lupton and Wilson[4] show in a frequently quoted but equally dated study how the kinship connections of the directors of the leading financial institutions not only interlock in the city but extend to include senior members of parliament and of the civil service. With the possible exception of the interest that has been shown in the use of boarding schools for the socialisation of their young and the possible effects that this has upon the development of personality, concern with the family life of the upper classes has largely been confined to a consideration of this arrangement of their financial affairs. Contrasted with the cool calculations of the upper class and its orientation towards the preservation of family wealth, is the characterisation of the warmth and spontaneity of working class family life as typified by the Young and Willmott[5] study of the East End of London where cultural and material deprivation has served to bind family members into a network characterised by the exchange of services, knowledge and care. Geographical mobility has been shown to disrupt the intensity of this network but not to result in its replacement by a community based network. Ties with kin are maintained although distance inevitably means that physical contact becomes less frequent and neighbours are likely to become sources of social contact and the exchange of services such as child minding, although it is still the family to which individuals turn for deeper rooted support.

Filling the vacuum between these two stereotypes at the polar ends of the class spectrum is the middle class family. Typified by Parsons as the victim of the increasingly mobile industrial society, likely to be cut off from effective contact with kin as a result of both geographical and social mobility, but portrayed by some as possessing the skills necessary to engage in secondary relationships of some considerable depth, the middle class family was the object of much sociological research in the 1960s both in America and Britain. A notable example is Bell's[6] study of the middle class families in Swansea. In this he showed how the middle class family is both alive and well and he reveals the importance of its male links inasmuch as they serve to transfer cash between fathers and their sons and sons-in-law, particularly on socially approved occasions such as the birth of children, Christmas and so on. These links are additional to and do not replace the social contact which continues between mothers and daughters. The impact of mobility, both social and geographical, may serve to dilute the strength but not the quality of both the male and the female linkages for where the families he studied have been geographically mobile it is obviously difficult for social contacts to occur with great frequency, whilst those who have experienced social mobility could not expect financial aid of the same magnitude as that received by their socially immobile peers. More recently, Goldthorpe and Llewellyn[7] have sought to test the hypothesis that social mobility is disruptive of kin relations and they conclude that once the effects of geographical mobility have been controlled for there is no difference, in terms of frequency of contact, either between the socially mobile and immobile members of the service class or between the service class and those who have remained in the manual Classes VI and VII. But the nature of the contact between kin differs between the members of these three groups inasmuch as whilst all of them turn to their kin at times of real need those who have experienced upward mobility into Class I do see less of their kin as leisure associates than do the stable members of either Class I or of Classes VI–VII.

CONTACT WITH KIN

There is little amongst the findings about the contact that parents in this sample have with members of their extended families to suggest that they differ significantly from those studied by Goldthorpe and Llewellyn. Although the distinction between contact with kin and their identification as leisure associates was not made, contact through work was excluded. The evidence in Table 3.1 suggests that the frequency of contact between the parents in the sample and their own parents and siblings is mediated by geography rather than by other variables, for social mobility serves to place neither physical nor social distance between the parents studied and their relatives. There is no reason to believe that the small number of parents in the sample who have been upwardly mobile have achieved this at the expense of the disruption of kin relationships. By way of illustration, one mother, the wife of a wealthy but self-made factory owner, suffered a mild heart attack just prior to the scheduled interview and was being cared for by her sister whilst the interview went ahead with her husband.

Such variations as are to be found in the contact with kin are typically the greater amount of contact with parents than with siblings, and the propensity for the frequency with which the mothers see their kin to exceed the corresponding contact between the husbands and the members of their extended families. This latter finding may be partly due to the greater amount of time that is available to women to engage in social contact during the day rather than to greater proximity, for the fathers tend to live closer to their own

TABLE 3.1 *Respondents' frequency of contact with their parents*

	Proximity							
	Within same town		*Up to three hours drive*		*More than three hours*		*Abroad*	
Frequency seen								
	Men (%) (58)	*Women (%)* (51)	*Men (%)* (22)	*Women (%)* (26)	*Men (%)* (15)	*Women (%)* (26)	*Men (%)* (10)	*Women (%)* (11)
Daily	22.0	33.0	0	0	0	0	0	0
Weekly	43.0	47.0	14.0	12.0	0	4.0	0	0
Fortnightly	14.0	14.0	9.0	19.0	0	0	0	0
Minimum monthly	14.0	0	9.0	35.0	0	4.0	0	0
Minimum quarterly	5.0	4.0	50.0	15.0	33.0	62.0	10.0	9.0
Once or twice a year	2.0	2.0	18.0	19.0	47.0	31.0	10.0	27.0
Rarely	0	0	0	0	20.0	0	80.0	64.0
Total	100%	100%	100%	100%	100%	100%	100%	100%

parents than do the mothers. This variation in frequency of contact is particularly marked amongst the spouses who have parents living in the same town which enables a third of the women but less than a quarter of the men to see their parents daily. However, even when visiting can necessitate anything up to three hours driving, it is the wife's parents who are likely to be seen more often than the husband's confirming that in this sense women of all classes remain more strongly bonded to their parents than do their husbands. The parents in this sample are less likely to be as close to their siblings, either in a geographical sense or in terms of frequency of contact, 32 per cent of the fathers and 27 per cent of the mothers have brothers or sisters living in the same town but in each case even weekly contact is the exception rather than the norm.

The numbers are too small to enable a full analysis of the relationship between class, social origins and contact with kin but an examination of the main groups within the sample, those who are stable members of Classes I and IV and those who have been mobile into Class I either from a non-manual or a manual background, shows that, once geographical proximity has been controlled for, there are no significant differences between these various groups with respect to the frequency of their contact with kin. A possible exception to this generalisation is the very regular contact that is maintained by the fathers who are stable members of Class IV. From Tables 3.2 and 3.3 it can be seen that not only to do these men live closer to their parents than do any other men in the sample, but they also see them with the greatest frequency. This could be the result of the occupational composition of Class IV, the self-employed farmers and proprietors, and it is possible that these fathers have been unable to disentangle purely social contacts from those generated by working in the family business. The fact, noted in the previous chapter, that some of the men are responsible for the management of family enterprises whilst the legal ownership remains in the hands of their widowed mothers could be a contributory factor to this difficulty in distinguishing between voluntary social contact and that which is almost an obligation enforced by the division between legal ownership and daily management.

However, in line with Parsons' thesis of the disruption of kin relations caused by mobility, interest turns primarily on the differences between those who are static and those who are mobile members of Class I, and there is no evidence to be gleaned from the parents of today's public schoolboys that social mobility serves to disrupt the relationship with the kin of either the fathers or the mothers.

TABLE 3.2 *Respondents' geographical proximity to their own parents according to social mobility and sex*

Proximity	Static in Class I		Static in Class IV		Non-manual to Class I		Manual to Class I	
	Men (%)	Women (%)	Men (%)	Women (%)	Men (%)	Women (%)	Men (%)	Women (%)
Same town	54.0	38.0	85.0	68.0	35.0	25.0	64.0	38.0
Within 3 hrs drive	24.0	19.0	8.0	11.0	31.0	36.0	9.0	38.0
More than 3 hrs drive	8.0	31.0	8.0	22.0	21.0	25.0	18.0	25.0
Abroad	11.0	10.0	0	0	14.0	14.0	9.0	0
Total	100%	100%	100%	100%	100%	100%	100%	100%

TABLE 3.3   *Frequency of contact with parents according to social mobility and proximity*

	Static in Class I		Static in Class IV		Non-Manual to Class I		Manual to Class I	
	Men (%)	Women (%)	Men (%)	Women (%)	Men (%)	Women (%)	Men (%)	Women (%)
	(20)	(13)	(11)	(6)	(10)	(7)	(4)	(3)
Same town								
At least weekly	70.0	77.0	73.0	67.0	50.0	100.0	75.0	100.0
Fortnightly	10.0	7.0	0	33.0	40.0	0	0	0
Minimum monthly	10.0	0	27.0	0	0	0	25.0	0
Minimum quarterly	10.0	14.0	0	0	10.0	0	0	0
Total	100%	100%	100%	100%	100%	100%	100%	100%
Within 3	(%)	(%)	(%)	(%)	(%)	(%)	(%)	(%)
hours drive	(9)	(8)	(0)	(1)	(9)	(10)	(0)	(3)
At least weekly	22.0	0	—	0	11.0	30.0	—	0
Fortnightly	11.0	13.0	—	0	11.0	20.0	—	0
Maximum monthly	11.0	38.0	—	100.0	11.0	30.0	—	33.0
Maximum quarterly	33.0	25.0	—	0	67.0	0	—	33.0
Once or twice a year	22.0	25.0	—	0	0	20.0	—	3.0
Total	100%	100%	100%	100%	100%	100%	100%	100%

FRIENDSHIPS

The above findings confirm the evidence already collected over the past two decades which refutes Parsons thesis but it is the importance of the non-kin based networks of the middle and upper classes which remains of particular interest to this research. In the various studies of the élites[8] and of the upper classes[9] attempts have been made to document the existence of an 'old-boy' network which locks together into positions of power and prestige those who share not only kinship but a public school education. O'Donnell[10] claims that the schools serve as a basis for the formation of social contacts which become 'self-help clubs' later in life but, of even more lasting significance, is the part that they play in socialising their pupils into the norms, values and style of life of the existing members of the élite and the upper classes. This facilitates participation in the boardroom and other loci of power which provide the formal meeting ground of the rich and powerful as well as in the more informal settings of the London clubs, friends' homes and events in the social calendar. Bechhofer *et al.*[11] look at the changing economic base of post-war Britain and suggest that the growth of bureaucratisation and the consequent enlargement of the middle class makes it increasingly difficult for all but a few to preserve their distinctive identity and to maintain such social networks. One landed member of the social élite explained how he has had to broaden his friendship network since marrying his second wife who is in 'the professional circles' and how inflation is making it increasingly difficult for him to preserve his distinctive life-style. An example of this is rising expense of membership of the London clubs and the consequent fall in the number of their members has been noted by Stanworth and Giddens.[12]

Both Bell[13] and the Pahls[14] have stressed the importance of friendship networks to the middle class and these stand in marked contrast to both the 'old-boy' network of the upper class and to the chance encounters with neighbours which form the basis of much of the non-kin based social life of the members of the working class. Friendship is an essentially spontaneous, unselfconscious act but it does require certain skills to both initially identify and contact those with similar interests and to subsequently sustain long-term friendships, frequently bridging great geographical distances. Members of the middle class have been represented as possessing a virtual monopoly of these skills. Thus Young and Willmott in describing working class community life in Bethnal Green[15] emphasised the importance of the 'doorstep community' with most of the social contact between non-kin taking place outside the home. Similarly, the Pahls contrasted the managers' wives who came from manual backgrounds and tended to have expressive friendships with neighbours, with the more educated and non-mobile members of their class who were more 'friend orientated'. Bell quotes Herbert Gans as saying that 'proximity is not enough to create intense relationships' and in mapping out the friendships on the estates that he studied, Bell found the attitudes, habits and aspirations of the residents to be more important than the siting of their houses when it came to forming friendships.

Friendships based on shared attitudes and habits are capable of withstanding spatial and temporal separation for Bell also found evidence of the existence of 'suspended primary groups', friendships which were dormant as the result of geographical mobility but which could readily be re-activated.

Consequent upon Parsons' earlier thesis of the disruption of the kin relations of mobile individuals is the more general 'dissociative' effect that mobility produces such that these people will be in a permanent state of marginality, caught between those whom they have outgrown and those who are unwilling to accept them as their social equals.[16] But the counter-thesis is that such mobile individuals will in fact tend to develop social skills in the course of their careers which will enable them to form congenial and supportive networks to replace those lost by the experience of mobility.[17] Goldthorpe and Llewellyn[18] distinguish between spare-time associates and good friends in their application of these alternative theses to Britain. They find that whilst there is little that differentiates the main groups whom they consider (the stable members of both the service and the manual classes and those who have been mobile into the service class) with respect to the number of spare-time associates that each is able to identify, there is a marked difference in the extent, source and composition of their friendships. The stable members of the service class reported the highest number of good friends and drew almost exclusively upon others in the service class for these friendships but their associates were more widely based. Those who had been mobile into the service class, did list more good friends than the stable members of the manual class, but they occupied an intermediary position between the two stable groups in terms of both the average number of good friends that each reported and the proportion of such friends who were members of the service class. It is interesting to note that Goldthorpe and Llewellyn found that the experience of downward mobility from the service class appears to have succeeded in dislocating early friendships, for the downwardly mobile report a smaller total number of friends and a lower percentage of service class members than those who have experienced mobility in the opposite direction. The interviews in this research confined the discussion to good friends rather than spare-time associates in the belief that it is the former who are more likely to form the basis of a social network which provides the sort of mutual aid which a public school education initiates. Parents were keenly aware of the distinction to be made between good friends and acquaintances when the interactional aspects of their social networks were being discussed and whilst they have a high degree of social contact with the latter, real friends are seen as those who have survived the test of time and distance. Occasionally a parent would come to doubt the distinctive value of such friendships, an example being the mother who was divorcing her husband and in the process found that 'ordinary people' had turned out to be very good friends to her.

In addition to omitting information about spare-time associates or acquaintances, the information obtained about friends, Table 3.4, is not strictly comparable with that used by Goldthorpe and Llewellyn inasmuch as the parents were asked to talk about good friends in general but not to identify and limit the discussion to any number up to three, although 5 per cent of the couples interviewed did volunteer that they had no good friends. Neither were the parents asked about the occupations of their friends in sufficient detail to enable these to be allocated to classes with any certainty but parents did report friends from a limited range of occupations, all of them non-manual, with a very strong emphasis placed on the professions.

The term 'professionals' was used by so many parents to describe at least some of their friends as to suggest that its use was being extended to include all those occupations which require some form of educational qualification and not merely to denote those that are strictly consistent with membership of a clearly identifiable corporate body, for in general it is the fathers who have had some further education who are the most like to include the term 'professionals' in

TABLE 3.4 *(a) Friends' occupations mentioned by respondents and (b) those mentioning friends with similar occupations to their own*

Friends' occupations*	(a) (%)	(b) (%)
The professions	62.0	83.0
Owners of small business	32.0	65.0
Middle management or clerical	19.0	—
Farming	17.0	83.0
Senior management	14.0	16.0
Owners of large businesses	10.0	23.0
Army	7.0	—
City	6.0	—

* These do not total 100% as respondents included several occupations in the description of their friends.

the occupational description of their friends. An accountant who is now a stockbroker said:

> Our friends do not just happen to be professionals – we are like them. . .

An alternative explanation of the widespread use of this term is suggested by the position of the father just quoted. Like him, many people who qualify in the professions are genuinely laterally mobile and move into management or entrepreneurship but are still thought of as professionals by their friends. This is just part of the complexity which characterises the manner in which people choose their friends and when another father said 'birds of a feather flock together' he was essentially correct for there is little to suggest that friends are chosen at random but rather that choice is constrained by a number of factors. Sixty per cent of all the parents interviewed used more than one occupational title to describe their friends but they tend to confine these to occupations which are either similar to their own, or which bear some relationship to their social origins. The clearest example of this is to be found in the description that the successful entrepreneurs, the owners of large business enterprises, give of their friends' occupations. It is only those who originate in Class I (the inheritors) who are linked through friendship to the owners of other large companies, although nearly a third of them do also have friends who own small businesses. The fathers who have been mobile into big business (the genuine entrepreneurs) confine their close friend-ships amongst businessmen to those who remain part of the *petit bourgeoisie* – the small businessmen – as do those who have remained part of this class.

The interplay between origins and current class position is also clearly to be seen when looking at those who number managers amongst their friends. Such parents are drawn from a cross-section of all the occupational groups represented in the sample but those who originate in the manual classes never include senior managers amongst their close friends and there is in general an inverse relation-ship between class of origin and the naming of middle managers and clerical workers as friends such that those with Class I origins are the least likely to do so.

The most endogamous of all occupational groups represented in the sample are the farmers and, it would appear, the professionals. Eighty-three per cent of each of these groups include others from the same or similar occupations when naming their friends and whilst 23 per cent of the former confine all their friendships to those with other farmers, nearly a half of the genuine professional members of the sample name only others who they in turn describe as 'professionals' but this may be the result of the elasticity of the term. The experience of social mobility, or lack of it, does not appear to affect the extent to which the professional fathers number other professionals amongst their friends for those who have been upwardly mobile as a result of their entry into a profession are as likely to describe their friends in these terms as are those who originate in Class I. There is insufficient detail to establish whether the professionals who have upwardly mobile are in fact forming friendships with other professionals who share this experience, but that this might be the case is suggested by the fact that it is rare for a professional who has had a full-time further education to include the proprietors of small businesses amongst their friends but those who have achieved their professional status by part-time study are much more likely to do so. This suggests that they are maintaining their social relationships with those of lower social origin and possibly therefore are friends with other professionals who have also been upwardly mobile.

Notwithstanding the addition that these findings make to the existing body of knowledge about the formation of friendships between factions of the middle class, it is the 'old-boy' network which centres on the city and the friendships of its members which lies at the heart of the interest in the friendships generated by the public schools. Various attempts were made in the previous chapter to distinguish and define those who inhabit the apex of Britain's class structure and a number of distinct but over-lapping groups were identified: an occupational élite, a social élite, a financial élite and finally an educational élite – those who had themselves received a public school education. A consideration of the interaction with kin of the members of these varying élites offers nothing to suggest that they differ in any way from the remainder of the sample for, once geographical distance from kin has been controlled for, the frequency of contact between members of the various élites and their parents and siblings is equal to that of the rest of those interviewed. However, there is evidence to show that the composition of the friendship networks of these various élites differs markedly both from those of the other parents and from each other. The occupational élites, in keeping with the fact that of all the élites it is the most representative of the whole sample, does not differ from the rest of the sample in the occupational spread of its friends but consistent with the fact that it is composed mainly of the chairmen and managing directors of large companies, a significantly higher proportion of its members include the proprietors of other large businesses amongst their friends.

The members of the financial élite, the upper class, are not unified in their choice of friends but vary according to what appears to be the source of their wealth. Levels of earned income alone do not serve to distinguish friends in occupational terms, except that those who earn less than £12 000 per annum do not have friends in the city and the relationship between income and friends with clerical or middle managerial jobs is an inverse one, high earners rarely have such friends. The smaller number, only 6 per cent of the respondents, who claim to have friends 'in the city' are most likely in occupational terms to be the higher grade administrators and officials, the senior civil servants and the managers in commerce and government, and in financial terms to be those with substantial amounts of investment income, in excess of £5000 p.a. The friendships of those who have been termed 'wealthy' – the owners of capital that exceeds £100 000 – reflects the influence of occupation and origins upon choice of friends, for those with capital in excess of £200 000 are much the most likely to have friends who are farmers and those with capital in the range £50 000 to £200 000 have as their friends the large proprietors. Those reporting friends who are the owners of small businesses divide between two categories of wealth holders: those owning £20 000 to £50 000 and those owning more than £200 000, the latter representing those who have been successful in their business activities but who have maintained their contact with their less successful peers.

It is the members of the social élite who display the clearest and most stereotyped pattern in their choice of friends, selecting them disproportionately from those who are in the city, are senior managers but not middle ones and are the owners of large business enterprises but rarely of small ones. In their choices of friends they provide a further example of the closed nature of the social network of which they are a part.

How the parents have been educated and in particular the form of their secondary education, is an important indication of whom they are likely to choose as their friends. It has just been noted how the members of the social élite, a collectivity which is virtually closed to the upwardly mobile and state educated alike, form their friendships with those from a select group of occupations and this finding is repeated in a consideration of how the couples where the husband has been to a public school choose their friends. The widespread practice amongst this sample of naming 'professionals' when describing friends has already been discussed and it is only those who have succeeded without any form of selective secondary education, private or state, who virtually exclude members of the professions from their list of friends. Conversely, the fathers who have had a public school education are significantly more likely than any of the others to include senior managers and the owners of large businesses amongst their friends whilst any mention of friends in the city is virtually confined to those amongst the public school educated who have been to one of the well known boarding schools, giving a glimpse of the 'old-boy' network which survives in the city where attendance at the right school is still considered to be of importance.

How important is education more generally in the choice of friends of those who are currently using the public schools for the education of their sons? Are those who are first generation parents excluded not only from the 'old-boy' network which plays an important part in our financial institutions but also from the larger network of the public school educated which operates at various points in the economy? It has been seen that friendship networks are largely composed of those who share similar occupational experiences and frequently similar class origins and it is the professions which have shown themselves to be the melting pot of the middle class, increasingly broad both in terms of the occupations that they encompass and the social origins of those who they include. Whether this melting pot conceals factions which are relationally segregated according to social origins, type of education and wealth cannot be fully determined from the available data. As Tables 3.5 and 3.6 show, parents acquire their friends in many different ways and have known them for varying lengths of time. Whilst 30 per cent of all parents identify school as the source of some of their friendships it is only one amongst many different sources and never the most important. School is of greater significance in the formation of lifelong friendships for those fathers (but not the mothers) who have been totally privately educated than it is for the remainder and this is reflected in the fact that 48 per cent of the fathers who have themselves been educated at a major boarding school do identify school as the place where they formed at least some of their current friendships.

Notwithstanding this and Bell's[19] assertion that attitude, habit and aspirations are more important than siting of homes when it

TABLE 3.5 *Origins of friendships and fathers' secondary schooling*

| Origin of friendship* | Fathers' secondary school | | | | |
	Boarding (%)	Other public school (%)	Other private (%)	State (%)	Total (%)
Current or ex-neighbour	55.0	31.0	42.0	44.0	42.0
Husband's or wife's work	18.0	39.0	32.0	29.0	30.0
School	48.0	39.0	26.0	24.0	30.0
Other (clubs, childrens' schools, etc.)	41.0	35.0	16.0	23.0	29.0
University	14.0	15.0	11.0	8.0	11.0

* Percentages do not total 100% as more than one source of friendship is mentioned by the parents.

comes to the formation of friendship, geographical proximity enabling regular contact is obviously important if not sufficient for the formation of friendships in general and by these parents in particular. The exceptions, those less likely to have formed close friendships with neighbours, are the farmers who are geographically very isolated and the university graduates, those who have been to Oxbridge are particularly likely to keep the friends made during their university days. Despite the importance of the friendships formed at public school, these obviously do not prevent the public school educated fathers from forming other close friendships later in life for Table 3.6 shows that they report as high a percentage of close friendships made in adult life as those who were educated in the state schools.

Thus the social contacts made at school take their place alongside many others which are the basis of the friendships that parents count as important today. This may go some way towards explaining why more than half of the men who have been educated at a public school share with a similar proportion of those who have not the belief that the type of education that a person has had does not matter when it comes to the formation of friendships (Table 3.7).

It is interesting to note that it is the fathers who are at the polar end of the educational spectrum who attach the most importance to the type of secondary education that an individual has received. This question was in fact prompted by one secondary modern school educated father who early in the interviewing stage described in great

TABLE 3.6 *Average length of time that close friends have been known and father's secondary schooling*

Length of time friends' known on average	Public school (52) (%)	Other private or state school (87) (%)	Total (139) (%)
Since school	11.5	13.7	13.0
Since youth or university	4.0	9.0	7.0
Long time	27.0	26.0	27.0
Mixture	27.0	14.0	19.0
Adulthood	31.0	37.0	34.5
Total	100%	100%	100%

TABLE 3.7 *Does a public school education matter?*

	Fathers' secondary school					
	Major boarding (29) (%)	Other HMC (17) (%)	Other private (15) (%)	State grammar (48) (%)	Other state (18) (%)	Total (127) (%)
No/other things count	31.0	53.0	53.0	46.0	34.0	42.0
No longer	10.0	12.0	0.0	4.0	6.0	7.0
Ambivalent	7.0	0	13.0	4.0	6.0	5.0
Yes	52.0	36.0	33.0	44.0	56.0	46.0
Total	100%	100%	100%	100%	100%	100%

detail the difficulty that he experienced in socialising with the other parents at his son's boarding school, feeling himself to be largely excluded by them. Whilst many other parents believed his perceptions to be totally without foundation or a thing of the past:

> people who mind about where you have been to school are diminishing as they are being out-numbered

was one grammar school educated father's reaction, others provided details of why they feel that type of education does still matter. In describing an evening he had recently spent with neighbours, one public school educated father explained how 'ex-public school people have dinner parties but others have cold buffets'. As trivial as such differences in custom are, they undoubtedly do place a strain on social relationships and therefore contribute to the erection of effective barriers between people. Although many parents are reluctant to acknowledge or to admit the importance of the form of education in the formation of friendships, Table 3.8 does show that even if they do not actually meet their friends at school they do show a marked tendency to select them from amongst those who share their educational experiences. The distinction made in Table 3.8 between friends who have had a public education and those who are predominantly privately educated is probably arbitrary for it reflects the terms used by the parents themselves.

This shows that effectively an 'old boy' network is formed of those who have been public school educated which serves to exclude, deliberately or otherwise, those who have not. The true significance of this lies in the actual effects of such exclusion rather than in whether it is the result of a deliberate attempt to restrict access to the rewards conventionally associated with public school education or merely an unintended consequence of people choosing to spend their

TABLE 3.8   *Reported education of friends and (a) fathers' secondary school, (b) extent of parents' combined education in the maintained sector*

	Don't know	*Public school*	*Mainly private*	*Mixed*	*Grammar*	*State*	*Total*
			Education of friends				
(a) Fathers' secondary school							
Major board (%)	6.5	26.0	55.0	13.0	0	0	100%
Other HMC (%)	0	7.0	48.0	18.5	11.0	15.0	100%
Other private (%)	6.0	6.0	22.0	39.0	0	28.0	100%
State Grammar (%)	3.0	0	23.0	22.0	20.0	32.0	100%
(b) Combined state education							
None (%)	1.5	14.5	55.0	21.0	3.0	5.0	100%
Mixed (%)	4.0	9.0	26.0	35.0	9.0	17.5	100%
Total (%)	5.0	0	13.0	17.5	21.0	43.5	100%

leisure with those who share a common subculture and way of life. However, findings such as these do suggest that the exclusionary class of modern capitalism is more narrowly based than that which is formed out of the fusion of property and credentials, as implied by Parkin.[20] They do not deny that property and credentials have fused but the fact that 70 per cent of public school educated but less than a quarter of the grammar school educated professionals have friends who are themselves predominantly privately educated does lend support to the long held view that a public school education cannot be dismissed as an important contributory factor in the formation of the exclusionary class. Any answer to the question of whether an 'old boy' network is effectively an exclusionary class in the sense that it seeks to restrict access to resources and opportunities must depend upon the nature of its interactional links but a final answer is beyond the scope of this book.

THE INTERACTION BETWEEN NETWORK MEMBERS

Both Coleman and Hobsbawm discuss the importance of social networks in the nineteenth century. Coleman,[21] in describing the burgeoning of the public schools in the second half of the century, refers to the growing importance of the old school tie and how it came to replace family connections, whilst Hobsbawm[22] includes the public school as one of a number of forms of educational institutions which generate the formation of networks

> the classical recourse of the bourgeoisie in trouble or with cause for complaint was to exercise or to ask for personal influence: to have a word with the major. . . the old school or college comrade, the business contact or kinsman.

Is there any evidence to be gleaned from the interviews with the parents to suggest that the old school tie is indeed an important source of mutual aid today or that the schools continue to dominate community life? It has already been shown in the previous chapter that class of origin and not a public school education *per se* was the key determinant of access to Class I positions at the time that the grammar schools were still in existence. Whilst it is difficult to disentangle the effects of education and of inheritance upon incumbency of élite positions, it would appear that access to such positions is primarily determined by family membership as opposed to type of education and therefore one needs to consider carefully the manner in which interaction between members of social networks who share a common educational background can be qualitatively superior to that which is fostered by the family network. Goldthorpe and Llewellyn[23] have looked in considerable detail at the relative merits of the social and kin based networks of factions of both the service and the manual classes and the role that members of each are expected to play in a number of scenarios, ranging from borrowing a tool to caring for young children during the absence of the mother, each one demanding an increased level of commitment to that which precedes it. In general they found that members of all the classes under consideration relied increasingly upon kin the more demanding the assistance needed. In line with some of the earlier studies comparing middle and working class families, that of Goldthorpe and Llewellyn contains the hint of a suggestion that the stable members of Class I, and to a lesser extent those who have been downwardly mobile from this position, are slightly less likely than their manual counterparts to call upon their kin even under the most demanding of the circumstances suggested, looking instead to friends, neighbours and other sources of assistance. Once again, the findings of this research are not strictly comparable to those of Goldthorpe and Llwellyn's inasmuch as the range of circumstances requiring assistance from kin or friends which were suggested to the parents were more demanding than those presented to the respondents in Goldthorpe and Llewellyn's study. It was somewhat difficult and rather unnecessary to ask parents who were ostensibly being interviewed about the advantages of a private education to whom they would turn if they needed to borrow a hammer and therefore they were only asked about giving and receiving help of considerably more substance: who would they be prepared to assist and to whom would they turn either if help was needed with the care of a relative for a minimum period of a week or if they needed to call upon a significant but not necessarily substantial amount of money. It was not possible to attach an exact value to the amount of money under discussion as people vary both in their attitude towards money and in the amounts that they have at their disposal, thus one hundred pounds may represent no less a sacrifice to one person than a thousand does to another, but if parents asked for an explanation of what was meant by a 'significant amount' assistance with the payment of school fees was given as an example. This rules out many of the forms of financial aid identified by Bell as well as any direct discussion about the sorts of advantages that membership of the 'old-boy' network normally brings but the questions about sources of aid were located in the context of the importance of family and friends in helping one to get along in life and some parents did volunteer information about alternative forms of assistance that they would be prepared to give and expect to receive, showing that help comes in many ways. In addition, information was obtained from the fathers about the amount and type of help that they had received in building their own careers and whilst this does go some way towards mitigating the effects of the absence of any direct questions about the value of the old school tie (the importance of which it has already been shown is under-estimated by the parents when discussing its role in the formation of friendships) it can only add a small amount to the limited assessment of the relative importance of friends and kin in the provision of mutual aid of varying significance.

Help in kind

Only 7 per cent of the couples interviewed are totally excluded from the web of exchange of services, relying entirely on the market or other agencies for assistance in times of need. For the remainder, the relationship between giving and receiving is not always a symmetrical one for nearly one in ten are prepared to give help in kind but do not expect to receive it, and conversely 7 per cent feel unable to give but do expect that their families or even their friends will provide assistance if called upon to do so. But the majority of parents, more than three-quarters, are involved in a network of reciprocity in which the family remains the single most important source of aid, even for those in the upper echelons of the class structure. More than 60 per cent of the respondents feel that they can look with confidence to a member of their extended family for help in times of need, but only a third of them would look to their friends for assistance of this nature. It is interesting to note the extent to which people show a greater readiness to offer help to non-kin than to expect or to ask for it: whereas more than four-fifths of those who are prepared to help members of their family are confident that they would receive similar help in return, little over a half of those who are willing to assist friends would seek reciprocation, indicating some of the uncertainties which underlie even good friendships. This reaches its apogee in the

TABLE 3.9 *The exchange of help in kind*

Would expect help from	Would give help to				*As a proportion of the total*	*Proportion of instances involving help from*	
	Nobody (25) (%)	*Family only* (59) (%)	*Both family and Friends* (59) (%)	*Friends only* (38) (%)		*Family* (114)	*Friends* (63)
Nobody	20.0	5.1	1.7	5.3	0.06		
Family only	36.0	79.7	47.5	13.2	0.49	∧ 0.63	
Both family and friends	4.0	1.7	39.0	0	0.14	>	
Friends only	12.0	5.1	6.8	73.7	0.21		
Pay	28.0	8.5	5.1	7.9	0.10		∧ 0.35 >
Total	100%	100%	100%	100%	100%		
Proportion of instances involving help to:							
Family (118)		< 0.65	∧ 0.54	>			
Friends (97)		<		>			

pattern of exchange between members of the social élite and their friends for whereas nearly a half of them are prepared to help their friends in times of need, only 5 per cent would in fact seek similar help, relying instead largely on paid help. Essentially it is those parents who originate in Classes I and II, the service class, who are significantly less likely than either their upwardly mobile counterparts or those who are stable in Class IV, to turn to their families in times of need. This is reflected in the differences between the members and non-members of the social élite and between those who have been privately educated and those who have not, but it finds its clearest expression in families where the father has been to one of the prestigious boarding schools for it is here that family bonds appear to be at their weakest. However, this is not true when it comes to readiness to give help to the extended family for the variations in the identification of family members as a potential source of help are not to be found here or amongst the friendship based mutual aid networks, in both these instances all the parents conform to an overall pattern that displays greater uniformity.

Another form of help in kind is assistance with embarking upon or building a career.

TABLE 3.10   *Percentage of fathers reporting any assistance in securing occupations*

	(%)
None	62.0
First occupation only	12.0
First occupation + 10 years later	5.0
Occupation 10 years after outset	1.0
Current occupation	2.0
Current and 10 years from outset	5.0
From outset of career to current occupation	13.0
Total	100%

Little more than a third of the fathers interviewed, Table 3.10, admitted to having received any help with building their careers, but when such assistance did come it was more usual to have received it earlier rather than later, although 13 per cent of the fathers have benefited from nepotism throughout their working lives. The form that help takes is either that of working in the family business or the use of personal contacts to assist in securing employment. It is the former which predominates and for this reason over 80 per cent of the stable members of Class IV have received help at some stage in their careers. Only 12 per cent of the fathers interviewed have been able to call upon personal contacts to assist them in their search for suitable employment and help was always confined to the outset of their careers. This usually took the form of an introduction by someone known to the family, such as the family solicitor, and only very occasionally were the fathers in this sample able to secure employment with a family friend or a distant relative. The use of personal contacts is virtually confined to the fathers originating in the service class who it can be presumed are the best endowed with such contacts. The small number who are stable members of Class II do not, by definition, have recourse to family firms to provide them with employment and are therefore totally dependent upon the use of family contacts and friends and distant relatives to help them climb the bottom rungs of their chosen careers. Those in Class I have benefited from both forms of assistance. The members of the social and the occupational élites are distinguished from the remainder of the sample inasmuch as they do receive more assistance with their careers but this comes at a relatively late stage and almost always takes the form of joining the family firm, suggesting that they have had to gain their earlier experiences elsewhere before being brought back as family employees.

In seeking to explore more carefully the role that a public school education plays in providing the necessary contacts for the enhancement of the careers of its pupils, one finds that it is indeed the fathers who have been to these schools who are the least likely to have proceeded unaided but yet again one finds that it is the family which emerges as the most important but not the exclusive source of assistance. Even at the outset of their careers where the use of contacts makes its sole contribution, twice as many of the fathers who were educated at the major boarding schools went into the family business (35 per cent) as made use of personal contacts (17 per cent). It is interesting to note how the fathers who were educated at the lesser known public schools have been able to combine both forms of help in building their careers. The fact that fewer of them than of their more illustriously educated peers had any help at the outset (36 per cent as opposed to 52 per cent) is due not to their inability to make use of personal contacts but to the fact that they are less likely to have joined the family enterprise at the outset of their careers. This is probably a reflection of the higher percentage of professionals amongst them who have needed to find articles with other firms, sometimes known to the family, before joining their own fathers, uncles or grandfathers in the family profession. Ten years after the outset of their careers an equal proportion, about a third, of all public school educated men were working in the family business be it in commerce, industry, farming or the professions. The fathers who were educated at the other private schools or at the grammar schools differ inasmuch as they are less likely to have had access to a family business at any stage of their careers, and this is particularly marked in the case of the grammar school educated fathers, but in particular they have rarely been able to make use of personal contacts in their occupational journey through life. The use of such connections by those who are public school educated can only be assumed but not proven to be based upon the old school tie but has to be viewed within the context of the markedly greater importance of the family as the source of this form of help in kind.

Financial Aid

No actual money has changed hands. Where it does come from is families do talk money. They set up trusts and act as each other's trustees. We have a trust in Jersey and a cousin who lives there is a trustee.

This, according to one of its members, is how the social élite arranges its financial aid. How widespread is this practice both amongst the members of the élite and more generally? The pattern of giving and receiving money is a complex one and, as Bell discovered, is surrounded by a sense of mystique and occasion. Thus the wife of the father just quoted, herself descended from the social élite, conceded that in times of genuine need help is forthcoming:

Three of his sisters have used state schools and have had no financial help but we would probably help if it was for a roof over their head or if they were starving.

and another father described the mutual aid pacts he had formed with his brothers, ensuring that in the event of the death of any one of them the family would be cared for. There is evidence, as can be seen in Table 3.11, that the parents are locked in a series of exchanges which, although on a much reduced scale to that which was found

TABLE 3.11 Giving and receiving financial help

Have given help to	Received help from						Have had from	
		Nobody						Inheritance As as proportion of total
	Expect none (94) (%)	Would look to Family (40) (%)	Would look to Friends (6) (%)	Family (24) (%)	Friends (2) (%)	Trusts (5) (%)	(8) (%)	(179) (%)
(a) Nobody	89.3	85.0	87.5	67.0	100	100	62.5	0.84
but would help:								
Nobody	50.0	20.0	0	20.8	100	40.0	37.5	0.38
Family	22.3	30.0	0	16.7	0	20.0	12.5	0.22
Friends	6.4	10.0	37.5	8.7	0	40.0	12.5	0.10
Either	10.6	25.0	50.0	20.8	0	0	0	0.16
Total who would help family	32.9	55.0	50.0	37.5	0	20.0	12.5	0.38
Total who would help friends	17.0	35.0	87.5	29.5	0	40.0	12.5	0.25
(b) Family	1.1	7.5	12.5	4.2	0	0	37.5	0.05
(c) Friends	9.6	7.5	0	29.2	0	0	0	0.11
Total	100%	100%	100%	100%	100%	100%	100%	
As a proportion of the total	0.53	0.22	0.04	0.14	0.01	0.03	0.05	

when considering the exchange of help in kind, does also indicate a greater readiness to give than expectation of receiving. A quarter of those interviewed exclude themselves totally from any giving or taking of financial help, but whereas just over a half of all the parents do not feel that they can turn to anyone for financial assistance, nearly two-thirds have either given financial help of some substance or would be prepared to do so. Again, the major discrepancy is between the numbers who have already received help from their friends or would look to them, less than 5 per cent, and those who would either be prepared to assist their friends or who have already done so, more than a third of those interviewed. The discrepancy between the giving and receiving of money within families is largely a result of the relatively early stage in their life-cycle in which this research found the parents. Although a fifth of the parents had already benefited from an inheritance, a family trust or the outright gift of money only 5 per cent of them had actually parted with any money to other family members, nevertheless more of them believe themselves to be prepared to give financial assistance if needed than willing to ask for it.

The giving and receiving of money is determined both by the ability and desire to do so and by actual and perceived need. There is a clear relationship between the help already received from the extended family, need and the ability of family members to provide financial support. Notwithstanding the widely stated reluctance to look outside the immediate family for financial support, where both partners in a marriage originate in either the service class or the *petit bourgeoisie* they are significantly more likely to have already profited financially than are those who originate in the manual classes or even than those who have intermarried across class. Similarly, need has proved to be of significance in activating family financial support, for amongst those with service class origins are fathers who have experienced downward mobility into Class IV and who, as a result, have probably required some financial assistance and they are indeed the most likely of all the fathers to have actually received such help from their extended kin.

Class I is a heterogeneous group of people with diverse origins who vary in their financial relationships with both their families and their friends. Contained within it are those who are second or even third generation members of this class who have had a public school education as well as many who have experienced upward mobility and who consequently are likely to have been educated at a grammar school or possibly a lesser known private school. It is the fathers within Class I who have been educated at the major boarding schools, the long established members of their class, who are the most likely to have actually benefited financially from their family membership both in the form of direct cash and as beneficiaries of family trusts.

Such variations with respect to having already received family money are not to be found when it comes to the readiness to seek help if it should become necessary to do so. Approximately a quarter of all the couples interviewed, irrespective of their social origins, would turn to members of their extended family for financial assistance should the need arise. There is no reason to believe that those in Class I who have already benefited financially have done so on account of need and thus, whereas the willingness to look to family should such a need arise in the future appears to depend upon the quality of the relationships within the family, the actual transfer of money is more likely to depend upon class position. It is amongst the established members of the upper and middle classes and in particular the social élite, those who have traditionally used the public boarding schools, that one finds confirmation of the existence of a well established financial web. The financial interchange with friends is more complex and the number of parents who would turn to them for help of this nature is too small to distinguish between them with any confidence but it does appear that there are some differences in the readiness to do so. Few of Class I as a whole and none of those who have been to a public school would be prepared to turn to their friends for financial help, it is only those who are stable members of Class IV or who have been upwardly mobile through the grammar schools who show any likelihood at all of using their friendships in this way.

When it comes to the giving of financial aid the picture is somewhat different for, as already discussed, there is a greater readiness to give, especially to friends, than there is to take and parents who are prepared to accept money from their families are more likely to give to their friends. Over a third of those who do not envisage giving financial help to anyone felt the need to qualify their position by saying that they do not possess the necessary resources to do so, but this is only partially supported by the available information about their financial status for whilst it is likely it is not inevitable that those with the highest income and largest amount of capital also show willingness to give help if required to do so. Financial wherewithal is not the only factor that is associated with readiness to provide financial assistance, for example more of the stable members of Class II, the poorest parents in the sample, both express a willingness to help friends and family alike if necessary and have already given such help to family members. Conversely, members of both the occupational and the social élites are amongst the highest earning fathers in the sample but they differ in their relationship with kith and kin. The occupational élite, many of whom have created their own financial success, are almost exclusively bound up with family in the sense that although little money has actually passed through their hands over a half of them said that they would help family members financially if called upon. Nearly as many of the social élite would do likewise but what distinguishes them from the occupational élite is the fact that they have already extended their support network to include their friends for a fifth of the members of the social élite have given financial assistance to friends. The social élite, drawn disproportionately from Britain's famous public schools, share with others who have been similarly educated and who are equally likely to be at least second generation members of Class I, this greater likelihood of having activated their friendship networks in order to provide material aid for its members.

What distinguishes the established members of Britain's middle and upper classes from both their more recent recruits and their less successful counterparts in the *petit bourgeoisie* is their relatively greater proven readiness to help friends financially and their corresponding lack of actual as opposed to declared support for their families. It is important to emphasise that the family remains the single most important source and object of help both in cash and in kind for the vast majority of parents using the public schools but, by definition, those parents who are clearly well established members of the *haute bourgeoisie* if not of the financial upper class are also members of families who are well placed financially and who are therefore unlikely to call upon other members for direct financial assistance. The fact that so few parents have looked to their friends for financial help or envisage doing so but appear to be as prepared to help them as they are to help family members is probably the result of their own lack of need rather than an indication of the total emptiness of social networks, of which that formed around the old school tie is only one example. The importance of social networks lies as much in their readiness to be activated as in the frequency with which they have been called upon to do so and this research shows that whilst it is still only a minority of the parents who are willing to activate their friendship networks in this manner the 'old-boy' network is one amongst a number which does have some real meaning for a substantial minority of the parents who are part of it.

COMMUNITY INVOLVEMENT

Whilst their critics may attack the public schools for their élitism and perpetuation of privilege, frequent reference has been made to the importance that the schools attach to instilling in their pupils the ideal of service. The 1968 Newsom Report, concerned with the boarding public schools,[24] identified this as one of their traditional functions whilst seventeen out of the twenty-two headmasters of such schools who were interviewed by Lambert and his colleagues in the early 1970s include a sense of service in their list of the primary goals of this form of education.[25] Lambert quotes one headmaster as saying:

> We try to get a boy to believe in what is bigger than himself – the school, the house and so on, and to make him serve these, not to live for himself, so that he realises that service to the community is the most important thing when he leaves.[26]

and he concludes that service to the community is one of the most important norms around which the schools seek to integrate their pupils such that it has come to replace the earlier emphasis that was placed upon training for leadership. It is difficult to identify the appropriate structures within the schools which are charged with the specific responsibility for achieving this, for all aspects of school life are permeated with the ethos of service but perhaps it is the chapel which is the most obviously associated organisational structure. In Chapter 1 it was noted that it is only within the last two decades that the schools, in response to the wider social changes, have both relaxed compulsory chapel attendance and made the effort to introduce community service in a more direct fashion, offering their pupils more opportunities to participate in community activities, occasionally instead of but more frequently as a timetabled alternative to the combined cadet force.

Apart from any consideration of the importance that parents attach to such activities or indeed whether these constitute one of the

TABLE 3.12 *Parents' involvement in community activities*

(a) Number of Activities	Husbands (%) (169)	Wives (%) (184)
None	23	41
One	37	38
Two	24	16
Three or more	16	5
Total	100%	100%

(b) Percentage engaged in varying activities		
Politics	11 (6)*	8 (3)
Parish council	4	2
Rotary club	8 (1)	—
Charity work	18 (11)	36 (8)
JP or school governor	8	3
Rural sports	12 (4)	3 (1)
Other clubs	44 (9)	17 (7)
Church	14 (10)	18 (10)
Professional association	26 (13)	3 (1)

(c) Fathers' involvement according to type of Secondary School	Major boarding			Others		
	None	Member	Office holder	None	Member	Office holder
Politics (%)	73	10	17	93	3	4
Rotary club (%)	90	10	0	93	6	1
Charity work (%)	73	10	17	85	6	9
JP/School Governor (%)	83	13	4	93	4	3
Rural sports (%)	70	13	17	93	7	0
Other clubs (%)	43	50	7	61	30	9
Church (%)	70	0	30	87	13	0
Professional association (%)	68	7	26	75	15	10

* Percentages in parentheses relate to office holding.

perceived advantages of a public school education, an analysis of the parents' own acts of service to the communities in which they live, Table 3.12, shows that only 18 per cent of the fathers and a third of the mothers are engaged in some form of charitable work, either as fund raisers or as direct providers of services such as meals on wheels or marriage guidance counselling. Whilst more than a half of the fathers so involved take positions of some responsibility in this work, usually holding office in a local charity, they tend to leave their wives to carry out the more routine tasks. However, participation in such acts of charity is not confined to any single groups of parents and there is no evidence to suggest that the public boarding schools have had the monopoly of instilling the notion of service into their pupils. Where the ex-boarding school fathers do show themselves to differ from their peers is in their declared involvement in the activities of the church; 30 per cent of these fathers as opposed to only 11 per cent of the remainder take an active part in church affairs, usually as church wardens, suggesting that enforced chapel attendance at school is the basis of a lifetime's habit which is difficult to break.

The information about the parents' attitudes towards compulsory community service and/or the combined cadet forces is incomplete but, such as it is, suggests that most of the parents are in favour of one or the other, either stressing the importance of contributing to the community or, more usually, the benefits to be derived by their sons. About a quarter of the parents are opposed to any compulsion to choose either one or indeed any of these activities and a small minority believe that it is the parents' responsibility to provide their sons with this form of moral training or even that such activities impede academic progress. Parents who have been educated at the public schools and who are therefore unlikely to have escaped instruction in the importance of service to the community are more likely to stress the serving aspect of the combined cadet force or of the social service activities that the schools offer but many of the others, such as this grammar school educated father, soon come to see the benefits to be derived:

> Originally we were against him being an army cadet because we felt that it would interfere with his work, but now we see how good it has been for him. . . it has made him try things that he would not otherwise have done or is afraid of.

The ideal of service is only one of several possible alternative interpretations of the importance that is attached to community service. Any consideration of the ruling class must include an analysis of the way in which its members enjoy power apart from that which is generated by their economic and occupational roles such that their wealth is linked to the state apparatuses by virtue of their subsidiary activities, for example as justices of the peace, school governors or activists in political parties. Morris and Newton[27] have traced the changing nature of the personnel involved in Birmingham's local political activities and show how control of the town hall is gradually being relinquished by the large manufacturers in favour of the bourgeoisie, not the small business owners and shopkeepers as suggested by an earlier study of Glossop[28] but those who are directly affected by many of the decisions made: the builders, the estate agents and the property developers. Bechhofer[29] found that, despite their strong support for the Conservative party, shopkeepers, in keeping with their anti-collectivism, have a low involvement both in local politics and in voluntary associations more generally. Few of the parents interviewed are involved in non-work activities which can be interpreted as linking them to the workings of the state, only 11 per cent of the husbands and 8 per cent of the wives have any stated involvement in politics, either national or local, and only a half of these play an active part in the sense of holding office. If industry and its interests are represented at all it is through its managers rather than its owners, but the numbers are small. It is those who are categorised as farmers and in particular the large landowners who take the most prominent part in political activities for 22 per cent of the farmers are active participants in party politics. That such involvement is seen as an act of public service rather than as bringing direct personal advantage is suggested by one such landowner:

> A lot of ex-public schoolboys have an enormous commitment to the community – they try to put something back into the pot.

The data supports this view to the extent that it does show a disproportionately large number (25 per cent) of his old school chums who are involved in party political activities and his altruism has to be contrasted with the view expressed by a member of the occupational élite, the upwardly mobile secondary modern school educated owner of a large manufacturing company, who resolutely resists all attempts to get him involved in any voluntary activities, believing that:

> before you know where you are all your time is taken up.

A similar but less successful father, a member of the *petit bourgeoisie,* explained that people with small businesses simply do not have the time to get involved. Even fewer parents, only 7 per cent of the fathers and 3 per cent of the mothers, are either justices of the peace or school governors but they represent a broader occupational spread than is found amongst the political activists and include farmers, the owners of large companies and the minor professionals.

In the main, those who seek to advance themselves occupationally do so by organising themselves collectively, joining their occupational associations. A quarter of the men belong to such associations and a half of them are active in the sense of being office holders. The farmers and the self-employed professionals are the most likely of all the fathers to belong to an occupational association but this is undoubtedly due to the way in which these two occupations organise themselves, providing a greater number of associations for their members to join. In itself, membership of an occupational association is unrelated to the route which has been travelled to reach a particular occupation but those who have been educated at the major boarding schools do provide a disproportionate number of the office holders.

Another way of enhancing one's occupational interests is through membership of the local Rotary Club. Nominally open only to men who have been invited to join them they provide an opportunity for local businessmen and professionals to meet socially and they form the basis of a local self-network. The number of fathers who are rotarians is too small to merit any detailed consideration but membership is much favoured by the *petit bourgeoisie* who lack a viable alternative forum for meeting the local burghers.

A further dimension of involvement in community activities is that which is associated with style of life. That the middle class in general are 'joiners' is now part of accumulated knowledge for joining organisations is one way in which the middle classes, constantly on the move in the search of occupational success, can replace the loss of early friendships. Table 3.5 confirmed the importance of the membership of organisations in the formation of friendships and this is particularly marked amongst those couples where the husband has been to a well known boarding school. The pattern associating the better educated and socially static managers' wives studied by the Pahls with an enhanced tendency to be friend oriented is repeated in terms of their membership of clubs for the Pahls found that 62 per cent of all the wives but only 47 per cent of those who had experienced upward mobility through marriage belonged to at least one club, the greatest divergence between the static and mobile wives being with respect to those who were frequent and those who were irregular attenders. Stacey[30] in her first study of Banbury discusses the importance of social contact as a reason for joining clubs:

> Banbury people do not engage in sport as an exercise in competitive athleticism but as an occasion for social intercourse.

She found that it was the men and not the women who were more likely to be the club members, a finding contradicted by the Pahls but supported by this research where 44 per cent of the men but only 17 per cent of the women belong to recreational clubs. Virtually none of the fathers belong to the gentlemen's clubs frequented by the directors of the financial institutions studied by Whitley,[31] the clubs that they belong to are mainly sports clubs, golf and squash being the most popular, which clearly meet a need for leisure pursuits. However, it is possible to envisage these clubs as middle class versions of the gentlemen's clubs of an earlier era, providing opportunities to form and maintain personal contacts which could coalesce to form a useful network. There is evidence from the findings of this research to suggest that the well established members of the upper strata are segregated relationally from those who could be termed *arrivistes* for whilst membership of recreational clubs in general is drawn from a cross-section of the sample, it is the fathers who have been educated at the public schools and the major boarding ones in particular who are more likely to belong to those clubs which have a national rather than locally based membership. That such clubs do not necessarily restrict their membership in any formal sense does not necessarily mean that informal methods of self-selection do not operate. A further example of the differences in life-style which separates those who have been to the prestigious boarding schools from the rest of the fathers is the continuing importance of land in their pursuit of leisure and this is expressed in the greater inclination to participate in country sports such as hunting and shooting. Hierarchies of status are found to be even more blatant in the country than in the town and affect the manner in which such activities are pursued for several of the tenant farmers who mentioned shooting as one of their leisure activities were at pains to point out that theirs is rough shooting for tenant farmers are not invited to join the local syndicates.

A total profile of the involvement of the parents in the life of the community shows that sexual and status differences still operate. The men are more involved in the various aspects of the community, participating in more activities and associations than the women, an average of 1.4 as opposed to 0.84, and in addition they take the dominant positions, holding an average of 0.58 of an office as opposed to the women's 0.22. The pattern of the types of organisation that the two sexes belong to varies inasmuch as the women are largely concerned with charitable activities and only to a lesser extent with the church and local clubs. These clubs, however, account for the leisure activities of more of the men than do any of the other activities listed in Table 3.12 with membership of the professional associations the next most frequently mentioned. However, given that the focal point of our interest in community activities is not the differences between the sexes *per se* but the role that the public schools play in fostering community involvement in general and forming the basis of an 'old-boy' network in particular, it is the differences between the public school and non-public school educated fathers in this sample that is of greatest concern. Those who have been educated at Britain's top boarding schools are clearly involved in more organisations and non-work activities than the remainder of the sample, mentioning an average of 2.33 such activities as opposed to the 1.1 of the other fathers. They simultaneously share in the general activities which characterise this predominantly middle class sample and participate in others which are relatively inaccessible to (or unsought by) those fathers who have not been to the top public schools and which therefore provide them with the last vestiges of an opportunity to interact informally with those whom they believe to be their social equals. Finally, these same fathers play a more active part in running Britain's community life for they hold a clearly identifiable position as distinct from simple membership in many of the organisations to which they belong, holding an average of 1.1 as opposed to 0.47 offices.

In conclusion, it can be seen that there are various ways in which the shell of an 'old-boy' network can be said to exist. There is clear evidence that, despite the occupational and economic convergence that has been brought about by the expansion of the service sector of Britain's economy, the social and community networks of those who are public school educated remain distinguishable from those who are not and this social segregation is achieved effectively and effortlessly. What is open to debate and further investigation is the precise significance of such networks for this research does clearly show the importance and undoubted efficiency of the extended family in three crucial areas of the parents' lives: helping them through minor and major crises; giving them financial support in the child-rearing phase of their life-cycle and acting as the single most important source of nepotism in the fight to secure a foothold in the world of work. A significant minority of those who have been educated at the top boarding schools do show a readiness to help their friends, most of whom have received a similar education to their own, in times of financial need but if the 'old-boy' network is the crucially important source of mutual aid and advancement that some believe it to be, the salient acts take place in the privacy of its member's homes and other informal meetings, beyond the relatively superficial scrutiny of declared sociological research.

4 The Long-Term Goals

CLASS IMAGES

The functionalist school of sociology, particularly as represented by Parsons and his disciples, draws heavily upon the assumption of a unitary value system believing that there is a basic consensus in society over its values and the means of achieving them. The conflict theorists portray this 'consensus' not as a free convergence of individual minds but as a dominant ideology imposed upon society by the ruling class. Central to the successful imposition of this ideology is the control of ideas, in which the media and the education system play no small part. What is at issue in this important debate between functionalist and conflict theorists is not whether people do indeed possess an integrated meaning system through which they come to impose order upon and make sense of their lives but how they come to acquire this meaning system initially. Does it emerge out of the internalisation of the norms of the primary groups to which individuals belong such that the raw materials of class ideology are located in the individual's primary social experiences, as suggested by Bott,[1] or is it imposed however subtly from above, as discussed by Parkin[2] in his consideration of the dominant value system and its moral interpretation of class inequality?

Like Parkin, Lockwood[3] (writing in 1966) screens out of his discussion of working class images of society any consideration of whether such images actually exist. He opens his paper with the assertion that ' . . . men visualise the class structure of their society from the vantage point of their particular milieux'. But by 1972 Mann,[4] in presenting his own research findings, questioned whether this is in fact the case. In drawing the conclusion that neither the workers he interviewed as a whole, nor any identifiable sub-group, possessed a coherent belief system he proceeded to observe that, together with those sharing in societal power, 'only those who seek to change the world need to encompass it intellectually'. Although referring specifically to manual workers, Mann succeeds in throwing open the wider question of whether or not individuals possess coherent meaning systems with which to encompass their daily experiences. The failure to intellectualise or to make explicit one's perceived vision of the world is insufficient evidence of the non-existence, even if only at the level of the subconscious, of some ordered view of the world. As opposed to the question of the very existence at a given point of time of an image which is internally consistent, there are the questions of whether such an image is stable or varies according to changing biographies and positions within the class structure and whether individuals who happen to share a common socio-economic position at a given point of study can realistically be expected to possess a shared view of the world given that they have different starting points and experiences. Miliband[5] in explaining how the nationalised sector of Britain's economy has remained under the control of the ruling class says that 'businessmen who enter the state system (as heads of the nationalised industries) may divest themselves of their stocks and shares but not of their view of the world'. By the same token, parents who have arrived at a similar class position from different social origins and who maintain their friendships with those who appear to have similar origins, are unlikely to have a shared view of the world and the part that education plays in securing access to positions within it.

The educational ideology emerging from a particular 'view of the world' will have an idea of the nature of the world into which people will have to fit, what makes or constitutes an educated person and hence the kind of educational experiences necessary to fit him (or her) into the world. Such an ideology inevitably includes a perception of the relationship between education and work; if the relationship is seen as contiguous the nature of work and the skills which it requires education to develop will be closely defined and consequently a greater degree of emphasis will be placed upon the need for education to meet the technical requirements of work. If, however, work and education are seen as relatively autonomous spheres of life the purpose of education will be defined as preparing people for life and developing the mind.

In seeking to explore the relationship between education and the macro-social structure there is a temptation to restrict models of society to class models and to assume that parents who use the private schools do so predominantly to advance or to consolidate the position of their sons in a class structure which is conventionally defined in terms of the social and/or technical division of labour, namely with ownership of the means of production and occupation. Even if education is not seen by all parents as an important determinant of position within the class structure defined in these terms, it will still be viewed by some as status conferring and by others as the means of reinforcing attitudes and ways of behaving which are highly valued. It is compulsory for all children to spend a minimum of eleven years in full time education before they seek their own place in the world. The content of this education is largely beyond the control of the parents as well as of their children and 12 per cent of the parents interviewed in this research stressed the importance of the freedom to choose a school which provides the form of education required and the facility to express opinions freely. One parent declared himself 'ready to defend (this freedom) to the end even if I never used the schools'. Bernstein[6] has argued that schools maintain and repeat the dominant cultural category in society and in capitalism this is class. The ruling class has a direct relation to the means of production but only an indirect one to education, hence it has to try and influence or control the state in order to perpetuate the dominant cultural category of class. Parents who choose to educate their children privately, at a cost of anything from £2000 a year not only have a greater degree of influence over the content and organisation of the education that their children receive, but in making this choice they must also possess a view of the nature of the world into which their sons are poised to enter. As part of the attempt to define the educational ideology(ies) held by the parents using the public schools they were asked to discuss their perceptions of the social class structure of contemporary Britain: whether in fact they believe that classes do exist and if so how many classes there are, what criteria are used to draw the boundaries between them and with what facility individuals can achieve and exchange position within the class hierarchy. Whilst Poulantzas[7] rests his analysis of social classes on the premise that classes designate objective positions within the social division of labour, independent of the will of those individuals who occupy them, such objective differences only acquire a hierarchical character and thereby become bases for stratification in so far as individuals recognise these differences, evaluate them and rank them accordingly. Yet there is no inevitable or necessary link between the objective bases of class and subjective aspects of stratification and whereas the behaviour of individual actors may be 'explained' by the former it is often best understood in terms of the latter. About one in thirteen of the couples interviewed do not perceive the existence of classes, either totally denying their existence or, more frequently, depicting an infinite number of individual differences in terms of money, interests, modes of behaviour and so on which fail to add up to any recognisable collectivities. The consciousness of these parents, who are located in the same objective class system as the remainder, is that of total freedom of social movement which gives rise to the belief in individual and parental responsibility for human action.

The use of the ideal-typical prestige model identified initially by Willner[8] and subsequently confirmed both by Bott[9] and by Goldthorpe and Lockwood,[10] has served as a heuristic device to highlight the way in which it is believed that non-manual or middle class people perceive society. This model emphasises society as an extended hierarchy of relatively open strata differentiated primarily in terms of prestige. Essentially the hierarchy is a ladder, built of many rungs, which is available for motivated people to climb and for others to fall down. This vision of the possibilities of individual mobility leads to a marked orientaton to the future with stress placed upon planning ahead and adopting attitudes appropriate to success, namely the sacrifice of short-term goals in favour of long-term benefits, such that hard work and orientation to the future become a matter of morality as well as expediency and the associated attitudes come to be highly valued for their own sake. The economic, status and power rewards identified by neo-Weberians as associated with positions near the top of the ladder constitute the social milieux of the majority of the parents who are able to afford to educate their children privately and it is this very experience of success and its rewards which fuels the belief that it is available to all who wish to achieve it. This view was expressed bluntly by a veterinary surgeon, the son of the fireman, when saying,

> As I have arrived in the middle classes I cannot see why other people cannot do it.

This is the very meat of the political philosophy of the New Right. Discarding all vestiges of *noblesse oblige* and looking back to the nineteenth century market liberals, those who subscribe to this philosophy have sought to and have largely succeeded in resurrecting the fundamental faith in the power of the market to provide opportunities for all who wish to succeed. This faith in the market extends beyond the belief in its capacity to provide the opportunities for occupational and economic success to include entrusting it with making the provisions necessary for educational success.

Since the writings of Bott, sociological research into images of society has mainly concentrated upon the occupational groups which constitute the working class and has sought to identify the variations both within and between these occupations with respect to the class images held by their members.[11] More recently Townsend's poverty study,[12] that by Roberts *et al.*[13] of suburban Liverpool and Fidler's[14] interviews with the business élite have updated Bott's early findings. Whilst Townsend confirmed the relationship between non-manual status and the use of the prestige model, both Fidler and Roberts show the diversity of images employed. Roberts found that only 15 per cent of his white collar respondents did in fact perceive society in terms approximating to a ladder or hierarchy composed of four or more classes. The use of such a model was normally confined to the sample members who were high earners, in professional occupations and who tended to hold relatively liberal views on social issues. Twelve per cent of the business élite interviewed by Fidler and 21 per cent of the parents interviewed in this research see society strictly in terms of a ladder which in the main is open to climbers but equally perilous for those who are prone to fall. The fabric of which the rungs of this ladder is constituted is varied and complex. About a half of the parents using the ladder model see them (the rungs) as composed of a single factor, money or, less frequently, occupation – 'the acquisition of money is now more important than the means of acquiring it' said one parent. The other parents use a combination of these and other factors to define the rungs, incorporating attitudes and ways of behaving; style of life and even self-definition such that an individual's position on the ladder is recognised only by himself. But for two-thirds of the parents invoking this model of society money and, for about 40 per cent, occupation feature as the important determinants of the way in which strata are evaluated and ranked. Education and attitudes were each mentioned by only a fifth of the parents using this ladder model, but by implication education is an important prerequisite for occupational and financial success. Just under a half of these parents do not see the ladder as totally unobstructed with the possibility of unimpeded mobility from top to bottom but as headed by an 'upper' class whose members can be distinguished by the inheritence of a title, position, money or land. Surprisingly this class is not seen as sealed from upward mobility by all of those who acknowledge its existence for a half of them believe that it is possible to gain entry by 'buying in'. But the important point to note is the number, almost two-thirds, of these parents who recognise the threat of downward mobility from the top class resulting either from the erosion of this class by fiscal action or from personal inability to manage wealth and inherited estates. Thus the upper class is seen as shrinking, to be absorbed into the ladder which is based upon ability and success.

Contrasted with the prestige model is the power model of society, distinguished by the image of society as sharply divided into two contending sections or classes and differentiated primarily in terms of the possession or non-possession of power. This model has been most frequently approximated in the images of the working-class and embodies a clear-cut division between 'them' and 'us'. The conditions giving rise to a clear identification of 'us' (the powerless working class) have been clearly spelt out by Lockwood,[15] discussed in terms of the subordinate value system by Parkin,[16] and identified most recently by Roberts[17] amongst the blue collar respondents. Although the literature on class in general and the public schools in particular has defined the objective bases of the complementary group in the two class models, the 'them' (the holders of power), attempts to isolate a group which identifies itself in these terms have been largely unsuccessful. Townsend[18] notes that while the great bulk of the population adopts class imagery which assumes the existence of an upper or ruling class practically no one claims to belong to such a class. In his entire sample only four people said they were in the upper class. Few of those interviewed by Fidler[19] were prepared to identify themselves as a part of the top class, seeing themselves as men who have to work for a living. Similarly, in this population of public school parents which the literature in its crudest and most popularised form describes as composed almost entirely of members of the upper class, only twenty-six couples or 14 per cent of the total use a two class model of society but few define it in the antagonistic terms with which it has come to be associated. Five couples drew a clear distinction between the classes in terms of the possession/non-possession of a valued commodity: extreme wealth, power, birth or private education and only one parent in inverting this model spontaneously identified herself as part of the new 'us'. Describing the beleaguered few remnants of the upper class who are born to money and have the standards of behaviour to accompany it, she bemoaned the sacrifice of these standards to those of the new ruling class, the workers. But for the majority of those adopting a two class model, the classes are seen not as antagonistic, divided by the possession of objective criteria such as power or money, but as legitimate, separated mainly by attitude and/or occupation. Typically, the boundary is drawn between the sheep and the goats, the leaders and the followers, the managers and the managed. From the vantage point of those who, by implication, are amongst the leaders access to leadership positions is not seen as restricted but as open to all with the necessary motivation to achieve them. The essential conflict between the two classes is reinterpreted as a conflict over values and attitudes and although education is rarely seen as a definitive attribute of class membership it is viewed by parents as the means of ensuring that their sons remain in the top class by virtue of their possession of the appropriate values.

The class model used by the largest single proportion, but not the majority, of Robert's respondents is the 'middle mass'. As its name implies, this model portrays the bulk of the population as centrally placed between the powerful few and a small underclass composed of the poor and the unemployed. Those of Robert's respondents who use this model identified themselves as part of the middle mass and felt secure in this position, neither fearing downward mobility into the underclass nor aspiring to reach the top which was seen as reserved for the privileged few. There was a recognition that the middle mass is itself differentiated but this was believed to be the result of inequalities of income rather than of ideological cleavages, divisions of interests or contrasts in life-style. Thirty-eight per cent of the parents using the public schools visualise the existence of three classes when they discuss the class structure of Britain today but their perception of the shape and content of these classes differs from that of Roberts' sample of Liverpudlians. The bottom class is rarely described as an underclass containing the poor and the unemployed but as formed from those who differ from the remainder of society either by holding distinct attitudes and interests or, somewhat less frequently, by doing manual work and occasionally both. For many of these parents the important difference between the middle and the bottom class is not one of financial resources but of how these are used and the different life-styles that this gives rise to and, of crucial importance, how access to the occupations which determine the level of these rewards results in turn from the possession of distinctive attitudes and values. The attitudes which are believed to characterise the bottom, frequently manual, class are low aspirations and the absence of any sense of responsibility as well as different standards of behaviour and modes of speech. The division between the bottom two groups of the tripartite class structure is a division of culture, virtually identical to that separating the two classes in the two class model used by the parents, the difference being that the parents who use the three class model are slightly more likely to perceive restrictions in the opportunity to move between the bottom two classes, recognising the difficulty of breaking out of the cycle of financial and cultural disadvantage in order to move into the middle class. However, the perceived possibilities of moving downwards, out of the middle class, are as real as for those holding a bifurcated view of society. The main difference between the two sets of parents is simply that in four cases out of five, those who see three classes do so by virtue of the addition of a clearly visualised top or upper class. For the majority, membership of the top class remains a question of birth, a belief in the existence of a small group of people who are still born to their position, bred to behave according to its culture and who inherit money, land or possibly a title to accompany it. However, parents who see the top class in these terms did have enormous difficulty in defining further what it is that is distinctive about its members. As one farmer put it: 'I can recognise them but I cannot define them'. A journalist, also believing that such a class still exists was nevertheless more perceptive and cynical in debunking the mystique which surrounds it:

> One of the criteria of the upper class is that they can only be upper class if you don't meet them.

Entry into this top class is invariably but not inevitably seen as difficult, especially by the women in the sample, but the possibility of losing class looms threateningly. Only a small number of the parents who add a top class to the middle and bottom classes do so on the basis of acquired wealth or power and it is rare for the few who define membership in terms of personal achievement to believe it to be closed to upward mobility, but this does not deny a recognition on the part of some parents of the difficulty of achieving success, nor of the precariousness of maintaining it and reproducing it in the next generation.

The small number of parents who see three classes but do not identify a distinctive top class do so by drawing a distinction between the main occupational groupings which comprise the middle class, thus endowing it with the diversity that makes many challenge the wisdom of using the term middle class as opposed to middle classes. The main dividing line that these parents draw is the one that separates the professionals and top managers from middle management and routine white collar workers. As a collectivity, the parents display some ambiguity about the position of the self-employed in this scheme, whether they fall into the upper or the lower faction of the middle class is an unresolved issue. In general, however, the barrier which divides the two factions of the middle class is barely visible for the possibility of movement between them is seen to be there for all who wish to grasp it or for those who fail to acquire the necessary aspirations and qualifications to secure their position.

A variation of the prestige model defined by Bott and included by Roberts is the identification of many (defined by Roberts as four or more) separate groups which are not ranged along a continuum of single or indeed multiple criteria of class determinants but are perceived as discrete units with clearly defined, if not inpenetrable, boundaries. This 'modified' prestige model, used by 20 per cent of the parents, includes variations within as well as between conventionally defined classes and therefore technically incorporates class factions as well as class divisions. The top class is always clearly defined as such and, as in the other models where it has been identified, this is usually done on the basis of hereditary factors and is believed by many to be sealed, particularly from the upwardly mobile. It is the use of multiple criteria to identify the remainder of the class hierarchy, lying beneath this apex, that furnishes the evidence of the complexities involved in defining classes and identifying factions within them. Although 61 per cent of the parents who employ a 'modified' prestige model to describe the class structure use money as one of the factors in the identification of at least one class or class faction, occupation is the most widely used criterion for making these distinctions such that the parents are in effect drawing subtle differences between occupational groups. However, in using occupation to distinguish between the bottom class and the one above, it appears that the parents are using the term less precisely than when they identify the class factions within the middle class. Virtually all of the parents recognise the existence of a working or lower class based upon manual labour but this is merely an epiphenomenon of the basic differences in earning power and attitudes such that 'working class' is a label which is used to describe the unison of manual labour either with lower financial rewards or with a different outlook on life, manner of behaviour and mode of speech than that which distinguishes the class above. Only a quarter of these parents further subdivide the working class in order to distinguish either the very poor or the feckless and the workshy from the bulk of manual labour, but all of the parents using the 'modified' prestige model are able to draw the finer distinction between those who, in occupational terms at least, they identify with most closely and whose subtle differences they can recognise more easily, namely the non-manual class. Here the use of occupation to make the distinctions is not as a label which is a convenient and recognised way of identifying fundamental cleavages of life chances or attitudes but as representing in itself an important source of differentiation between sections of the middle class. The distinction drawn by the majority of these parents is the one between the routine non-manual occupations, including middle management, and the senior managerial and professional occupations which are generally perceived as based upon the possession of recognised symbolic skills, namely qualifications. It is the consequent enhancement of market capacity and the commensurate rewards that these qualifications bring which enable those who enjoy them to engage in life-styles which are essentially different from those of the remainder of the middle class.

It is the women rather than the men using this more sophisticated model of the class structure who identify the way in which the need for educational qualifications as a prerequisite for joining the ranks of the professionals results in somewhat more restricted opportunities for social mobility than is characteristic of the other models identified. Whilst 83 per cent of the men using this modified prestige model believe that mobility in an upward and downward direction is easy to achieve, only 69 per cent of the wives share this belief, education serves to secure class position but also makes it harder to achieve initially. One mother, a teacher in a private school explained how she believes that position in the class structure is heavily dependent upon educational opportunities which in turn are associated with class of origin. Not only does a private or a grammar school education open the door to certain occupations, it also effectively denies access to others. This mother claimed that a child who had been to a private school would never be accepted for an apprenticeship and it is in this way that classes reproduce themselves from one generation to the next.

Given the difficulties, outlined at the beginning of this chapter, of eliciting models of society from respondents as well as the doubts which have been cast upon the very existence of such models, what conclusions can be drawn about the way that the class structure looks to parents who are paying large amounts of money for the education of their sons? Tables 4.1 land 4.2 summarise the main findings discussed so far.

Whilst some parents are unable to name discrete classes but see strata ranged along a continuum of money and occupation with free movement in both directions, others do make clear-cut divisions, frequently using occupation to denote differences in outlook, life chances and financial rewards. Yet this dichotomisation of the

TABLE 4.1   *Parents' perceptions of class bases and opportunities for mobility according to number of classes perceived*

	None or Cells (14)	Two (26)	Three (71)	Four (38)	Many Layers (39)	Total
Percent of respondents	7.5	14.0	38.0	20.0	21.0	100%
Percent who see a clear top class	—	19.0	79.0	95.0	44.0	67.0
Percent of those who base remaining classes on one or more of the following:						
Money	—	12.0	38.0	61.0	67.0	47.0
Occupation	—	42.0	48.0	76.0	41.0	53.0
Education	—	27.0	25.0	32.0	23.0	29.0
Attitudes	—	50.0	63.0	55.0	20.0	50.0
Life-style	—	23.0	25.0	26.0	10.0	25.0
Self-defined	—	21.0	18.0	10.0	8.0	19.0
Percent who see opportunities for mobility in the general class structure						
Husbands:						
Perfect	—	71.0	66.0	74.0	88.0	74.0
Up easy, down hard	—	19.0	17.0	9.0	3.0	12.0
Up hard, down easy	—	0	11.0	9.0	9.0	9.0
None	—	10.0	6.0	8.0	0	5.0
Wives:						
Perfect	—	71.0	57.0	56.0	87.0	66.0
Up easy, down hard	—	19.0	25.0	13.0	6.0	16.0
Up hard, down easy	—	0	12.0	13.0	6.0	9.0
None		10.0	7.0	19.0	0	9.0

Table 4.2   *Perceptions of nature of top class**

Class based upon	Percent of respondents
Inheritance	73
Money	17
Land	16
Birth/breeding	28
Titles	13
Acquisition	27
Occupation	6
Power	7
Money	14
Total	100%

Perceptions of opportunities for mobility into and out of the top class	Class basis		
	Inheritance (%)	*Acquisition (%)*	*Total (%)*
Husbands			
Perfect	33	58	40
Up easy, down hard	3	13	6
Up hard, down easy	21	19	20
Closed	42	10	33
Total	100%	100%	100%
Wives			
Perfect	27	56	34
Up easy, down hard	8	21	11
Up hard, down easy	26	13	24
Closed	39	10	31
Total	100%	100%	100%

*Based on the total of 126 sets of parents who recognise the existence of such a class

parents may well be more a matter of degree than of kind for those who are able to identify distinct classes do also, in the main, recognise possibilities for considerable social mobility between them which, though tempered by the perception of some restriction on free movement, rarely amounts to the belief that class boundaries are impenetrable. Only slightly more of the parents see the opportunities of upward mobility as exceeding those for movement in the opposite direction and it is this belief in the existence of freedom of movement which makes it as vital for individuals to strive to maintain the class position into which they are born as it is for those from below to seek to move upwards. The barriers to upward mobility are not normally seen as structural but as cultural, the absence of the necessary ambition and determination to succeed and it is this lack of orientation to the future which is seen to divide the bottom class from the rest of society. Whilst there is some acknowledgement of the different level of financial reward associated with membership of the bottom class, there are also parents who specifically deny that such rewards are a determinant of class, often stressing that members of the working class earn more than those who lie immediately above them. Many parents emphasised the importance of their sons acquiring the necessary outlook on life to enable them to remain within the middle class and their discussion of the possibilities of downward mobility made it clear that they believe that the absence of such an outlook will leave the boys vulnerable to losing class position.

All the parents who do not use the ladder model to describe the class structure do clearly distinguish a bottom class and about a half of them draw a further distinction between the professional and managerial middle class and the routine middle class. These parents are very conscious of the ordering of occupations and the financial rewards that accompany them and only marginally fewer of them than of those using the ladder model perceive opportunities for mobility between the factions of the middle class. Whilst education as a criterion of class membership is mentioned with surprising infrequency it is plausible to conclude that the parents are as anxious for their sons to receive an education which reinforces the value placed upon ambition and the need to work for success as for them to gain the qualifications necessary to enable them to enter the professions.

Any perception of restrictions on individual movement, such as they are, are associated with mobility between the apex of the class structure, usually termed the upper class, and that which lies beneath it. A third of the parents do not believe that a clearly recognisable upper class exists and their vision of the world into which their sons are poised to enter is one of opportunity for relatively unrestricted movement and achievement, an opportunity which is there for all to grasp. Amongst those parents who still recognise its existence, there is an element of confusion about the precise nature of the top class. Essentially it is seen by the majority as a class into which one is born rather than climbs and as such is not strictly a financial class. Only a quarter of the parents recognising the existence of a clearly defined top class do so on the basis of acquisition, usually of extreme wealth but occasionally of the power to control the fortunes of others. Three-quarters of them, or half of the total sample, still use the criterion of inheritance and therefore of long established membership to identify the top class but they do not see it as totally sealed from the remainder of the class structure. There is a clearly perceived danger of losing membership of this top class either by its very erosion or by the failure to cope with the increasing difficulty of maintaining the life-style with which it is associated. Despite its essentially hereditary nature, nearly as many parents do believe that it is possible to move into this class as it is to fall out of it and even if this cannot be achieved over one generation then it is possible over two, taking time to acquire the life-style and breeding that accompany it. It is tempting to conclude that a public school education is seen as a vital part of this process by at least some of the parents who are currently using it; whilst it is a minority of all parents who believe that such a class both exists and opens its doors to those who are not born into it, it is those who have themselves had this form of education who are the most likely to define membership of the top class in hereditary terms and as totally closed to any new blood.

Despite the fact that the clearest line of cleavage between classes is the line that is drawn beneath the top class and those that lie beneath it there is little evidence to support the view that the top class is viewed in antagonistic terms. Less than a fifth of the parents interviewed see the top class, however it is defined, in terms which could be described as conflictual rather than legitimate. Whilst there is a limited amount of resentment of the large incomes received by those at the top of the incomes league, whom it is believed have sufficient muscle to ensure their rewards, only a handful of the parents who still identify an hereditary upper class believe that it is symbolic of undue privilege and command over resources. The very existence as well as the actual membership of this class is seen as legitimate, the general feeling being that it is increasingly difficult to manage wealth today, whether it is held as landed estates or in more liquid forms, and those who have succeeded in preserving family wealth intact have done so by dint of sheer hard work and ability, hence the emphasis on the possibility of movement downwards from this class. Its manners and behaviour, termed 'breeding' are clearly admired and if there is any recognition of conflict between classes it is essentially a conflict not over the distribution of rewards in society but over values – the values ascribed by these parents to the working class. These values are seen as both different and inferior to their own and those of the top class and are to be avoided by their sons at all costs, failure to do so would result in a loss of class position, downward social mobility into the working class.

There is a remarkable degree of convergence in the class images held by the parents who make up the population of those who use the public schools today. The material condition of virtually all of these parents is one of above average financial and occupational success and their consciousness appears to be shaped by this rather than by their divergent past experiences. The parents have arrived at this common point from very different beginnings and show a marked tendency to seek out those who share their early experiences, yet this does not appear to affect the way in which they perceive the class structure. The parents who have achieved upward mobility into their current class position share very closely in the perceptions of those who are second or even third generation members of their class. Having either experienced upward mobility or witnessed it, both believe that such opportunities as well as very real dangers of downward mobility still exist today. In recognising the danger of downward mobility, those who have managed to maintain the class position of their birth are as likely as those who have been upwardly mobile to believe that their current success is due to their own efforts rather than to the prevailing structural conditions. Whilst the evidence from the Oxford Mobility Study does little to support the view that there was any significant chance of downward mobility amongst the generation of parents being interviewed, this does not inevitably match their own experiences. Many simultaneously witness new blood coming into the schools and are able to relate instances of friends and relatives who had themselves been privately educated but who cannot afford to pay for their own children's education. The few in the sample who have themselves experienced downward mobility are the least likely of all the parents to believe that society is open to the upwardly mobile. Despite all their differences, the members of this population are fundamentally united in their perception of the social order which has afforded them their privileged position.

PARENTAL ASPIRATIONS

It has proved difficult to disentangle parents' hopes for their sons futures from their actual expectations. Parents who were interviewed had sons at different stages in their school careers and obviously those with sons nearing the end have a clearer idea not only of their academic capacity but also of their likely future than those whose sons have just entered the schools and who can therefore afford to nurture their hopes for a little while yet. The majority of the parents interviewed, 75 per cent, possess or possessed a stated desire for their sons to proceed to university, a third had their sights clearly set on Oxbridge or Sandhurst. Conversely, very few, only 6 per cent denied the desirability of a university education and the remainder reserved their judgement about their sons' possible university careers. However, parents were not as forthcoming when it came to identifying their aspirations for their sons' occupational careers. Whilst some may well dream of membership of the upper or ruling class their responses were far more realistic. In a world which is seen as open to individual failure and success according to merit and ambition it is pointless and possibly dangerous to cherish dreams whose translation into reality cannot be ensured. Over half of the parents stated that the choice of career is up to the boy himself and this is not something that can be decided or even hoped for by his parents. Many parents mentioned that by giving the boy a good education they had discharged their moral duty as parents and that it is now up to him to make the most of the opportunities that this presents. Whilst recognising that parents are reluctant to express hopes and aspirations the achievement of which they feel is genuinely beyond their control, it is difficult to accept that the investment of such large amounts of capital as is necessitated by the payment of public school fees does not carry with it some vision of the future. Yet 19 per cent of the parents would not be drawn about the type of occupation they at least hoped for if not anticipated, and a half of these also refused to identify what occupations they would consider to have been a waste of the money spent. Thus nearly one in ten of the parents gave no indication of any of the parameters of their occupational aspirations for their sons. The other half, in common with all the parents who would identify the lower limits of their aspirations by naming the occupations that they would deem to have been a waste of the education, identified manual work or no work at all (perpetual studenthood or layabout) as the future which would disappoint them the most. Very few parents were as honest as this father, a middle manager in a large industrial firm:

> If they left it to us to plan it they would go to university and one would come out in medicine and the other in law. But I am not going to beat them into it, the time will come when they are going

to make their own decision. . . we will have given them the opportunity.

Eventually, 35 per cent of the parents did name the professions or a job requiring a qualification as their ultimate hope; 16 per cent envisaged that their sons would have an entrepreneurial career, in the family business or farm in half the cases, and 21 per cent mentioned a variety of other non-manual occupations such as engineering, journalism or government service.

Cooper[20] in his description of Eric the schizophrenic described how he was to be 'to an unusual degree the vehicle in which his parents lived out vicariously. . . all their past wishes and frustrated needs'. The parents interviewed in this research do not appear to have many such wishes and needs, at least in occupational terms. Few fathers expressed any marked dissatisfaction with the position that they had reached although 15 per cent would have preferred to have been in the professions rather than in business or public administration. Although there was some evidence of a desire for gentrification the main concern for these parents, with their perceptions of the danger of downward mobility being only slightly less than the opportunity for upward mobility, is that there is only one way for their sons to go – downwards – and parents with privileges will do whatever is necessary and possible to ensure that their children do not slip. There is evidence to show that these parents have been largely successful in maintaining the class position of their elder sons but this is limited evidence as there are only forty older brothers who have already left school. Of these, 13 per cent have already entered one of the major professions, 10 per cent have embarked upon careers in management or banking and a third are still in higher education, although only 8 per cent are at Oxbridge. The remaining few are evenly spread across the other non-manual occupations although one is in an apprentice-ship, one is a salesman and four are unemployed or doing casual work. The girls, of whom there are more, are similar to the brothers inasmuch as they are just as likely to be in higher education and indeed at Oxbridge but occupationally appear to be reproducing the careers of their mothers, being largely concentrated in the minor professions of teaching and nursing as well as in clerical and sec-retarial work. However, given the great reluctance with which parents did express their aspirations for their sons' future occupations it is important to resist the temptation of forging too close a link between education and parental ambition in occupational terms which precludes a consideration of other dimensions of the value of education.

PURCHASING PRIVILEGE

Peter Jay, speaking on television, [21] once said:

> I don't believe in private schools but I am a parent and want to do the best for my children.

Do these parents share his view? As part of the general questioning on the legitimacy that they attach to the class structure they describe, parents were asked to discuss the fact that the majority of children in this country are being educated in the comprehensive schools which they had rejected for their own children and as a consequence are being denied the advantages afforded by a private education. They were questioned about their support for the then recently announced Assisted Places scheme as well as their views on the Labour party's proposal to abolish the private sector.

Table 4.3 shows the widespread but not unanimous support that exists for the Assisted Places scheme. Many parents believe that the children who are being educated in the comprehensive schools are getting a raw deal and that the extension of the educational advantages of a private education that the scheme offers will help them to grasp the opportunities for individual success which, in the eyes of the parents, do undoubtedly exist. Some of the parents can also see benefits in the scheme for their own children for it brings into the schools others of high academic ability:

> We would never like to see capable people kept away from. . . it is the academic stimulation that carries other boys on.

About a third of all the parents believe that it is the children of average rather than exceptional ability who are losing out by the denial of the particular advantages that a private education offers and of all the parents they are the most ambivalent towards or even opposed to the Assisted Places scheme. It is the grammar school educated fathers who are particularly likely to express concern about the fate of the above average children destined to receive their education in the comprehensive schools, possibly sensitive to the loss

TABLE 4.3   *Support for the Assisted Places scheme*

	Husbands (%)	Wives (%)
In favour	61	57
Ambivalent	16	28
Against	22	14
Total	100%	100%

of opportunity which enabled many of them to achieve upward mobility, and they are the most unequivocal in their support of the scheme.

There are several different reasons why parents are not whole-hearted in their support of the Assisted Places scheme or indeed oppose it. Designed as it is to select the academically able who would otherwise be unable to enter the private sector, it offers nothing to appease the parents who are concerned about the average child and many who are opposed to it feel that the extra resources should be devoted to improving provision within the maintained sector. Several of the privately educated fathers oppose the scheme, or at least have doubts about it, because they feel that children selected for entry to the private schools in this way would feel out of place, that the discontinuity between the culture of the school and that of the home would be too great, a view shared by many of the mothers irrespective of their secondary education. Strangely, it is the university educated parents who, as a group, are least in favour of the Assisted Places scheme, the mothers fearing that the children will be out of place and the fathers concerned that the money would be better spent in the maintained sector.

Whilst parents generally welcome the extension of the advantages of a private education through the Assisted Places scheme, their feelings about the abolition of this sector do not match those expressed by Peter Jay.[22] They are overwhelmingly against its abolition and at best a few of them could be said to have mixed feelings on the subject; 16 per cent expressed a limited degree of sympathy towards such a proposal, recognising the inequity of a market system which coexists with provision by the state, but feeling that the provision made by the former is currently superior to that offered by the latter and that the private sector should only be eliminated by falling demand resulting from improvements in the provisions of its maintained counterpart – these parents believe in abolition by market forces rather than by statute. Those, the majority, who are against abolition stress the importance of freedom of choice and the fact that they are paying twice for this privilege. In so far as any of the parents recognise that the continued existence of the private sector has an effect upon the organisation and content of education in the maintained sector they naturally see this as a force for good rather than evil, providing academic and moral standards for the maintained sector to emulate. What they fail to acknowledge is that by educating their children privately they are pre-empting access to the very opportunities that they believe are the result of this form of education, which could be jeopardised if there is any large scale expansion in the number of assisted places, for there is only limited room at the top. This danger would have been magnified by the dilution of the scarcity value of a private education had more competitors been introduced into the fight to improve life chances through the introduction of educational vouchers, a policy much favoured by the 'privateers' in the Thatcher government[23] but which now appears unlikely to see the light of day.

The description so far of how the parents perceive the class structure within which their sons' education is taking place is but an arid shell, lacking any consideration of the dynamics of the relationship between classes. Reference has just been made to the manner in which parents convey the impression that opportunities exist for all those who are both ambitious and able to succeed, and to their failure to acknowledge that competition for the restricted and indeed diminishing 'room at the top' is inevitable such that the success of one individual is at the expense of another. Some parents deny that such conflict between classes or competition between individuals is inevitable, believing that it is possible to increase the total national wealth in order to produce more winners without corresponding losers; they see the improvement of educational standards, in line with those already prevailing in the private sector, as an important part of this process of 'increasing the size of the national cake'.

Sentiments such as these were expressed by approximately 10 per cent of the men and 17 per cent of the women in their responses to the question 'who gets a raw deal and who gets a good deal in Britain today?' By identifying only losers these parents are indicating their belief that the failure of some to gain an equitable share of this country's resources is the result of an overall shortage (of resources) or possibly of disorganisation rather than to the benefit of a specific class or group of individuals. In naming the losers in these circumstances and indeed more generally, parents appear to adopt a parochial rather than global perspective on inequality, identifying those with whom they are most likely to come into contact. The men tend to recognise as losers those who are poorly rewarded relative to their effort or worthiness in the financial or labour markets, whereas women are more likely to stress those who lie outside or on the fringes of these markets: the elderly, the handicapped, those trapped in the inner city and single parents. In a similar vein, a further 12 per cent of parents identify winners without corresponding losers, those who gain at the expense of society in general rather than any specific section of it, but such winners are to be found at all points in the social structure.

The remainder of the parents do believe that there are identifiable inequalities in our society but accept that inequality is inevitable. One father described this as the natural outcome of 'the law of the jungle' which he finds infinitely preferable to the 'law of the zoo', which dictates that everything must be done for the individual, to be avoided at all costs. What is important to these parents is the notion of equality of opportunity such that the belief that equality is inevitable does not mean that they necessarily endorse the particular distribution of rewards that they can perceive. Only 16 per cent of the parents fail to identify any desirable change in the distribution of resources, indicating that they believe that the inequalities which are to be found in Britain today are both inevitable and legitimate. About 60 per cent of the sample are able to delineate recognisable areas of either antagonism between classes where one class has clearly used its power to triumph over another, or competition within class where one faction has succeeded in monopolising social and economic opportunities at the expense of others. In two-thirds of the cases where it is possible to clearly identify such areas they appear as antagonism between classes rather than as competition within them (Table 4.4).

Just over a fifth of the parents believe that the beneficiaries of our unequal society are those who occupy positions near the top of society's reward system and there is a tendency but not an inevitability to identify those who have acquired their wealth or power in what appears as unacceptable ways: the speculators, the tax evaders and the pop or football stars, only rarely is mention made of those who inherit position or money. For every one parent who sees these gains made at the expense of those in the routine middle class, the hard

TABLE 4.4   *The parents' perception of inequitable distribution of resources and power*

Losers	Winners Speculators, establishment, wealthy, inheritors (%)	State scroungers, trade unionists (%)
Take responsibility, work hard	7.4	12.1
Genuine poor, elderly, inner-city residents	14.9	8.9
Total	22.3%	21.0%

workers, the exceptionally able or those who are prepared to accept responsibility, two parents locate the losers at the lower end of the class structure amongst the deserving poor: the low paid who are engaged in manual or clerical work, those who are on fixed incomes or are genuinely deprived by virtue of physical or social handicap. But a more or less equal number of parents see the victory in the bid for an unfair share of resources as belonging to the trade unionists or those who exploit the provisions of the welfare state, the social security scroungers, women are more likely to identify the latter group and men the former. It is rare for those who are being taxed on high income to be seen as losing out to these working class groups, it is either those in the middle – symptomatic of latent conflict between the worthy middle class and the over powerful trade unionists; or the genuinely poor or hard working who are being exploited by the less deserving members of their own class. Thus whilst there is some recognition of the undue privileges associated with membership of the upper class and the way in which these are used to the detriment of the middle classes, class conflict in so far as it exists in the eyes of these parents is predominantly but not exclusively a conflict between specified sections of the working class and of the upper and middle classes rather than a more generalised conflict between the owners of capital and the owners of labour.

The voting pattern of these parents is overwhelmingly Tory, as can be seen in Table 4.5. Seventy-three per cent are regular Tory voters and just over 10 per cent normally support this party, occasionally defecting to the Liberals (the SDP had not been formed when the

TABLE 4.5 *Parents' voting habits*

Current voting pattern	Husbands (153) (%)	Wives (164) (%)
Don't vote	3.3	1.2
Vote		
Tory	71.9	74.4
Reluctant Tory	4.6	3.0
Tory/Liberal	10.5	8.5
Liberal	3.9	4.3
Labour	2.0	4.3
Floater	3.9	4.3
Total	100%	100%
Voted Labour in the past	(%)	(%)
Never	76.1	82.7
Once	4.0	3.6
Yes	20.0	13.1
Total	100%	100%

fieldwork was carried out but may well now be attracting those who call themselves 'reluctant Tories' and who at the time were searching for a realistic alternative).

These figures provide stark confirmation of the observation made by the father that one needs to avoid the 'law of the zoo'. The Tory voters are as likely as the rest to identify the poor and the handi-capped as the victims of a system which rewards those who have either capital to invest or labour to sell, but however inequitable society may appear the correct solution is to be found in the enhance-ment of individual opportunities to compete rather than in increasing state power to protect the least powerful; hence the support for the Assisted Places scheme but not for the abolition of the private sector. Whilst current Tory voters are not significantly more likely to see either the trade unionists or the social security scroungers as having benefited unduly from the umbrella of the state, those amongst them who have never voted Labour in the past are more likely to see inequity in these terms. Of course voting patterns reflect many different interests and votes are not only about social issues of general concern but also about personal interests and needs. Both voting patterns and general attitudes towards equity do furnish some slender evidence to suggest that parents' norms and values are shaped more in terms of the point at which they have arrived than from where they come. This is highlighted by the fact that, whereas nearly 50 per cent of the fathers who have been mobile into Class I supported the Labour party in the past, there is no difference between those who have arrived and those who originate in Class I with respect to their current support for the Tories.

Class II is the group of fathers who deviate most markedly from the rest of this population, both in terms of being grossly under-represented and in terms of levels of income and ownership of capital. These fathers are the least likely of any to have had any private, let alone a public school, education and whereas a dispro-portionate number of those who have managed to gain higher qualifi-cations have done so by route of Oxbridge, most have had to resort to education outside the university sector. Possibly as a consequence of their current and past struggles the members of Class II are the least likely of any of the sample members to vote for the Tory party. The inequity of society appears to them as the victory of the top income group over those who lack power by virtue of their lack of education or their immigrant status; slightly more of these fathers than of the remainder are in favour of the Assisted Places scheme and are ambiguous towards rather than definitely opposed to abolition of the private sector but they are equally as concerned about the importance of preserving individual freedom of choice.

Class I contains more of the highest earners and of the best educated in terms of both university and public school education, but it is very diverse in terms of its composite occupations and the relationship of their members with other classes. Those with financial interests to protect are indeed the most solid in their support of the Tory party and they believe that the injustices of society are those perpetrated towards wealth by excessive taxation. Those who work in industry whether as the owners of capital or as its agents, the managers, employ largely unionised labour and therefore have the most direct and potentially antagonistic relationship with the union-ised faction of the working class. It is these fathers who are the most likely to name the trade unions as those who have used their power not at the expense of capital but to the detriment of the weak groups in society, particularly the elderly and the deserving poor. Along with the farmers, they are significantly the most unflinching in their support of the Tories.

The day-to-day working conditions and experiences of those in industry stand in marked contrast to those of the professionals, for whereas they and the self-employed professionals are largely motivated by profit their actual work situations are very different. These differences are reflected in the way that the professionals, whether self-employed or not, identify the inequities associated with capitalism. A higher proportion of the professional fathers emphasise the mobilization of power by the wealthy to the detriment of those who sell their labour and are prepared to work hard and take responsibility (presumably themselves) as well as the low paid. Their voting patterns confirm these attitudes inasmuch as they are the least likely of any group to consistently vote Tory but they do not stray very far in their partisanship, usually vacillating between a Tory and a Liberal vote. Despite their different modes of access to Class I, most of the self-employed professionals are born into it whereas the employees are more likely to have been upwardly mobile, the professional fathers differ little in their political orientations and their beliefs about the nature of inequality in Britain today.

The largest single occupational category in Class I found in the public schools is that of administrators and officials, the situs of their work does vary but many more of them are employed in commerce than in government. Like their peers who are employed as professionals, their own backgrounds vary but they share the relatively liberal attitudes of all the professionals rather than the conservative ones of those engaged in industry, and like all the groups who together make up the Class I parents these attitudes are unrelated to class of origin.

Class IV is constituted of two very different parts of the *petit bourgeoisie,* the farmers and the owners of small retail and manufacturing businesses. Both share the very high rate of self-recruitment into this class, over 70 per cent of the membership of each has inherited its class if not occupational position, yet each is markedly different in its political outlook. Both have been the subject of detailed research which highlights the differences between the two occupations.[24] The shop-keeping faction of the *petit bourgeoisie* is characterised by insecurity and uncertainty, caught between the demands of capital and labour. The farmers have been discussed within the context of a value system which is traditionally associated with land such that their normative and relational patterns differ from those entrepreneurs who are the owners of industrial and financial capital. Farmers work in close proximity to their employees and class relationships are defined in terms of moral obligation and paternalism as opposed to coercion and conflict. In economic terms the members of the *petit bourgeiosie* in this sample represent something of a convergence between the ideal-typical farmer and shopkeeper: although the farmers are indeed the owners of large amounts of capital by virtue of their stock as well as their land, they have been allocated to Class IV because they are mainly working farmers with a small number of employees; the proprietors of small businesses are probably atypical of their occupation inasmuch as they own significant amounts of capital, mainly in the range £10 000 to £50 000, and can afford the fees of a public school; yet the differences in the attitudes and voting patterns of the two groups do reflect their very different normative frameworks. The business proprietors display their feelings of marginality by being far more likely than the farmers and indeed the whole sample to mention both the high income groups and the trade unionists as the winners in our unequal society, whilst seeing those who work hard and are subject to heavy taxation as the losers. The farmers are unlikely to see society in conflictual terms, more of the them stress its equitable nature, but as a group they do express an above average concern for those on fixed income and those without work. One of the few farmers who can more accurately be described as a landowner, for although he works his 600 acres with five employees he does also own land which is tenanted, was singularly unwilling to discuss the class structure outside the rural scene. He clearly represents the 'stewardship of land' discussed by Newby[25] and the only group who he would identify as doing too well in society were those who inherit land but fail to preserve it for the benefit of society. In failing to respond to attempts to discuss the subject more widely he described his position as feudal and himself as ill-equipped to discuss matters beyond the rural community with which he is familiar.

Following the re-election of the Thatcher government, with its policies designed to appease populists both within the party and the electorate, Peregrine Worsthorne wrote in the *Sunday Telegraph*[26] calling for a return to the paternalistic values upon which the party was founded, values which it was argued have been preserved by a few institutions such as the old public schools and Oxbridge. Do the parents in this population, who are drawn disproportionately from both institutions, provide any evidence to support the assertion that they are the custodians, and indeed uniquely so, of such values? There is, in fact, very little which serves to distinguish those with a grammar school or university education from the majority of their more illustriously educated peers. Those who have been educated in a public school and particularly in one of the top ones, are more likely to identify a top class on the basis of inheritance and to carry forward with them a sense of responsibility towards their weaker brethren, showing a concern for the plight of the elderly and the handicapped rather than for those whose working conditions are arduous, but these are the only attitudes and beliefs which serve to distinguish some of the public school educated fathers from the remainder. Neither in their perceptions of the whole of the class structure and its legitimacy, nor in their faith in the different political parties to rectify society's wrongs do those who have been born to privilege differ from those who have married into it or achieved it in their own right.

The attempt to locate parents in class terms on the basis of their own subjective identification was soon abandoned in the face of the previously discussed tendency for individuals to place themselves in the middle of any hierarchy. Townsend[27] discusses the manner in which people seek to distinguish themselves clearly from the upper class as a strategy to deny an unfair recourse to resources in society whilst simultaneously wishing to disassociate themselves from the non-achievers below. This tendency reached its apogee in this research when a member of the occupational élite and one of the few hereditary peers in the sample each denied his position at the apex of the class structure. The latter, using a strictly money ladder model to rank people declined to place himself anywhere near the top for, despite his inherited land, he feels impoverished by his relative lack of liquid assests; whereas the member of the occupational élite who is both public school educated and in the top bracket of all forms of income and wealth sees himself strictly as a member of the middle class by virtue of his exclusion from royal circles. These two fathers illustrate clearly the clash between land and entrepreneurship which has bedevilled Britain's class system since the industrial revolution. Whilst entrepreneurs have aspired to but never fully achieved the style of life of the landed classes, the owners of land feel constantly threatened by new money and its associated values. Dahrendorf has argued only recently[28] that this is the basic weakness of the entrepreneurial class with its lack of confidence in its own life-style and values and the associated need to constantly emulate the landed class. This is the basis of the particular appeal of Thatcherism and the New Right which have provided a normative framework to liberate the entrepreneurs from the chains of tradition-alism. The findings of this research suggest that in addition to the support received by the New Right from the entrepreneurial and service classes, it is able to draw increasingly upon the landed class which is becoming bourgeoisified with the result that parents who come from a variety of backgrounds to meet at or near the apex of the class structure differ little in their norms and beliefs. It is their more recent and shared experiences which unite these diverse groups who still recognise the differences between them but are increasingly coming to share a common perception of society.

5 Why a Private Education?

Debates about the value of education abound in all parts of society. Economists differentiate between public and private goods and education is an oft-quoted example of a good which straddles the two arenas. Given its undoubted intrinsic qualities, education could be seen as an item strictly for private consumption but in practice it has proved impossible to disentangle this from its public investment aspects. Functionalists and Marxists are agreed that formal education performs two key functions for society: it provides 'qualified' people to participate in the division of labour of an advanced industrial economy and, possibly of even greater importance than the technical competence it bestows, it serves to foster the discipline necessary for the acceptance of the established relations of production and obedience to the existing authority relationships in the workplace. Thus education has the public benefit of providing society with a disciplined as well as a trained workforce whilst simultaneously giving additional private benefits to those in receipt of greater amounts of it, for there is a positive if not perfect relationship between the length of time spent in education and the level of material and status rewards.[1]

Parents, when making decisions about their children's education have a clear, if not always sharply defined, view of the social order for which their children are destined. As discussed in the previous chapter, most of the parents interviewed do perceive a distinct class structure in Britain. Whilst the majority perceive the apex of this structure as based upon inherited factors and therefore relatively closed to upward mobility, over three-quarters see social position within the remainder of the hierarchy as based upon a combination of attitudes, occupation and money, enabling social mobility to be achieved with relative ease in a downward as well as upward direction. Whilst education *per se* fails to define classes, it is ascribed a significant role in determining class access. Three-quarters of the

125

parents want, or at least hope that their sons will proceed to university and although somewhat reluctant to specify their aspirations for future occupations, the professions or other occupations requiring an above minimum level of education appear to be at a premium. Taking these findings together, it would not be wrong to surmise that at least one of the main purposes of education, as seen by the majority of parents, is to facilitate access to desired positions within the middle, if not the top, of the social class hierarchy.

Before considering in detail the kind of educational experiences which parents feel will be of value to their sons in preparing them for entry into this class hierarchy with its attendant dangers of downward social mobility seen as little less than the opportunities for movement in the opposite direction, it is necessary to consider the sources of information about the maintained sector available to the parents who are rejecting it in favour of the private alternative. On what are their views based? From where do they gain their knowledge about the state education which they are rejecting in favour of the private sector? Whereas nearly half of the fathers and of the mothers had themselves been privately educated, knowledge of the state counterpart is not confined to half of the couples interviewed. The extent of the educational exogamy discussed in Chapter 2 is such that familiarity with the maintained sector of education and not ignorance of it is the norm. The experience of such an education has been a remarkably successful one, for the fathers at least, for it has been shown that for the fathers who have experienced upward mobility into their Class I positions such mobility is associated not with a private education but with a state one. In addition therefore, to asking how useful parents' own educational experiences are when it comes to making decisions for their sons one needs to consider the reasons why there is the lack of faith in contemporary provisions that is exhibited by the successful, state educated fathers.

State education has undergone a marked change since the time that these parents were at school. There have been significant alterations both in the institutional character of secondary schooling in the form of the transition from a predominantly bipartite structure to predominantly comprehensive education and, of possibly even greater significance, in the actual experience of learning. The move towards comprehensive reorganisation was fuelled by the demonstrated failure of the 1944 Education Act to significantly widen access to academic education. These provisions, notably selection on the basis of merit as opposed to parental means, were aimed at satisfying the dual demand for efficiency and equity by drawing upon the available pool of untapped talent to simultaneously stimulate Britain's economic growth and satisfy the desire to promote equality of opportunity. Marsden[2] documents clearly the essentially conflicting ideologies which have come together to stimulate the growth and development of comprehensive secondary education. He discusses how the particular organisational form which each gives rise to will depend upon the combination of ideologies produced by the participating actors involved in bringing the schools into being. The ideal-typical forms he names as: the 'meritocratic school' which is grounded in the belief that society should be stratified according to talent rather than inherited position, resulting in the streamed comprehensive; and the 'community school' which is based upon the desire for a wide diffusion of power in society, enabling local democratic decision making, resulting in the need for an unstreamed learning situation and calling for a radical alteration in the learning process.

Attempts to monitor the results of comprehensive reorganisation are confounded by this lack of unity in the organising principles and their resultant forms; the fact that education is a locally provided service with varying rates and patterns of change such that some local education authorities maintain an element of selection whilst others do not; and of course the continued existence of the private sector and (until 1976) of the direct grant schools. In general, it would appear that the comprehensive schools have found favour with neither their supporters nor their critics, the former are disappointed by their failure to reduce inequality whilst the latter claim that they have succeeded in lowering the educational standards of this country. Ford[3] in a study of a streamed inner London comprehensive school evaluated its achievements in terms of four criteria: the greater development of talent, as measured by examination results; the greater equality of opportunity for those with equal talent, as measured by differential class access to the top streams; widening childrens' occupational horizons; and increasing social interaction across class and ability. Her evidence suggests that the school that she studied failed singularly to achieve any of these aims and merely served to reproduce the divisions of the tripartite structure, albeit under one roof. Meanwhile, starting in 1969, a series of attacks were launched on the educational system from the political right by the new notorious Black Papers.[4] In criticising the comprehensive schools they laid particular stress on the way in which the diversion of resources away from the very bright child to the average child would

be to the detriment of the former who would be unable to escape to
the private sector. In a consideration of the likely outcome of the
abolition of streaming, Bell,[5] a former grammar school headmaster,
discussed the levelling down pressures on children wishing to work
which the mixed ability teaching groups and the anti-academic ethos
of the schools would foster and he argued that this would be to the
detriment of Britain's economy which needs a highly educated workforce. By 1977 a preliminary analysis of the comparable results from
the comprehensives and the bipartite schools was published in the
Black Paper of that year[6] and the inevitable conclusion was drawn
that academic standards were indeed falling.

Amongst the most recently published research into the effects of
the reorganisation of secondary schooling on educational performance is that carried out by the National Children's Bureau which is
monitoring the progress of a group of children born during one week
in 1958. Its findings provide little in the way of support for either side
of the antagonists in the war over comprehensives; its latest report[7]
deals with the performance of the children at GCE ordinary level and
whilst this shows that the total impact of reorganising secondary
schools into comprehensives is minimal, with the possibility that the
children of average ability who came from middle class homes and
went to comprehensive schools fared slightly less well than their
grammar school educated peers, its value is reduced by the lack of
homogeneity which characterised comprehensive schooling at the
time of the research.

Whilst findings such as these do little to confirm the fears of parents
whose children were destined for the grammar schools, they have low
visibility as compared to the moral panic over the impact on Britain's
educational standards of progressive education and the new sociology
of education that has been generated by the media and right-wing
politicians. Progressive education, with its emphasis on child-centred
teaching methods, seemed to be a necessary accompaniment to
comprehensive reorganisation for it was believed that equality could
not be achieved merely by altering the structure of education, it had
to be accompanied by a change in pedagogy. The Bennett Report[8]
was only one of a number of the virulent attacks on progressive
education and its effects on the attainment of primary school pupils
which were widely reported in the right-wing press.

At the end of the 1960s what has come to be known as the 'new
sociology of education' launched its critical attack upon the 'received'
view of what is problematic in education and why working class

children are failing to achieve in middle class terms. This received view was manifested in the concern to maintain the traditional goals of education, the reproduction of inequality, whilst seeking to share access to unequal positions more widely between unequal social groups. The new sociology of education draws on two sociological perspectives, the interactionist and the phenomenological. Emerging from the first are those studies which have focused upon the inter-action between pupils and teachers and shown it to be charac-teristically traditional and conservative with a heavy emphasis on authoritarianism. Keddie[9] documents the manner in which, in a large comprehensive school, the teachers use conservative categories to organise both educational knowledge and their perceptions of the pupils' abilities. In many cases this pattern prevailed despite the teachers concerned subscribing formally to an educational policy which dictated both integrated curricula and no streaming. Drawing on its phenomenological roots, this new sociology questions what actually constitutes appropriate knowledge in terms of content and the manner in which it is organised. The earlier writings of Young[10] are essentially devoted to a consideration of what counts as educational knowledge and to showing how all knowledge is socially and historically constructed, relative to a particular time or social context. Thus what constitutes an educational curriculum is merely a particular selection and organisation from a plurality of potential available knowledges. This process of selection invokes the stratification of knowledge, placing a high premium on the academic curriculum as opposed to daily life or common experience. Consequently, professional teachers, particularly those who have undergone a period of training in academic subjects, are endowed with high status and a rigid distinction is maintained between teachers and taught.

Bernstein, drawing upon the writings of Marx, Durkheim and Mead, discusses the management of knowledge and this is articulated most clearly in his paper 'On the Classification and Framing of Educational Knowledge'.[11] Here he distinguishes between the manner in which knowledge content can be classified either into discrete subjects with clearly defined boundaries or into packages where the boundaries between disciplines are not sharply drawn. The former he labels the 'collection' type and the latter the 'integrated' type. He proceeds to differentiate between strong and weak framing of knowledge, thereby codifying Young's concept of the stratification of knowledge: strong framing refers to highly stratified knowledge, with a clearly drawn boundary between what is considered appropriate educational knowledge and what is not, with the result that the teacher has a limited range of options of what to teach but increased power in the pedaegogical relationship as the pupils have no control at all over what is taught. Where framing is weak both the teacher and the pupils have increased power to determine the material to be included in the classroom situation, how the day will be structured and so on. The organisation of knowledge into either collection codes or integrated codes will result in different socialisation experiences for both the teachers and the pupils. At the time of writing, Bernstein described the English education system as collected, with strong subject loyalty. In secondary schools at least this collection code was accompanied by strong framing.

In his later writings, Young proceeds to translate his earlier ideas into a 'sociology of education relevant to teachers' which therefore has to 'start with classroom practices and on those who produce constraints'[12] and gradually his work was incorporated into the teacher training courses at London's postgraduate insititute of education and beyond. Bernstein's later writings represent a shift from his earlier micro-level of analysis to a macro-one. What happens in the classroom is not isolated from the social context within which it is located and Bernstein seeks to discover the origins of the dominant power and control relations within the school.[13] In so doing he moves closer to the inspirations of Marx by linking the education superstructure to the economic base of capitalism. He is concerned to show how the distribution of the education codes described in his earlier work[14] is systematically linked to the anticipated part that the pupils will play in the social division of labour of production. Thus in secondary schools the 'less able' (working class) pupils are more likely to be exposed to integrated codes and weak framing, whilst their 'more able' (middle class) counterparts are socialised into collection codes and strong framing and are therefore poised to embark upon university careers and corresponding occupations. The stronger the role of education in its approximate reproduction of the workforce, the stronger the grip of the mode of production upon the education codes. If the relative autonomy of education is preserved, the power of production is maintained indirectly through the forms of middle class control realised in the codes of education.

Bernstein's writings serve to provide a useful bridge between the new sociology of education and the varities of Marxist writings which assert the political nature of education in capitalist economies. Such writings seek to establish a correspondence between society and schooling such that education is essentially concerned with social reproduction. These writings vary with respect to the primacy that each ascribes to the economy in determining the education superstructure. Bowles and Gintis[15] posit a one to one correspondence between capitalism's social relations of production and the authority relations that can be found in educational establishments and they describe how the relationships within the school are designed to ensure that pupils are well socialised for the future roles in the system of production.

Bourdieu[16] discusses the screening and consequent selection which is carried out in schools. Whilst this process invokes the use of academic criteria in a way which is acceptable to societies whose ideologies are increasingly meritocratically based, the effect is the same as if social or ethnic criteria were used. Thus the education systems of capitalist societies succeed in converting social hierarchies into academic ones and fulfil the function of legitimation which is more or less necessary in today's social order. Common to the writings of Bernstein, Bowles and Gintis and Bourdieu is the way in which they see the schools as disguising the true process of social reproduction. Giddens,[17] in a somewhat different context, identifies the selfsame feature of contemporary capitalist societies, the pressure upon the established upper class(es) to remain invisible in a society where the ideology of equality of opportunity prevails.

Given that at the time of writing education remains a locally provided and controlled service which gives a unique autonomy to its teachers, it is difficult to assess the full impact that such ideas have had upon the actual experience of schooling. The most widely publicised attempt to implement them and the response that this evoked is the William Tyndale episode where the headmaster and a group of teachers sought to radically alter the learning experiences of their primary school pupils. The fear that there are many William Tyndales which never see the light of day has provoked a backlash, the full magnitude of which is just beginning to be revealed. The early Conservative attacks on comprehensive reorganisation contained in the Black Papers were followed by a number of proposed changes by the first Thatcher government. The abolition of the Schools Council on which the teaching profession was well represented and its replacement by an Examination Body and a Curriculum Body where the weakened position of the teachers has resulted in the National Union of Teachers' declination to make any nominations; the withholding of a small proportion of the Rate

Support Grant to local authorities to be used to fund specific grants for education development schemes;[18] and the proposals contained in the 1983 White Paper on Teaching Quality[19] to radically alter the selection, training and deployment of teachers are all examples of the Thatcher government's firm intention to exercise greater control over what is taught in schools, how it is taught and by whom.

However, the critique of the current state of education which is reflected by these proposals and publications is not confined to the political right. The spate of reports appearing in the mid to late 1970s which were concerned with the effects of progressivism, identifying low standards,[20] subversive teaching[21] and disruption in schools[22] were taken up by the Labour government of the time. It was Callaghan who, as Prime Minister, launched the 'Great Debate in Education' in 1976 when in a speech at Ruskin College he issued his call for a core curriculum in basic subjects. This was followed by the publication of a Green Paper[23] by the Secretary of State for Education, Shirley Williams, which, in its statements about the Secretary of State not abdicating from curricular responsibilities, hinted strongly at a possible swing of power to the centre. Eggleston[24] in asking whether teachers had effectively increased their power in making curriculum decisions (such that there were at least some grounds for advancing the sorts of policies outlined in the Green Paper), is optimistic in his answer for he concludes that ' . . . the reflexive curriculum, based upon interpretations of teachers, seems to be in ascendency'. Certainly the Mode 3 examinations in CSE and GCE have given teachers increased control over the curriculum. Others, however, are less optimistic about the power of the 'new sociology' of education to radically reshape teachers' thinking and practices. Demaine[25] sees the writings of the 'new sociology' as 'empty of specifics and pitched at such a high theoretical level as to be confusing . . '. This view is shared by members of the Centre for Contemporary Cultural Studies who, in describing the failure of the teachers who were trained in the 1970s in this new sociology of education to challenge the Fabianism of the left, identify how the combination in these courses of

> high abstraction and crushing detail, as well as distance from the everyday world of the schools has served to inoculate teachers against such "experts" with the consequence that the newer forms of socio-educational analysis are no more attractive or accessible to practising teachers . . . [26]

Amidst this confusion, parents have little opportunity to assess for themselves the full impact of the new sociology of education and of progressive teaching. There are a number of limited ways open to them to either renew or initiate familiarity with what is actually happening in the maintained sector of education in order to establish a basis for rejecting it for one or more of their children. These range from the first-hand experience resulting from the use of the maintained sector either for the sons under discussion (since removed to the private sector) or for their siblings, through a professional or possibly voluntary involvement with the schools and/or second-hand experiences related by friends and relatives to third-hand information gleaned from the media. For some parents merely being the employer of state educated labour is a sufficient basis for the wholesale condemnation of its provisions. It is paradoxical that it is one of the few fathers who was himself educated at a secondary modern school who should have concluded, in discussing the employees in the small garage that he owns:

the state is a waste of time – they come out at sixteen as complete duffers.

RECENT CONTACT WITH THE MAINTAINED SECTOR OF EDUCATION

The 190 sets of parents[27] inteviewed had an average of 2.6 children each producing a total of 498 children between them (Table 5.1).

These children ranged in age from 3 to 43, thus encompassing the potential for a wide range of educational experiences. Of the 498 children 232 are boys who were actually in the schools used in the survey at the time of the interview, seven were under school age,

TABLE 5.1 *Number of children in the family*

		(%)
1	child only	7.4
2	children	44.2
3	children	32.1
4	children	12.6
5+	children	3.7
	Total	100%

leaving 259 who were receiving or had received their education in schools other than those used for the study. Their parents' contact with the maintained sector of education could therefore be nil, confined to the primary sector or extended to the secondary one which is currently being rejected for the boys under consideration. Any assessment of the impact that direct knowledge of the maintained secondary schools (through their use for other children) has upon the parents' decision regarding these boys is complicated by the fact that the available alternatives vary not only between parents in different parts of the country but also within families as provisions alter for children of different ages. Analysis of the available information shows that eight of the boys now in the public schools (equal to 4 per cent of families) had in fact been to a maintained secondary school prior to entering their present schools and therefore the decision to educate them privately was based upon direct knowledge of the alternatives.

> We initially thought it would be a good thing for the boys to 'muck in together with their friends' at the local comprehensive and we sent . . . for a year but it just did not work . . . a disaster . . . a year's boredom . . . left to his own devices.

In addition 20 per cent of the parents did have or had had other children in the maintained secondary sector, 11 per cent at comprehensive schools and 9 per cent at a grammar school. On the basis of these figures there is scant evidence to support the view that the decision to reject state education at the secondary level is the result of direct experience of any substance, either through the children immediately concerned or through their siblings. Eleven per cent of the parents did say their decision was the direct result of a poor experience with the maintained sector, but not all of these experiences were with secondary schools for approximately half of the boys have spent some time at a state primary school and this may have influenced at least some of their parents in the choice of a secondary school. Table 5.2 and 5.3 show the type of primary school education received by the boys currently in the public schools and the stage at which they entered their present schools. These tables show a remarkably conventional pattern of entry into the public schools, with relatively little transfer from the maintained sector at the age of eleven.

TABLE 5.2 *Primary school education*

	1st boy (190) (%)	2nd boy (36) (%)
Totally private	55.8	58.3
Predominantly private (i.e. since infants (7–8)	12.6	11.1
	68.4	69.4
Predominantly Maintained (i.e. a year or two in private prior to change)	11.6	22.6
All state	19.5	8.3
Total	100%	100%

TABLE 5.3 *Stage of entry to present school*

	1st boy (190) (%)	2nd boy (36) (%)
From the preparatory dept	15.8	31.0
Aged 11	22.6	13.9
Aged 12	1.6	0
Aged 13	58.9	55.5
6th form	1.1	0
Total	100%	100%

Whilst this suggests that many parents have used the state primary school as a pre-preparatory school with their sons destined for the private sector regardless, others, such as this mother may have genuinely turned to the private sector only after their disappointment with what they found at the primary school:

We started A—off at the state school as we had never been to one ourselves and did not know what they are like. Having seen what they are like no way . . . I would rather go out to work.

Some support for this possibility is provided by the evidence contained in the tables illustrating how experiences similar to this have resulted in fewer of the younger brothers entering the public schools at the age of eleven with a corresponding increase in the use made of the preparatory departments.

Regretfully information about the type of primary school education of the older siblings is incomplete and this makes it impossible to assess how many additional families have some direct knowledge of the maintained primary sector which they could have used in deciding upon the type of education to choose for the sons under discussion. A cross-tabulation of the primary school education of these boys with the known educational experiences of their siblings shows that as well as the 24 per cent of families who have had at least one child at a state secondary school, 30 per cent have had some experience of the primary school education offered by the maintained sector. Conversely, 19 per cent of the parents are known to have had no direct experience of the provisions of any part of the maintained sector before deciding to use the private sector, leaving approximately a quarter of the families for whom no relevant information is available (Table 5.4).

Thus a maximum of a half of the parents interviewed would appear to have chosen to educate their sons in the private sector despite their lack of any direct experience of the contemporary state alternative and, of even greater significance, three-quarters of them had no first-hand knowledge of the provisions at the secondary level which they have rejected. In discussing their decision to turn their backs on the state schools, 18 per cent of the parents did mention either the lack of a grammar school in their area or the uncertainty that the boy

TABLE 5.4 *Summary of parents' contact with the educational provisions of the maintained sector through their own children*

Level of education	
Secondary: With sons currently at public schools	4.2
With other children at a grammar school	9.0
With other children at a comprehensive school	11.0
Total secondary contact	24.2
Primary: with sons currently at public school	30.0
Total contact	54.2
No contact	19.0
No information available	26.8
Total	100%

would gain a place, as a factor in the decision. Most of the few parents whose other children had been grammar school educated explained the difference in their treatment of their children in terms of the fact that they could not afford to educate all their children privately and where a grammar school education had been a realistic option for the other children but not for the boys under discussion they were using the private sector to compensate. Typical of such parents is the engineer, father of five children who said:

I would not have looked at independent education if the grammar school still existed in this area. R—is tailor made for the grammar school – the worst thing that happened to the education system in this country was the passing of the grammar schools.

A comparison of the sort of secondary education provided for male and female siblings does show a small, although statistically insignificant, tendency for more girls than boys to be educated within the maintained sector.

TABLE 5.5 *Secondary education of the boy's siblings*

	Comprehensive	Grammar	Private	Total
Boys (%)	11.0	6.0	83.0	100%
Girls (%)	17.0	10.0	73.0	100%

When asked to explain the different forms of education used for these children, a few parents did reveal sex-typed attitudes towards boys' and girls' education. The parents of girls not in private secondary schools were more likely than the parents of similar boys to stress the individual nature of each child and the need to provide the sort of education best suited to their individual needs. Over a third of the admittedly small number of parents using the comprehensives in which to educate sisters admitted that they could not afford to send all their children to private schools and so, as one privately educated couple, members of the social élite, explained:

People are beginning to move girls into the comprehensives whilst continuing to use private schools for the boys.

Or, as a secondary modern educated father bluntly put it:

I don't feel inclined to spend money on educating the girls.

INDIRECT CONTACT THROUGH RELATIVES AND FRIENDS

A more tenuous contact with what is happening in the maintained sector of education is established through the experiences of friends and relatives. An almost equal number, approximately 40 per cent, of the husbands and the wives have relatives who are currently using the maintained system in which to educate their children, but, totaling the experiences of the relatives of the husbands and the wives shows that only 17 per cent of the couples have relatives who are educating all their children outside the state system and this has to be contrasted with the corresponding estimate of 50 per cent of these parents. Social networks are composed of friends as well as kin and the parents are more likely to have (or to choose) friends whose attitudes towards the state sector correspond with their own for just over a half of the couples interviewed have friends who were educating their children predominantly within the private sector. No distinction has been made between use of the primary and the secondary sectors of the maintained sector but a quarter of the couples' friends are educating their children exclusively within the private sector. Combining statements about the education of the children of friends and relatives shows that 45 per cent of the parents belong to a social network where private education is the predominant mode of educating the children. Parents who feel that they are at odds with their friends and relatives in this respect were at pains to explain why their behaviour differed and essentially two types of explanation were invoked. On the one hand finance: whilst some parents stressed that their friends and relatives would like to educate their own children in a like manner but could not afford to do so, others clearly stated that they believe them to be acting selfishly in choosing to spend their money on items of consumption rather than investing it in their childrens' future. Alternatively, other parents believe their friends' actions in rejecting private education to be politically inspired and some gleefully told of friends where the political convictions of at least one of the partners concerned had initially led them into the maintained sector but who are gradually returning to private education following their actual experiences with the comprehensives. Thus friends in particular would seem to be an important point of reference for parents when choosing the education of their children and this is obviously a subject which is widely and frequently discussed.

A MEASURE OF ISOLATION FROM THE MAINTAINED SECTOR

Although the evidence presented so far does not add up to a substantial involvement, either directly or indirectly, with the maintained sector of education such that the decision to educate children privately could be described as the result of considerable knowledge and careful consideration of the state alternative, it would be equally misleading to portray these parents as a group of people who are traditionally isolated from the maintained sector, locked into a social network and style of life characterised by the virtually exclusive use of private education. In only twenty families, 10.5 per cent of those interviewed, have neither of the parents nor any of the children ever been to a maintained school and in only another 25 has the combined experience of the parents' and childrens' education been that of a predominantly private education. Only 26 out of the total of 45 families (14 per cent of all the parents) where private education is the norm have friends and relatives who are educating their children in a similar fashion and could thus be described as highly isolated from the maintained sector of the education in terms of their own education and that of the children of this generation. They stand in contrast to the greater proportion of parents who are 'moving into' the private sector despite their previous distance from it, for only a fifth of the 58 couples whose own combined educational experiences were predominantly within the maintained sector have friends and relatives who are joining them in their use of private education.

THE ROLE OF THE MEDIA

Even if the parents have had the opportunity to learn about the maintained sector of education through their own experiences or those of their friends and relatives, this is inevitably narrowly based and they are ultimately dependent upon the media for a more broadly based view of whether or not there is a crisis in education. The power of the media in shaping the perceptions of the parents can be gleaned from an interview with Mr and Mrs X. Living in the inner city, the parents of two boys at a major day school, neither has been state educated and nor have they had any substantial contemporary state contact either directly through their own boys or indirectly through the experiences of their friends and relatives. Yet the wife explained the decision to 'go privately' on the following grounds:

> State schools in this area are appalling . . . they really are black-board jungles and one would have to be very brave parents to feel that one's own home background and educational levels in helping one's children were such that they [the children] could survive [in the state schools].

At least the next parent can claim some 'expertise' for arriving at a similar conclusion. He represents the polar opposite to the parents just described, living in the far reaches of the home counties, the father of a son with a local authority place at a medium sized boarding school and a daughter at a state boarding school, he and his wife received their education exclusively in the maintained state sector, both at grammar schools, and have friends and relatives who are mainly using state schools for their children's education. This father believes that:

> If we just had the comprehensive schools we might as well go to war with the Russians and be blown up because I don't think this country would last till the end of the century.

Not all parents are as wholehearted in their condemnation of the maintained sector as the two just quoted. There is evidence amongst some parents of uncertainty and indeed confusion not only over what had already taken place but also of what is yet to come. These interviews took place after the Thatcher government had made clear its increasing reliance on the private sector, having already announced its intention to cut government expenditure on state education whilst simultaneously investing more into the private sector in the guise of funding the Assisted Places and having placed the voucher system on the agenda for discussion. With all these question marks hanging over the maintained sector it is hardly surprising that some parents should choose to play safe by buying an education whose short term future seems secure and which provides an educational environment which at least has the advantage of familiarity. As one state educated mother, married to a private but not public school educated father, put it when discussing teaching methods:

> I would rather they did not experiment with my son thank you.

THE ADVANTAGES OF A PRIVATE EDUCATION

The reasons that parents give for choosing a private education for their sons are many and varied and number between one and nine, with an average of 4.4 reasons and a standard deviation of 1.9 reasons. Answers came at varying levels of abstraction and ranged from a generalised commitment to private education and the need to 'do one's best' to a very precise view of the specific advantages that it would bring. The history of the emergence and development of the public schools within the private sector is fraught with the tension between their academic and traditional functions. The origins of these schools were discussed in the first chapter and were shown to lie amidst the endowed grammar schools which were established in order to give their pupils a classical education. It was only as the schools enlarged their curriculum to include a general liberal education, no longer enslaved to instrumental ends, that upper class parents began to seek entry into them. The Newsom Report[28] identifies the traditional values of the Edwardian days espoused by the schools themselves: service to the community, leadership, initiative and finally self-reliance. These have been expanded in recent times to embrace but not to be replaced by the goal of academic success. More recently, Scott,[29] in his discussion of the upper classes in Britain today identifies three possible advantages that a public school education can offer to those seeking access to and acceptance by these classes. Undoubtedly there is a need for academic skills, the necessary certificates to prove technical competence but in addition there is the importance of cultural integration to ensure a shared set of values and beliefs, and finally inclusion in the 'old-boy' network with its distinctive style of life and useful social contacts. Whether or not the schools are uniquely successful in meeting any of these functions singly let alone in combination is not the issue, for what counts is whether or not the parents believe this to be the case.

From the evidence to hand, it would appear that the parents, both as a collectivity and as individuals, do believe that the schools confer a multiplicity of advantages when compared to the state alterntive and these are listed in Table 5.6.

From this it can be seen that academic advantage stands out as the single most important reason for choosing a private education, mentioned by 52 per cent of the parents with 12 per cent giving it as the only reason. Academic success is essentially about getting examination results–O levels, A levels and entrance to the universities and the

TABLE 5.6   *Reasons for choosing a private education*

Advantage	Percent of couples who mention these*
Better academic results	52.0
Character and discipline training	48.0
Children treated as individuals	46.0
Better teachers and/or methods	40.0
Fuller education	36.0
Size of school and/or classes	34.0
Get on better in life	28.0
Mix with a better type of child	27.0
Develops confidence and/or independence	26.0
Stretch and/or develop children	22.0
Polish children	18.0
Do one's best	17.0
With children who want to learn	13.0
Freedom to choose	12.0
Family tradition	9.0
Better facilities	8.0
Old school tie	8.0
Boarding need	6.0

*These do not total 100% as parents gave an average of 4.4 reasons.

professions, for as we have seen a university education is the immediate goal of many of the parents.

> Everything is on the margin . . . the answer is that I believe that if my son, by going to a public school . . . gets a five per cent better chance of going to a university and therefore of getting a degree . . . he may just need that five per cent as that may be the difference between success and failure

explained a member of the financial upper class. Direct experience of the provisions of the state, albeit at a primary level, clearly contributes to the belief in this aspect of the superiority of the private sector for 70 per cent of the parents of sons who had been to a state primary school as opposed to 45 per cent of those who had not give academic results as a reason for using private education. An examination of the socio-economic and educational background of the parents emphasising this advantage reveals little that is distinctive about them and they would appear to be drawn equally from the whole population using the public schools. The notable exceptions to this conclusion are the fathers educated in the non-selective part of the state system (themselves a small part of the total parents) and the self-employed in business, both of whom are more likely to mention the importance of academic results, but in general their importance and association with the private sector is widespread.

This common endorsement of the importance of academic results, shared by parents of varying backgrounds, could be construed as a legitimation of a range of other motives which underlie the choice of a private education but it does suggest that the public schools are having to respond to changing demands from their clientele and as a consequence are relinquishing some of their control over their ability to define the content of their own curriculum. Smith[30] identifies how, with the gradual erosion of the traditional organisation of learning in the comprehensive schools, new norms are beginning to challenge those which have traditionally governed education, placing a far greater emphasis upon unstructured learning. Yet these new norms are operating within a macro-social structure which is placing increasing value on credentialism to determine access to key positions within the division of labour; therefore whilst some schools within the maintained sector of education may be redefining the rules which govern the race to success, the definition of the winner of the race remains unaltered. Smith suggests that the winners under these new rules will be those who can succeed in this new, largely unstructured environment. For those parents, however, who can afford the fees it is not necessary to enter their children for a race which is governed by these new rules, the simple solution appears to be to withdraw them from the maintained sector where the new rules have reached their apogee and place them in a learning environment whose norms they both recognise and endorse. In this way the parents simultaneously contribute towards the continued use of credentialism as the method of selection and ensure that they maximise their sons' chances of success in the macro-economic structure. The schools for their part, however reluctantly they are responding to new markets and new demands from their traditional market in the effort to meet their ever rising costs, have come to inherit the mantle of the largely defunct grammar schools and are beginning to return to the form from which they originated. At the same time, they too are playing a part in sustaining the meritocratic ideals of the 1944 Education Act into which an increasing number of their parents were socialised and thereby are retarding possible change in the maintained sector.

If academic success is the principal long term goal of the parents, and by the same token of the schools, one needs to turn one's attention to the perceived means of achieving this – in what ways can the private sector be said to facilitate academic success? Answers to this question, as seen through the eyes of the parents, fall into three main categories: the nature of the teachers and what they can do for the children; the facilities at their disposal and the other children in the school.

Forty per cent of the parents mentioned superior teachers and/or their methods as an important advantage of a private education. They believe that the subjects taught and the methods used are more traditional and less experimental and that the teachers are simply 'better' in terms of qualifications, greater dedication and accessibility and less transient. Some parents recognise that this is facilitated by better pay and less stressful working conditions, but a handful do specifically mention the morals, politics and general demeanour of the teachers as important, conveying a strong impression that they see the teachers in the maintained sector as not only inept and selling their pupils short but as politically motivated in their attempts to foster revolution. Thus whilst the state was seen as 'a great place for experimentation by any crank educationalist who comes along' by many of the parents, fear of political indoctrination was voiced by a few. The general belief in the superiority of the teachers was confirmed by one parent, the deputy headmaster of an inner-city comprehensive school:

> there are poorer teachers in the comprehensive schools . . . [they] have been underpaid for so long that the quality of the staff is poor.

What the parents appear to want is for the teachers to give their children the individual attention which they feel the maintained sector cannot provide, and this is particularly marked amongst the parents of boys who had a state primary education. Forty-six per cent of the parents mentioned that their children are individuals who need to develop at their own rate and approximately a quarter of these parents feel that whilst the maintained sector caters for children who are very bright, their own sons need the individual attention and encouragement of the teachers to develop their full potential; a further quarter indicated that they believe their sons to be of above average intelligence and as a consequence their progress would be retarded if they remained within the state system. The remainder gave no clear indication as to where they feel their sons fit into this hierarchy of intelligence but merely emphasised the importance of individual attention and getting to know the children in depth, thereby maximising the opportunities available to the teacher to tap the potential talent of the individual child.

In addition, 22 per cent of the parents were very specific about the methods to be used in propelling their sons towards their ultimate goal, stressing the importance of continual pushing so that they are stretched to achieve ever expanding goals. This method of securing academic results is particularly favoured by fathers who have been educated in the maintained sector and whose consequent distance from and lack of familiarity with the private sector possibly makes them unaware of the methods used. A typical parent of this ilk is the police officer who appears to be wholehearted in his condemnation of the comprehensive schools for failing to drive the children on. In discussing the schools in his area he vehemently rejects the developments that have taken place in education pedagogy:

> Many of the schools that I come into contact with as a policeman should be closed down. The teachers are totally unfit to be called teachers, I would call them childminders . . . it is the teachers' job to drive children on, not to be loved by the class.

Yet on closer examination of his attitudes towards contemporary education provisions, one is alerted to the extent to which both he and his wife have placed private education on a pedestal, possessed of complete faith in its power to further the individual in his career. In turns out that this father is not really rejecting the contemporary provisions of the state which he has attacked so strongly, but is looking to the private sector to provide opportunities which he feels his own secondary modern education has denied him:

> Looking back my whole life has been wasted as my education was so bad . . . I had to educate myself . . a lot could have been avoided if I had gone to a decent school and I suppose that was at the back of my mind when I decided to send—

Stretching and developing the child is not always down to the individual teachers but needs to be seen within the overall context of the facilities that the schools can offer. Parents do recognise that the teacher's job is made easier by the relatively small size of the classes that they have to teach. A third of them mentioned the daunting size of the comprehensive schools and/or, more usually, that the class sizes are too big to enable the sort of education that they desire. In the main, few parents believe that the private schools offer better facilities *per se* and in fact many specifically mentioned that these schools are superior in spite of the undoubtedly better facilities that many comprehensives have at their disposal and they voiced their regret or even disgust that these expensive facilities are put to such poor use. Thus it was rare for parents to see better physical ameni- ties, as distinct from size of classes, as an important means whereby academic success can be achieved and it is the parents who do not place as much emphasis on academic results who are the more likely to mention better facilities as an important advantage of a private education.

Finally one needs to consider the effects of the presence of the other boys in the school. Thirteen per cent of the parents consider their presence to be a distinct asset, one of the many advantages of a private education. There is the feeling that parents who are prepared to invest large sums of money in their sons' education must be strongly committed to it and this inevitably rubs off on their sons, to the advantage of the boys being educated with them. A few of the parents believe that their own sons benefit from being educated with (other) clever boys who provide a competitive and stimulating envi- ronment but in general parents who mention the other boys in the school as one of the advantages of a private education believe that they contribute to an environment where education in its traditional form is valued by all and where the majority of pupils expect to remain at school until the age of eighteen.

That the parents are correct in their view of the schools as provid- ing better academic results is beyond debate, what is at issue is the extent to which this is the result of the schools and what they have to offer and how much is the result of the nature of their pupils and the families from which they come. Kalton[31] had acces to the GCE O and A level results of the 6 per cent of public schoolboys in his sample who were known to have failed their eleven plus. He concludes that it is the better teaching at the public schools rather than the boys' IQs which helps the schools to play their part in monopolising the top positions, for he is able to show that amongst the 6 per cent of eleven plus failures 72 per cent gained four or more O levels as compared with 67 per cent of the grammar school boys in the same year. He fails, however, to control for the length of time that the boys remain at school and it may be that the difference can be explained by the fact that fewer of the grammar school boys were able to remain at school long enough to sit for their O levels.

In response to the question 'does type of school matter?' Halsey, [32] comes to the conclusion that boys of the same social background at the public, direct grant and grammar schools had very similar GCE O level records and whilst those at the public and direct grant schools were more likely to stay in school beyond O level the differences were not great. He concludes that 'parents who had a choice between the three types of school would have gained very little for the expenses of fees at the private school'. This may not necessarily be the case for the parents of children who would not have won a grammar school place but evidence for this is scanty. His conclusion serves to illustrate Bourdieu's argument that the purpose of education is not to transmit academic, or more generally technical, skills, but to legitimate the reproduction of cultural capital. That access to the private schools is determined predominantly by the possession of economic as well as cultural capital emphasises the fact that cultural capital has not succeeded in displacing economic capital as the mechanism of reproduction but is merely placed alongside it as another option open to parents in the process of transmitting their own advantages to the next generation. The demise of the grammar schools enhances the power of the private schools to ensure that cultural capital in its present form is both preserved and passed on.

Whilst acknowledging the importance that parents undoubtedly attach to academic results, the occupational and economic success of their sons and the part that they perceive that the private schools play in this process, one needs to consider more carefully the interrelationship between these variables. At one level is 'everything about opportunity' as one parent suggested and if so is such opportunity linked exclusively to academic results or are there other ways in which children can be helped to succeed? Is the concern with opportunity confined to economic and occupational success such that education and position in the class structure are conterminous or do parents perceive any non-insrumental benefits to be derived from this form of education? In beginning to answer these questions the parents and their responses need to be divided into various categories. There are those (about 16 per cent of the parents) who articulate their essential concern for their sons to get on in life and their belief that this will be achieved by getting academic results:

'The first thing that an employer asks for is qualifications' said a grammar school educated managing director of a large contracting company, a member of the occupational élite. To these parents can be added the far larger number (36 per cent) who stressed the importance of academic results without specifically mentioning their wish for their sons to 'get on' but to whom such a motive could be imputed, making a total of 52 per cent of the parents who clearly state or appear to believe that their sons will get on better life if they have good academic results. A small minority of parents (13 per cent) also indicated that they attach great importance to their sons getting on in life but they do not give any indication that they link success to academic success, there are other ways in which the schools will help their sons to succeed. The remainder, about a third, of the parents gave no indication that they are using the schools in their pursuit of such instrumental goals and a fifth of them specifically denied that their sole or even most important function is academic with its implications of economic and occupational success. Neither this, nor the fact that the schools are seen as offering other advantages even by those parents who place a premium on academic results, should be allowed to be obscured by the emphasis that is laid upon the academic opportunities that this education affords.

Both Jencks[33] and Collins[34] before him have provided data to confirm the importance of length of schooling and formal qualifications in securing access to high status occupations, even after social origins have been taken into account. However, both Collins and more recently Parkin[35] have analysed the growth in the practice of using credentials as the means of occupational selection and they challenge the assumption that it is the academic content of education which is actually necessary for successful performance in the majority of occupations which recruit in this manner.

Collins considers how both functionalist and conflict theories can be used to explain the variety of ways in which education and stratification are linked. The usual way in which education is portrayed as being of value in industrial society is to link skill requirements with technical change, hence Collins' discussion of a technical-function theory of education with its assertion that education (and by implication academic results) is a functional prerequisite for the technical requirements of work in industrial society. Drawing upon American research of the time, Collins fails to find sufficient evidence to support this theory either as applied to entry into manual work or into the majority of non-manual occupations. Certainly training in specific professions could be considered to be vocationally relevant but evidence comparing particular degrees of success with particular kinds of occupational performance or success is not generally available and Parkin quotes Berg[36] in saying that there is 'no evidence to show that variations in the level of formal education were matched by variations in the quality of work perform-ance'. Soderberg[37] shows that 40 per cent of American engineers in the early 1950s lacked college degrees, suggesting that technical skills were acquired on the job. Similarly, Goldthorpe[38] in his cohort analysis of social mobility in Britain shows how such mobility was conditional upon the expansion of the service class such that the earlier cohorts in the sample were able to achieve upward mobility prior to the expansion of higher education in the 1960s. Several fathers amongst the users of the public schools serve as examples of the pattern identified by Goldthorpe having either reached or remained in Class I without any post-school qualifications or with the help of only part-time further education. In turn, Blaug[39] has ques-tioned whether expenditure on education does in fact stimulate economic growth. Thus there are sufficient grounds for doubting whether expenditure on education does contribute to economic development beyond the provision of mass literacy and this in turn throws into question the value of many of the provisions of the 1944 Education Act which was born out of the belief in the need to expand education in order to maximise national efficiency. Collins concludes that the technical-function theory of education does not give an adequate account of the evidence and education therefore needs to be considered as a status commodity rather than as a mark of achievement such that existing power groups use it to monopolise positions in the way that Bourdieu[40] has suggested.

In developing the alternative theory to link education to stratifica-tion, the conflict theory, Collins like Parkin draws upon the writings of Weber rather than of Marx. Conflict is essentially over 'rewards' – economic position, power and prestige. The struggle to achieve these tend to be between 'associational groups' rather than individuals such that the existing owners of these rewards will select their new mem-bers from amongst their own status group. Criteria are necessary to identify group members and the function of education can be viewed as teaching particular 'status cultures' both inside and outside the classroom. Such a culture may be explicitly expressed and recognised as such both by the schools and the parents, hence the emphasis in the public schools on service to the community, leadership and so on; or it may remain implicit as Collins suggests so that it constitutes the actual content of academic education and has become overlaid with technical importance. In this argument the educational requirements for employment which have been so widely accepted do nothing more than recruit employees who share the élite culture. Parents who stress the need for academic results may simply recognise that they are part of the status culture of those recruiting into the desired occupations, normally the professions, and therefore a necessary qualification for success.

There have been relatively few attempts to specify the precise content of such a status culture. Anderson[41] identifies the cultural supremacy underlying the hegemony of the 'upper class' which is not articulated in any systematic major ideology but is diffused in a miasma of commonplace prejudices and taboos. He stresses that the fusion of landed, industrial and commercial capital which has resulted in the creation of a single hegemonic class is still dominated by the culture of the landed section. Parkin points to the absence of a universal acceptance of a unitary culture and discusses the potential for intra-class antagonisms as social attributes come to be singled out as the basis of exclusion in the process of social closure. Any group attribute can be used for this purpose and he reminds us that it was necessary for the new middle classes to challenge the established values of the landed class in their effort to gain political power; therefore the homogeneity of the hegemonic culture emphasised by Anderson will not necessarily be evident in any detailed examination of the content of the status culture of the top group. This culture is manifested in many different arenas and will find expression in the advantages that parents ascribe to a private education. It has been shown that the importance of academic results is subscribed to equally by all the different groups of parents and an examination of the other advantages perceived should reveal still further the extent to which there is the cultural homogeneity claimed by Anderson.

At the heart of the stereotype of the British public school lie their 'expressive goals,' so labelled by Lambert.[42] These are the qualities or attributes which are seen as ends in themselves – the values of behaviour, morals, taste and expression – the goals most frequently mentioned by the headmasters of the schools interviewed by Lambert and his colleagues. Lambert sums these up as 'laying stress on character training towards an ideal pattern of moral, religious and cultural ends which put a greater emphasis on serving the community than the pursuit of individual success'. His findings show that whilst the parents he interviewed support the goals formulated by their headmasters they have added to them the one of academic success. This pattern of parental goals appears to reproduce itself in these research findings, for as Table 5.6 shows, the second most frequently mentioned advantage of the schools is the very character training referred to by Lambert. However, a scrutiny of the responses within this category reveals that they bear little resemblance to Lambert's expressive goals, only a minority of parents stated a wish for their sons to 'be imbued with the serving spirit', or become outward looking and socially responsible which are characteristically associated with character training in these schools. The overriding concern of the parents is with the notion of discipline and self-discipline, punishment and respect for authority, a strong emphasis on the recognition that we live in a world with rules and the necessity of learning to cope with this as soon as possible . . . discipline, old-fashioned discipline, the order, the work'. Such sentiments are the essential ingredients of what Dale[43] terms 'populism', an important strand of the philosophy of the New Right which found early expression, in educational terms, in the Black Papers. This is the meaning that the vast majority of today's clients of the public schools attach to the term 'character training'; this is the content of their culture and the meaning of the attitudes which they believe distinguish the lower class from those who lie above it. The only parents who deviate from this interpretation of character training are the members of the social élite, the remnants of the old traditional landed classes or those who have joined them, who are much more likely to use the term in the sense described by Lambert.[44]

Anderson's reference to the actual content of upper class culture and the values into which the sons of the rich are being socialised by the public schools[45] reveals how ostensibly expressive goals actually become laced with threads of instrumentality. He stresses the cultural emphasis upon leadership which is based not on skill but on style and values, not on training but on natural aristocratic superiority. What Anderson is in effect describing is the means whereby leadership is secured and how instrumental goals are transformed into expressive ones. Only 14 per cent of the parents mentioned the importance of character training without linking it to either academic success or to getting on in life and they are the parents who give the clearest indication of pursuing the strictly expressive goals identified by Lambert. Over twenty years ago Vaizey described the process in which public schools translate instrumental goals into expressive ones:

The public schools train people to accept the cultural norms which they exist to perpetuate . . . As a result, whole numbers of people walk about convinced that they are wearing themselves to the bone for the public good; they are really walking about keeping the Establishment going.[46]

Bowles and Gintis[47] analyse the manner in which intra-school experiences are designed to ensure that individuals will fit neatly into their future productive roles. Whilst such an analysis is conventionally associated with the mechanism whereby subordinate classes are socialised into their exclusion from élite or indeed service class occupations, preparation for these roles is equally dependent upon preparatory socialisation for the 'natural aristocratic authority' described by Anderson does have to be learned. The public schools are still characterised by their organisation around the house system, the whole ethos of which is changing only gradually as the power of the prefects is reduced. The traditional purpose of the prefectorial system is the preparation for the exercise of authority through a training to initially submit to it and gradually to administer it such that those occupying intermediate positions within the house hierarchy are both subject to and hold authority simultaneously. This is founded upon the belief that one cannot rule others until one has been ruled oneself. One of the élite fathers in the sample not only clearly remembers his own experiences at school but unquestioningly accepts their efficacy. During a discussion of the way in which the schools develop the boys' characters he described his days in the army:

For those of us who joined up during the war who had been to public school it seemed a relative relaxation . . . you know those chaps, so called working class people, it [the discipline] nearly killed them.

By expressing the hope that their sons would have occupations within the non-manual sector of the economy, parents are undoubtedly indicating their preference for positions that involve a degree of responsibility and control but to conclude in the way that Anderson does that this conforms closely to the ideal-type of leader who controls others by maximising the differences between the ruler and the ruled would be to overstate the case. Only a handful of the parents acknowledge that they believe a private education will help their sons to become leaders and to control others, for the majority of those who are primarily concerned that their sons should succeed in the world emphasise the importance of getting a good job and/or learning to submit to rules in the manner already discussed. This is not to say that a distinction cannot be made between submitting to the rules of life and accepting one's part in the larger order of things and submission to authority exercised by others but for some parents it is difficult to divorce controlling others from controlling one's own fortunes:

> You either tell others what to do in life or for ever more get told what to do

was the view of one father.

Another important facet of a public school education listed by the headmasters interviewed by Lambert as well as by the parents in this survey, is the individuality and personal independence that it fosters, enabling a boy to retain a legitimate identity and self-reliance despite his concern for and absorption into the community. Salaman and Thompson's[48] study of the process of officer selection into the army clearly shows how such qualities stand the candidates in good stead. They cite how two candidates, a bright working class boy and an average public schoolboy, both failed an assignment. The first attempted to resolve this by seeking advice, the second by maintaining his confidence in himself. In the subsequent discussion it was the second candidate who earned the approval of those making the selection, an approval of his coolness. Evidence from the CBI to the Public Schools Commission, quoted in the first chapter, stressing the importance of self-reliance and self-confidence, suggests that the army is not unique in placing a premium on these qualities.

Confidence and independence, seen as one of the perceived advantages of a private education, is one of the few ways in which it is possible to differentiate between the parents using the schools for this is not mentioned equally by all the parents. It is those in Class IV, the *petit bourgeoisie,* who appear to be looking to the schools in far greater numbers to provide these qualities. Fifty per cent of those who originate in Class IV as opposed to less than a quarter of all the members of Class I mentioned the development of confidence and independence as an important way in which the schools can help their sons to succeed, a typical example being the mother who believes that a distinct advantage of these schools is the way in which they foster the ability to:

put people down, which is something we can't do but would like
M—to be able to do if he wants to.

Those who have experienced downward mobility into Class IV,
despite their failure to maintain class position during a period of
economic expansion, do not in the main share this need for confidence and independence to be developed by the schools, for only a
fifth of them mention this is an advantage of private education. A
corresponding distinction between the static and the upwardly mobile
members of Class I is not evident, occupational success breeds
self-confidence, however this success is achieved. It is those parents
who have yet to experience this degree of success on their own behalf
who are more likely to be looking to the schools to help their sons in
this way. The owner of a small business who has prospered sufficiently to enable him to pay the fees, or a farmer who has inherited
his farm, typically has highly personalised relationships in his work
and does not have to grapple with the complexities of the relationships characteristic of service class occupations, he is probably fearful
of having to do so but recognises the importance to his son of
believing in himself and possessing the ability to convince others of
his worth.

The overriding concern of the parents to secure their sons' positions in the world of work must not be allowed to obscure the fact
that education and work are not always viewed as intimately bound
together. Even some parents who stress the importance of academic
results do not believe that this is all that matters in life and the chance
to experience the fuller and broader education that 34 per cent of the
parents interviewed believe that the schools offer is another example
of what is meant by the expressive goals of the public schools. Many
parents view the maintained schools as nine to five institutions,
leaving the pupils to pursue their own interests outside this period of
time. The private schools, by contrast, with their numerous activities
– societies, music, sports, chess, metalwork and so on, are seen as
providing their pupils with the chance to sample many different
aspects of life, an opportunity which could only be gained with great
difficulty elsewhere and which will maximise their enjoyment of life:

Training for the three day week . . .

observed one farmer.

The value of this fuller education was particularly likely to be
stressed by the members of the social élite and even the grammar

school fathers who are married to mothers who have had a private as opposed to state education are significantly more likely to mention the importance of a fuller education, indicating that this is part of the content of the high status culture. However, even amongst the parents mentioning the advantage of this fuller education are to be found a few who recognise the instrumental value of exposing their sons to this culture for a few parents said that the experience gained from these activities would not only enrich the boy's future personal lives but would help them to 'mix with others later in life'.

Specific reference has yet to be made to 'gentrification', the motive of the newly emergent wealthy nineteenth century industrialists for using the public schools which contributed to their overwhelming popularity and consequent expansion during the second half of the century. The motive to 'get on' in occupational terms was not part of this quest on the part of the new wealthy class to educate their sons in these schools, for they had already got on exceedingly well. What they sought, through the use of the schools, was acceptance by the existing landed classes and to achieve this an approximation of their standards of behaviour as well as styles of life was believed to be necessary. Coleman[49] devotes considerable attention to the evolving definition of 'gentlemanliness', originating with the ability to 'live idly and without manual labour' and gradually incorporating a 'moral code' merging with the gentlemanly code of honour which provided the basis for a 'luxuriant undergrowth of unwritten and unspoken rules of behaviour'. Gradually this code became embedded in the culture of the public schools such that in a speech to Old Etonians in 1916 Lord Plumer, himself an Etonian in the 1870s was able to say:

> We are often told that they taught us nothing at Eton. It may be so, but I think that they taught it very well.[50]

There is a concern on the part of some of today's parents not only with the inner man in terms of the character training, discipline, confidence and future style of life made possible by the fuller education offered, but also with outer appearances. Whilst few of the parents confirmed the opinion expressed by one of them, a prep. school headmaster, that what they are in fact paying for is:

> for their sons to meet a high standard of person on the staff – high personal standards which the children can absorb – accent, lack of pornography and not drinking in excess.

nearly a fifth of them were concerned that their sons should be 'polished' by their teachers. 'A whole general air, a certain something that will help when he goes for interviews' was the hope of one socially ambitious farmer's wife. But in general there is a certain down to earthliness about the parents' desire for 'gentrification' or more accurately preservation of personal standards with a strong emphasis on correct manners and speech.

> We don't want a little Lord Fauntleroy – we want someone with discipline, a bit of grip, good basic education and good manners . . .

is the wish of another farmer.

'To speak English, not what left wing trendies think necessary' said an upwardly mobile solicitor, one of the few parents making direct reference to the political nature and characteristics of the teachers.

This concern with outward experiences and standards of behaviour is reflected in the anxiety about the other pupils who their sons are mixing with. Few of the parents, only 8 per cent directly mention the importance of the social contacts which Scott[51] identifies as the crucial element of a public school education and of interest is the way in which they do not refer exclusively to the national network of élites as described by one old boy:

> R—has opened lots of doors for me . . . purely wearing the right tie, people recognise it . . . it opens doors but it never puts you through them.

but also to the local business community:

> One is paying the money to give a social advantage over other people – one can get as good an education at a good comprehensive but even in this day and age when you tell people the boy is at B— [a minor public school] the eyebrows still go up a bit.

Not all parents share the two views quoted above, a third, also on old boy of a well known public school bemoaned the fact that such an advantage was a thing of the past, for this doctor at least the meritocratic age has well and truly arrived:

> The level of A Levels has got so extreme now that you are only getting the brightest academically getting into medicine, which is a

shambles. I think it is very bad thing . . . you used to be able to get in the back way – you could just be a decent chap who played rugby . . .

Such concern as is expressed about the social characteristics of the boys who their sons are likely to meet at the schools is more to do with allaying fears of them being pulled down than with ambition for them to climb up. The characteristics referred to are not related to academic prowess but to social attributes. The desire for sons to mix with 'their own type'; the wish to avoid the bullies in the comprehensive schools or to meet the more interesting type of child who goes to these schools, all of these are sought after attributes of their sons' peers. For a few parents, living in or near the inner cities there is a genuine fear not only of bullying but of corruption, leading to vandalism. The pitfalls of trying to engineer the social contacts of one's children are made abundantly clear by two very different types of mothers, the first a third generation member of Class I, the daughter and wife of large industrialists, whose family has always used the private sector to meet its educational needs; the second a Class IV secondary modern educated mother, trying to build up a small business from home with her similarly educated husband:

We want him to get away from the local scene and meet a broad range of people, yet we feel that a disadvantage of this form of education is that he is meeting too narrow a range of people.

and

The advantage of an independent education is to get him away from the local boys who speak badly. One disadvantage is that the local boys don't want to play with him now – he has no-one to play with.

Endeavouring to provide answers to the questions posed earlier in this chapter, namely questions about the parents' precise motives for rejecting the state sector, is complicated by the fact that they associate the schools with many different advantages and vary considerably in the manner in which they combine them. Marsden,[52] in one of the very few of the earlier attempts to discover why parents pay fees, outlines the many stated reasons for doing so but concludes that 'parents are inevitably but not always willingly drawn into a web of snobberies and social exclusiveness'. A careful analysis of the tape

TABLE 5.7 *Analysis of the parents' motives for using private education*

Motive		Percent of couples
No clear motive		8.0
Anti-comprehensive schools		3.0
Boarding need		4.0
Individual attention		2.0
Family tradition		9.0
Only	4%	
+ other reasons	5%	
Do one's best		9.0
Only	3%	
+ other reasons	6%	
Get on better in life		28.0
Through: Academic results	6%	
Character and discipline and/or polish	10%	
Academic results and character, discipline and/or polish	5%	
Contacts and/or label	5%	
Only	2%	
Academic advantage		23.0
Only	14%	
+ character and discipline	3%	
+ other reasons	6%	
Develop character and foster discipline		14.0
Only	4%	
+ others	10%	
Total		100%

recordings of the interviews with the parents using the schools today shows how their particular combinations of advantages vary and gives a clearer picture of the primary motive that each set of parents has for making his choice. These motives are summarised in Table 5.7.

Although 44 per cent of the fathers have been privately educated only a handful of parents fully acknowledged that family tradition is the sole reason for using a private education, the fact that their families have always used private schools is sufficient reason for continuing to do so and to probe for any deeper explanation would be to distort the truth.

> I would have to be very financially embarrassed before I would
> contemplate a state school

was the way one such father expressed it. To these parents must be
added the 5 per cent who also mentioned family tradition but went to
considerable pains to justify their choice, giving additional reasons.
The mother of a boy at a well known boarding school with a second
son and a daughter also in the private sector gave many reasons for
her choice but concluded by saying:

> I was not free to choose a state school. As soon as I started looking
> at state schools I actually became aware of all sorts of feelings
> inside me – that I seemed programmed to choose private schools. I
> don't think that I did have a free choice.

Thus nearly one in ten of the boy come from homes which can be
termed 'traditional'. Private education is used exclusively for the
education of the children, both primary and secondary, and this is
part of a general culture and life-style which is shared by these
families' friends and relatives.

In a somewhat similar vein there is some evidence of what could be
termed 'blind faith' in the power of the schools to optimise life
chances. Three per cent of the parents merely stated that they felt
that they are doing their best for their sons, whilst a further 6 per cent
could be drawn to state what it is about this sector of education that
actually constitutes doing one's best. Thus 9 per cent of the parents
can be said to have a generalised rather than clearly articulated
commitment to private education. Whilst such faith is not confined to
any particular group of parents it is more frequently associated with
those families who have experienced social mobility, albeit in an
upward or a downward direction. Such parents can best be portrayed
by the grammar school educated father who is now highly placed in
local government, incidentally an authority whose education depart-
ment is one of the few that continues to provide a fully fledged
tripartite structure:

> Not knowing enough about the system [the private system] one
> assumed that there must be something more to it that one did not
> know about, and so if one could struggle to enable one to do it one
> should take a chance and put them in in the hope that there is
> something extra.

However, familiarity with the system is not necessarily a reason for losing this blind faith, as indicated by this father, himself educated privately and married to a teacher in their sons' school:

> To a large extent it is the salving of personal conscience, deciding to pay for a child. It is this feeling of doing the best that you can for them . . . there is a great deal in the decision making process that I do not think is rational.

In addition to these parents, a further 8 per cent gave so many reasons for deciding to educate their sons privately as to make it impossible to discern their true motives for doing so. One is tempted to add these parents to those who freely admit that they are simply doing what they believe is the best for their children, such that a total of 17 per cent of the sample could be said to have a generalised, even if not blind, faith in the powers of the private sector. It may well be that there is a genuine belief that they are sending their sons to schools which offer every single advantange and included amongst these are both a more pleasant environment – 'why use furnished digs if you can afford a five star hotel?' asked one father – and the ability to confer advantage over others.

If one adds to all of these parents those who are vehemently opposed to the comprehensive schools without actually stating what it is that education should be doing, and those who have a boarding need for family reasons, then a third of the parents can be seen to have a commitment to or need for private education which obviates the possibility of any further analysis.

A further 28 per cent of the parents are more obviously concerned that their sons should get on in life and they believe that there are a number of ways in which the schools can help them to do this, of which the academic results are but a small part. These parents are somewhat similar to the 23 per cent who place a virtually exclusive emphasis on the importance of the academic results but they differ inasmuch as they have a very clear idea of what constitutes 'getting on', namely entry into the professions or, mentioned less frequently, into business or other service class occupations. The parents who indicate that it is the disciplined environment which is the main difference between the private and the maintained schools and give this as their reason for choosing the former, similarly clearly indicate, somewhat surprisingly, that their choice is motivated by occupational success. Unlike those parents who stress the importance of their sons getting on in life, they are not as specific about their vision of the future for they emphasise the importance of making money or of entering business or managerial occupations rather than specifying the professions or other named occupations but like them they recognise the components of the status culture identified by Collins[53] and wish to ensure that their sons are eligible for selection. Parents who are motivated solely by the search for good academic results, alongside the traditionalists and the few parents with a boarding need, are the least likely to be drawn about the occupational future that they envisage for their sons. Their main concern is with the academic results and these could almost be viewed as an end in themselves, a belief in the importance of technical competence, good academic results are an insurance against all future occupational eventualities allowing career decisions to be deferred.

In conclusion, one of the most remarkable features of the reasons which parents give for choosing a private education for their sons, and indeed for their imputed motives for doing so, is not the reasons or motives themselves but the extent to which they are shared almost universally by parents from the diverse range of backgrounds represented in today's public schools. Particularly noticeable is the way in which Class I parents where the father is second or third generation within this class, and thus more likely to have had a private education, can barely be distinguished from those where the father has been upwardly mobile into Class I and therefore is unlikely to have had this education.

A similar examination and comparison of the total educational experiences of the fathers leads to virtually the same conclusion. Obviously those fathers who have had a substantial amount of private education themselves are more likely to mention traditional reasons for providing this form of education for their sons, but helping them to get on in the world appears as the prime motive of the majority of all the fathers, irrespective of their own education. The only exceptions to this are not to be found amongst the privately educated fathers but amongst those who have been to a grammar school, more of whom are likely to emphasise the importance of academic results than of getting on in the world.

In reviewing the findings of the Oxford Mobility Studies, Roy Hattersley[54] notes that:

the inequality of British society is, in part at least, preserved and perpetuated by the ease with which the recruits to the 'service class' assimilate its standards and values. Recruited young, direct from the expanding ranks of higher education, reaching positions of power and prosperity by a route both straight and well defined, these new men adopt the attitudes and identity of the 'service class' with a speed and facility not possible for their pre-war counterparts.

In the absence of many pre-war counterparts in this survey, the findings can only vindicate the first part of Hattersley's assertion, there is indeed little with which to distinguish between the established and the newly arrived members of the service class.

Isolating the mothers in terms of their own education produces different but complimentary findings. Here one finds that the mothers who have been predominantly privately educated share with such men the greater tendency to have largely traditional motives for choosing a private education but they differ far more sharply from their state-educated sisters not only in this obvious respect but also in their greater reluctance to mention 'doing one's best' or indeed 'enhancing the opportunity for getting on in the world.' The motives for educating boys privately are more clearly associated with their mothers' educational patterns than with those of their fathers. This can be understood in terms of the very different experiences and expectations of men and women. Both the content and the level of these women's education differs from that of their husbands: far fewer of them, 13 per cent as compared with 31 per cent, have had a university education and those who do work outside the home are rarely destined for the upper echelons of the service class but for the typically female occupations within Classes II and III. Thus the convergence in motives that can be identified between the men of different social and educational backgrounds is not as sharply reproduced amongst the women for they have not participated personally in the post-war thrust in upward mobility. It is in this way that the mothers bring their own distructive cultural capital to bear upon the decision to use private schooling.

The failure to distinguish succinctly between the motives of the different class factions and thereby to identify the stereotypes of public school parents which are prevalent in the literature might initially appear to be an indictment of the research – a failure to come to grips with the issues and to recognise what people are saying.

There is a strong desire on the part of all researchers for their findings to fall into neat patterns, and indeed a temptation to ignore those that fall outside. Such patterns, however, probably bear little relationship to reality. The initial expectation that parents should have a clearly thought-out vision of the nature of today's (complex) class structure, where they expect their sons to fit into it and how, if at all, the schools are going to facilitate this, all of which in turn varies according to the particular combination of their own backgrounds and education is a case in point. While it is not unreasonable to formulate such clear patterns in the light of the very considerable expenditure that this education calls for, this does deny the complexities of the stratified society in which we live: the considerable degree of social mobility experienced by the parents themselves and envisaged by them for the future which in turn give rise to variations in individual experiences and the acknowledged uncertainties about the future.

The high level of commitment that the parents show to the private sector does not mean that they are unaware of the disadvantages that are associated with this form of education, quite apart from any specific criticisms that they have of the individual schools. Seventy-three per cent of the parents mentioned at least one associated disadvantage and these are listed in Table 5.8.

This clearly shows that, counter to the conclusion drawn in the last chapter, some parents have thought about the way in which the schools are alleged to preserve a class divided society and in particular how differentiated forms of schooling become stratified such that those who receive their education in the different parts evaluate themselves and

TABLE 5.8 *The potential disadvantage of a private education*

	Percent of couples who mention these
Narrow social mix, danger of boys being snooty	36.0
No local friends, not part of the community	27.0
Facilities are poorer than those offered by the state	18.0
Public opinion is against these schools and the boys may suffer	12.0
Narrow outlook, the boys are too protected from the world	11.0
Not co-educational	9.0
Boys suffer financially/feel obligated to their parents	5.0

*These do not total 100% as some parents gave no disadvantage whilst others gave several.

are evaluated by others in hierarchical terms. This is expressed at varying levels of specificity: a few parents are aware of the way in which the very existence of private schools perpetuates the class structure and how possibly they are the root cause of industrial strife, but in the main fears are more specifically related to the effects of this divisiveness on their own sons, some fear that the boys will carry feelings of superiority with them into the world of work and others that they will be working in a climate of public opinion where a private education will constitute a handicap. Of more immediate concern, especially to the mothers, is that the boys are seen to have difficulty in forming or sustaining local friendships and are isolated from involvement in the local community. Parents who express these anxieties do not deny that inequality between social positions is inevitable but confirm their perceptions of Britain as an open society where credentials are used increasingly to fill these positions. There is an inherent tension between the parents' desired educational ends and the appropriate means of achieving them for they are confident in their belief that the incumbents of service class positions are distinguished by the very qualities that they have stressed as important but not in the ability of the maintained sector to endow its pupils with these qualities. In turning to the private sector, the parents are seeking to enter into a partnership between home and school where the values of two institutions can be assumed to be in harmony rather than in competition. Those who recognise the social divisiveness of a private education are anxious lest their sons, the hoped for future members of the service class, are seen to have acquired the necessary qualifications by illegitimate means.

6 Choosing a Public School

Up to this point the discussion has deliberately freely interchanged the adjectives 'private' and 'public' to describe the schools which provide an alternative to those in the maintained sector for they share in common the use of the market to recruit the majority of their pupils. Yet, as discussed in the opening chapter, there are substantial differences which both distinguish the public schools from the remainder of the private sector and differentiate between them. Such differences are manifested in the internal structuring and organisation of the private sector as well as in the specific social and political responses that the different schools evoke. What remains to be considered is how closely the parents' evaluation of the schools takes cognisance of these differences. In rejecting the maintained sector in favour of the public schools are they choosing the private sector *per se* or a particular type of school within it. By the very design of the research the parents interviewed are drawn from a cross-section of public schools which are themselves distinguished by their long standing independence from the state, those which have never been subject to direct grant regulations, and it is necessary to consider why these pupils come to be in the particular school in which this research finds them. Is this the result of a deliberate choice by their parents, and if so what factors influence this choice; do the parents have the complete freedom of choice which they value so highly or has it been constrained in any way and finally how would they respond to further constraints? Answers to these questions will go some way towards discovering whether parents seek to maintain their own distinctive social identity by educating their sons in separate establishments, each perceived as having its own subculture but which collectively have come to be known as the 'public schools'.

BOARDING OR DAY EDUCATION

In particular the role and the function of the boarding school needs to be examined in greater detail than hitherto. Only 6 per cent of the parents mentioned boarding as a distinct advantage of a private education and only half of these appear to have a boarding need as their primary motive for using the private sector, yet as Table 6.1 shows, over half of those interviewed are in fact the parents of boarders.

It is to the boarding schools that much of the literature on the subject of public schools has been devoted and to which the label 'public school' is most frequently attached. Public day schools do to some extent model themselves on their boarding counterparts but it is the boarding which enables the schools to attempt a more complete control of their pupils' lives and minds in pursuit of their ends and therefore it is necessary to consider in what ways, if any, the parents of boarders differ from those of day boys both in terms of their socio-economic characteristics and their normative aspects.

In simple occupational terms there is no statistically significant difference between the boarding and the day parents and the fact that Class IV parents are disproportionately represented amongst those using the boarding schools is solely the result of the over-representation of farmers in the sample, none of whom use day schools. Not surprisingly the boarding schools are able to attract the 'wealthier' parents, their parents earn more and possibly therefore are more successful within their chosen occupations. In addition, they are significantly more likely to own capital in excess of £100 000 but yet again this finding is distorted by the disproportionate number of farmers whose wealth is tied up in their land. It is in examining the

TABLE 6.1 *Distribution of boys (by family) in the different categories of public schools*

| Boy | School | | | | | | | |
| | Boarding | | | | Day | | | |
	Major	Medium	Minor		Major	Medium	Minor	Total
Boarder	47	20	35		5	1	0	108
Day	3	5	6		21	31	16	82
Total	50	25	41		26	32	16	190

relationship between the parents' own education and their choice of school that a clear picture begins to emerge, for tradition clearly plays a part in the choice of a boarding education. Parents whose educational experiences have been mainly in the private sector and who are therefore likely to be at least second generation members of their class are the most likely to choose a boarding school for their sons, as can be seen from Table 6.2. It is the expansion in the number of day places, necessitated by the rising costs of boarding, that has succeeded in attracting many parents who are largely state educated and unlikely to have considered a boarding education.

TABLE 6.2   *Choice of day or boarding according to parents' education*

Sons' Education	Parents' Combined State Education		
	Predominantly State (96) (%)	*Mixed* (25) (%)	*Predominantly Private* (66) (%)
Day	52	39	32
Boarder	48	61	68
Total	100%	100%	100%

It is not merely the fact that the parents' own education has been largely within the private sector that predisposes them towards boarding their sons, but their familiarity with boarding, for it is the actual experience of boarding which appears to heighten parents' quest to provide their sons with a similar experience. Of the parents who have themselves been mainly privately educated, 86 per cent of those who boarded, as opposed to 52 per cent of those who have not, now board their sons. Not only are the parents of boarders more likely to have boarded themselves but they also take the decision about private education earlier for as Table 6.3 shows, nearly 80 per cent of the boys who board had a predominantly private primary school education.

Thus it is within the sub-sample of boarders that one is most likely to encounter the parents who are seeking to reproduce their own educational experiences as closely as possible in those of their sons. Does this mean that the parents of the boarders are merely following tradition, giving relatively little thought to their decision to reject the maintained sector as concluded by Marsden,[1] or are they looking for

TABLE 6.3   *Relationship between sons' primary and secondary education*

| | Type of Secondary Schooling | |
| | Boarding (108) (%) | Day (82) (%) |
Type of Primary School		
Boarding private	51.0	6.1
Day private	28.0	50.0
Mixed	4.0	8.5
State	17.0	35.4
Total	100%	100%

different qualities in the schools than those sought by the parents of day boys? The available data lends some support to both these possibilities. The parents of boarders do give fewer reasons for their decision to use the private sector and over twice as many of them (13 per cent) as of the parents of day boys (5 per cent) appear to be motivated by tradition. However, boarding schools do appear to act as lenses, bringing into focus the different and diffuse forces which constitute parental motives for choosing private education, for whilst both sets of parents share in common many of the advantages that they ascribe to the schools, a comparison of their predominant motives does suggest that these differ. Whilst 'getting on in life' and the academic results remain the dominant motives of both sets of parents, in addition to those who use the boarding schools primarily for their boarding facility, and those who see private education in general and boarding in particular as part of their own subculture (the traditionalists) more of the boarding than of the day parents stress the importance of discipline and character training as a single advantage without adding it to the other benefits to be derived from a private education. Composed of a higher proportion of those who have been state educated, the parents of day boys concern them-selves to a greater extent with how the desired results are achieved and in particular they attach more importance to the actual teaching methods; the parents of boarders are more likely, probably as a result of their greater familiarity with this form of education, to put their trust in the schools to achieve the desired results and not to concern themselves to such an extent with the detail of their day-to-day organisation.

BOARDING AS AN ISSUE

In the same way as parents expect many different things from a private education in general, so the parents of boarders display considerable diversity in their reasons for favouring this form of private education, varying with respect to both overall philosophy and pragmatism. The issue of boarding education serves to polarise not only individuals who might otherwise be politically insensitive to the debates about private education, but also societies which display considerable variation in their use of boarding education. Boarding schools are relatively closed institutions and as such are able to function more effectively both as agencies of socialisation and as substitutes for the physical care functions of the family.[2] It is for both these reasons that Israel and Russia use boarding as a method of providing education on a larger scale than is to be found in Britain, both societies have been created out of distinct ideologies and both have a high proportion of married women who work. Much of the wholesale criticism that the public schools evoke is the result not of their political function of locating people within a stratified society but of their perceived potential as boarding schools to damage the psychological development of their pupils. A psychotherapist in the sample expressed his violent dislike of boarding schools, believing their perverting effects to be the cause of many of his patients' problems.

Those who defend the boarding schools are likely to use cultural terms to do so, stressing their superiority in transmitting the core value of 'upper class' culture, moral training. It is argued that by isolating their pupils from the pernicious influences in the outside world, the boarding school is able to control their whole existence, which is clearly directed towards the desired ends.

The parents' attitudes towards boarding are shown in Table 6.4 and these appear to be strongly influenced by their own experiences of boarding for there is a positive correlation between their sympathies towards boarding and the extent to which they have experienced it. This is particularly pronounced in the case of the mothers, for fathers who have never boarded are more likely to adopt pro-boarding attitudes than are such mothers. Eleven per cent of the boarding parents said that boarding is the norm in their families, they had never thought of any other form of education and would not do so. In these families all the fathers, and 90 per cent of the mothers are in favour of boarding. Essentially, however, the unspoken debate

TABLE 6.4   *Couples' feelings about boarding*

	(%)
Both parents against it	29
Mother more pro than father	10
Both have mixed feelings	8
Father more pro than mother	15
Both parents pro boarding	38
Total	100%

between the parents interviewed reflects the debate at a societal level between those who feel that boarding schools are superior to the family in providing the required moral training and those who feel that at the very least it undermines family life and at worst is psychologically damaging. Fifty-three per cent of the boarding parents stressed the benefits of being away from home in terms of the development of the personal characteristics which are the essential ingredients of the high status culture already discussed,[3] with its emphasis on independence and facing up to problems. A few see the intensity of family relationships as potentially damaging, a view shared by Laing and Cooper's work on schizophrenia,[4] but not by many of the parents of the day boys. A virtually equal proportion of day parents, 55 per cent, stress the importance of family life as their reason for not boarding their sons, in particular they believe that as parents they have an important role to play in the socialisation of their children and this is not something to be delegated to the paid staff of the boarding school. In choosing a boarding education parents may well be placing what they believe to be the long term benefits before the immediate happiness of their sons. One such father commented on his wife's concern that the boys should be happy and enjoy themselves:

> They go to a public school for a number of reasons, one of which is not to be blissfully happy.

Whilst this debate about the proper role of the family in socialising its young is an important and possibly the most vital element around which the decision to board revolves, there are other more pragmatic reasons which influence the parents' decisions. One of these is the necessity rather than the desirability of seeking an alternative agency to discharge some of the welfare functions of the family. The most obvious case in point is where the father has been posted abroad and there is either a perceived lack of suitable education or the posting is transitory and involves frequent moves; the boarding school is Britain's answer to America's world-wide chain of schools which serve her expatriates. Twelve per cent of the boarding parents gave working abroad as the reason for boarding their sons and this figure is undoubtedly deflated by the fact that it was only possible to interview the parents who were in Britain during the period of the fieldwork.[5] Twenty-six per cent of the boarding parents pointed to the incompleteness of their family structure, being a single parent or the lack of siblings; or to its 'pathology', having an elderly relative living with them; or to their busy lives which make it difficult to give the boys adequate attention, as the reason for boarding. A quarter of them see the environment of the boarding school as more conducive to learning thereby emphasising the importance that they attach to this education in developing technical skills. Frequent mention was made of supervision during homework, combined with careful control of the amount of time spent watching television. The television began to emerge as a hidden enemy over which many parents feel that they have no control but which can be defeated by the structured environment of the boarding school. In addition, the communal life of the boarding school appeals to many of the parents and a quarter of them mentioned either the opportunity that they provide to be part of a closed community or their sons' need for constant companionship from boys of the same age, not always easy to find at an isolated rural address.

The actual practice of using a day or boarding education does not always match the parents' feelings about the desirability of doing so. Nearly a fifth of the couples who favour boarding in principle do not board their sons and correspondingly a fifth of the couples who declare themselves to be against boarding are in fact using such schools. A number of factors stand between the parents' beliefs and their practices, geography and cost being prime examples. A quarter of all the boarding parents but a half of those who are against boarding mentioned the distance between their homes and the nearest secondary school as an important factor in their decision to board their sons, indicating that it would be impossible for the boy to travel the distance or claiming that too much travelling is tiring and therefore counterproductive. Conversely, over a quarter of all the day parents and a half of those who are in favour of boarding gave the expense as a reason for not using a boarding school. Finally the boys' needs and wishes are of some account for a third of the families who are in favour of boarding and nearly two-thirds of those who are ambivalent towards it mentioned the boy's reluctance to board, as did a quarter of the parents who are against boarding in principle. Eighteen per cent of the boarding parents indicated that they would use only this form of education for their sons but 62 per cent of their day counterparts exclude the possibility of even considering boarding.

PRIVATE OR PUBLIC SCHOOLING?

Boarding provision is only one axis along which the private schools vary, for it has already been shown that they are differentiated in a number of ways. In one sense an important feature of any system which thrives on the principle of the market, with freedom of choice as an important part of its philosophy, is the individuality of the commodities it sells: free choice implies that there are differences which people are free to choose between and this challenges the temptation to categorise. Some well known boys schools do not belong to the Headmasters' Conference and therefore fall outside the conventional definition of a public school not because of unacceptable low academic standards but because they wish to retain their individuality and not join what is effectively a club with rules. Despite the autonomy of each of the private schools there is sufficient common ground between some of them to enable them to unite under the umbrella of the Headmasters' Conference and within conference it has been possible to stratify the schools into 'leagues' according to their informal standing, a ranking which correlates strongly with the size of the school. Thus in Table 6.1 the major schools are normally those with the largest number of pupils and by the same token the minor public schools are the smallest, with the two categories separated by the medium sized and ranked schools.

Parents who have rejected the maintained sector and decided upon either a day or a boarding education are still involved in a series of decisions when selecting a particular school. These are decisions which are in turn constrained by a number of variables, not least by their own ability to pay the fees and their sons' ability to meet the schools' entrance requirements, largely academic. Before seeking to identify the factors which affect the choice of a school, it is necessary to examine the manner in which such a choice is made and the extent to which it is constrained. There are a number of routes which lead the parents to the actual schools that they are using: 56 per cent of them succeeded in obtaining places for their sons in the school of their original choice and a further 10 per cent in a school of their first choice, albeit a revised one. Conversely, 21 per cent of the boys are not in schools that their parents originally wanted and 13 per cent are in schools which at best can termed 'a realistic first choice', the original one probably having been amended in the light of the parents' revised estimations of their sons' ability to gain admission to the preferred school. This strategy of revising choice is necessitated by the common practice of nominating the school of first choice prior to the boy sitting the Common Entrance Examination which determines entry to the majority of the schools under discussion. The scripts are then sent to the nominated school for marking and the boys who fail to reach the required standard have to take their chances in gaining admission to those schools which still have unfilled places.

Schools vary with respect to the extent to which they are being used by the parents who had chosen them originally. In general, the day schools are more likely to contain the parents who claim the school as that of their first choice, whilst the boarding parents are likely to have amended their choice or to have been compelled to compromise. Given that the entry to the schools is largely on the basis of academic selection, one would expect the more prestigious major public schools to have the first 'pick' and therefore to contain the highest proportion of pupils whose parents chose them originally. However, 81 per cent of the parents in the minor day schools as opposed to 65 per cent of those in the major ones claim to be using the school of their first choice and the major boarding schools contain the highest proportion of parents who amended their original choice, with the result that it is the parents in the medium and the minor boarding schools and, to a lesser extent, those in the medium day schools who have been the most severely constrained in their choice of school.

There is a variety of reasons why parents are unable to use the school of their original or first choice. Just over a half of these parents either anticipated (27 per cent) or witnessed (25 per cent) their sons' failure to gain admission, making a total of 22 per cent of the total sample whose sons failed to secure a place at the school of their parents' choosing on the grounds of insufficient academic ability, and this is particularly marked amongst the pupils of the minor and medium boarding schools. About 14 per cent of the parents not using the school of their first choice would have preferred their sons to have gone to a direct grant school and therefore are not seeking a public school education in the strictest sense of the term whilst over a half, about a fifth of the total sample, would have preferred a more major school. The parents who expressed a preference for a more major school are not confined to those whose sons failed to secure a place at one of Britain's major public schools, for 9 per cent of the parents using such schools wanted one of even higher standing, namely one of the Clarendon Nine.[6]

The practical details of money and geography play a part in the choice between day and boarding education and they constrain the selection of a particular school both in this manner and more generally. Thirteen per cent of the parents, all of them using day schools, named as a preferred school one which is beyond their financial grasp, either unable to afford boarding fees or even the higher ones of another day school. One in ten of the parents amended their original choice of school on the grounds of geography and this is particularly likely to have occurred amongst the parents using the major boarding schools, a quarter of whom expressed an original preference for another school but finally decided not to use it in view of its inaccessibility or distance. Many of these parents had originally intended to send their sons to 'the family school' but revised this intention in the light of their desire to be more involved with the boys' schooling and to spend more time with them during their increasingly frequent exeats.

The degree to which the parents of the day boys, and particularly those in the minor schools, have been able to match their experiences to their aspirations is the result at least in part of their lower aspirations. These in turn devolve from their relative newness to the private sector and consequent lack of familiarity with the finer details of the available alternatives. This is compounded by the fact that so many day parents have ruled out the possibility of using a boarding school for their sons such that their realistic choice is limited to what is available in the immediate vicinity and the schools of their ideal choice are likely to have been discounted at a very early stage, there is no point in naming Eton as a preferred school if one lives in Manchester and does not wish one's son to board.

By contrast, the parents of the boys in the medium and minor boarding schools have compromised substantially in their search for a suitable school and they frequently articulated their disappointment at the failure of their sons to secure a place at a more major school. It is the public school educated fathers amongst them, and in particular those who have been to a well known boarding school, who are the least likely to be educating their sons in the schools of their original preference, their familiarity with the differences in the relative standing of the schools has served to render them more discriminating. Whilst only 17 per cent of the state educated fathers expressed a wish for a more major school for their sons, 41 per cent of those educated at a major boarding school, 23 per cent of those from another public school and 39 per cent from a private school expressed such a wish. Similar differences are not to be found with respect to the manner in which the mother has been educated, suggesting that fathers who have been privately educated are instrumental in selecting their sons' schools. Disappointment at their sons' failure to secure a place at the school of their original choice is markedly pronounced amongst the fathers who belong to the social élite, who are themselves overwhelmingly public school educated. Forty per cent of them as opposed to a quarter of the remainder of the fathers expressed a preference for a school of a higher standing.

What these findings show is the parents' willingness to compromise in their search for a public school for their sons. What they are unable to show (as a result of the design of the research) is for how many parents the failure of their sons to gain entry into their preferred school has resulted in the decision to return to or remain within the maintained sector. It is possible, however, to make some estimate of this from the responses of these parents who have been successful in securing some form of a public school education for their sons. They were asked to identify the unacceptable alternatives within the private sector, the schools which they would reject in favour of state education (Table 6.5).

Eleven per cent would have used the maintained sector in preference to any school other than the one currently being used but it was the parents of boys in the minor public schools who showed themselves to be the least likely to do so. A further 23 per cent of the parents identified the status of the private schools that they would not use: 10 per cent a school outside the HMC: 7 per cent a minor public school and 6 per cent various other individually named public schools. Thus, by implication, an estimated three-quarters of the parents using the public schools are prepared to remain within the private sector, considering schools outside the HMC and hence the

TABLE 6.5 *'Minimum' acceptable alternative private schools in preference to the state secondary schools*

Schools	Parents mention these (%)
None	11.0
Only an HMC school	10.0
Not a minor public school	7.0
Total only wanting to use a public school	*28.0*
Not other named public schools	6.0
Would not exclude any private schools	66.0

conventional definition of a public school if necessary. For only a quarter of the parents in this sample is private education confined to one within a public school, and they are particularly likely to be the parents who stress the advantages of instilling confidence and developing social contacts. Given the high percentage of parents of day boys who were either unwilling or unable to consider a boarding alternative, the potential leakage to the maintained sector would appear to be considerably greater from the day users of the private sector, the boarders having left themselves far more room in which to manoeuvre. This is confirmed by looking at alternative schools that parents would have used if they had not succeeded in gaining admission to the present one, 5 per cent of the boarding but 19 per cent of the day parents said that they would have used a school in the maintained sector.

THE FINAL DECISION

It has been argued that a characteristic feature of the market is the distinctiveness of the commodities which it sells, enabling the maximisation of its cardinal feature – freedom of choice. Thus, at the end of the day parents have to decide, either as their first or as their acceptable choice, upon the particular school to which they are going to entrust their sons' education, at a not inconsiderable cost to themselves. The ranking of the schools within the HMC, which one mother unwittingly referred to as 'a caste system', has stood up in a large measure to the test of reflecting the parents' own views as expressed directly by their stated preferences and indirectly by the way in which those who are the most familiar with the system cluster in the major schools. Barely any of those who use a major school for their sons expressed a preference for a lesser one and of those who are in the medium and minor schools, the stated preference of both groups was overwhelmingly in favour of the major schools, very few of either group stating a preference for another medium school. The satisfied day parents in the minor schools are those who have restricted their horizons, partly as a result of their strong aversion to boarding. What are the salient factors which determine how parents make their final choice, how do they come to use a particular, individual school?

As in all the other choices that have been considered many reasons come together to determine the use of a particular school and these vary according to the type of school chosen and whether or not it is the first choice (Table 6.6).

Proximity is both the most frequently mentioned reason and the commonest deciding factor when choosing a particular school. As important as this is to the parents who use the major boarding

TABLE 6.6 *Factors affecting the choice of a particular school*

| | Main Factor | | | | | | Mentioned as a factor | | | | | |
| | Boarding | | | Day | | | Boarding | | | Day | | |
	1 (%)	2 (%)	3 (%)	1 (%)	2 (%)	3 (%)	1 (%)	2 (%)	3 (%)	1 (%)	2 (%)	3 (%)
Proximity	22	24	40	29	53	60	40	44	78	65	88	88
Advice of prep. HM	0	44	32	8	3	7	10	40	34	12	3	9
Father's family school	27	12	5	4	3	0	26	14	7	12	6	6
High Standard	13	4	0	17	3	0	30	8	15	46	22	13
Not too academic	4	0	5	4	3	7	15	32	37	8	34	13
Acceptable price	4	8	8	17	16	0	10	16	10	17	16	0
Known in the community	13	4	3	13	13	0	34	32	22	17	27	56
Boy liked	7	3	3	4	6	13	18	20	17	18	16	19
Total †	100%	100%	100%	100%	100%	100%	*	*	*	*	*	*

* These do not total 100% as parents mentioned more than one factor.

  1 Refers to Major

  2 Refers to Medium

  3 Refers to Minor.

† Only the most frequently mentioned factors are listed.

schools, causing some of them to alter their original choice, tradition remains their most frequently stated main reason for selecting these schools. Twenty-seven per cent of the parents who use a major boarding school gave the education of the father or occasionally of 'the family' as their reason for choosing it but only 22 per cent are lured by its proximity. The advice of the headmasters of the preparatory schools has a crucial role to play in guiding the parents towards the medium and minor boarding schools which are the least likely of all the categories of school to be the school of their parents' first choice. No fewer than 44 per cent of the parents in the former category and 32 per cent of those in the latter relied upon their sons' former headmasters when making their final decision, although proximity was the main factor in the choice of 40 per cent of those in the minor boarding schools. Conversely, it was rare for the parents of day pupils to rely on the headmasters in this way. As a third of the day pupils have entered their public schools directly from the maintained primary sector it is unlikely that they will have recourse to the advice of their headmasters to the same degree and indeed some are likely to encounter active opposition to their decision to remove the boys to the private sector. But, given the relative proximity of the day schools, the parents are in a better position to know of the school's existence and characteristics, even if only from the local grapevine and 13 per cent of parents choosing major and medium day schools for their sons referred to their local reputation as the main factor determining their choice.

Given the importance that parents attach to academic results, it is somewhat surprising that so few of them, less than a quarter, mentioned the academic reputation of the chosen school, and how even less of them gave this as the main reason for selecting it. Certainly parents using the school of their first choice are twice as likely as those who are not to mention its academic reputation, but even for the parents in the major day schools this, along with price, came second to proximity as the main reason for choosing them. This could mean either that parents who use the public schools are confident of their academic superiority to the maintained sector alternative, or that the frequency with which the advantage of academic results was mentioned as a reason for choosing a private education is merely a legitimation for the other reasons discussed. There is the temptation to glibly use this second explanation, particularly in explaining the behaviour of people who are merely perpetuating the tradition of their own education, but it would be wrong to ignore the parents' belief that we are living in a changing and increasingly open and competitive society where formal qualifications are at least a prerequisite for all those who wish to succeed and where the inheritance of occupation and class position is on the wane. As one father, educated at a well-known boarding school but no longer able to educate his children at boarding schools since giving up his own business to become the financial director of a multi-national company put it:

> We are all anxious about our children and ninety-nine per cent of us do not have a business to pass on.

Table 6.6 shows that there are other parameters to parents' choice of a particular school but, with the exception of price, they rarely feature as the deciding factor and it can be concluded that the majority of parents are highly pragmatic in their selection of a particular school. Its individual qualities are taken into consideration but are rarely crucial when it comes to the final decision. Apart from the few who choose a school for reasons of family tradition, parents are looking for schools which are near, which they can afford and which are known to them or have been recommended. In the main they have succeeded in their quest for proximity for less than a quarter of the day boys live more than five miles away from their school and, contrary to Lambert's finding that 64 per cent of boarders live more than fifty miles away from the school,[7] about three-quarters of the boarders live within approximately an hour's drive of the school. This search for a 'local' school on the part of the boarding parents is a departure from tradition and emphasises the very different view that they take of boarding than that which is presented in the stereotype of the boarding parent. Parents are not, in the main, abdicating their responsibilities to the schools and in explaining the importance of choosing a local school they stressed their desire to be able to attend various school events as well as the boys' preference to spend time at home rather than at a local restaurant during their exeats.

In some cases the search for a school which is near is tempered by the traditionalism of the parents or the academic limitations of the boy, but overall the headmasters are faced with the daunting task of having to meet a demand from parents who want many and differing things from a school but whose choice of a particular one is rarely determined by the belief that it uniquely can meet these demands. The schools have to be all things to all parents if they are to survive in the marketplace and in this they have largely succeeded for in general the parents appear to be very satisfied with the education that their sons are receiving. A third of them declined the invitation to offer any criticisms of or disappointments with their chosen schools and a few, 4 per cent, expressed the reverse opinion, namely that the total experience has been better than hoped for. The deputy head of a large comprehensive school who was looking for an essentially grammar school education for his son had feared the emphasis on masculinity conventionally associated with the public schools and was relieved to find that most of what he had anticipated and discounted as the price of a really good academic education had not in fact materialised. Only two parents had actually removed their boys from their schools during the course of the interviews but both have remained within the private sector. Two-thirds of the parents did voice one or two criticisms of their chosen schools and these are listed in Table 6.7.

These criticisms are unrelated to whether or not the school is the one of first choice and it is interesting to note how closely the list mirrors the list of advantages, underlining the features of the schools which parents believe are important and for which they are paying. Failures with certain aspects of the academic provision; insufficient discipline; disappointment with a particular member of staff (occa-

TABLE 6.7 *Criticisms/disappointments with schools*

	*Percent of couples**
Aspect(s) of academic provision poor	17
(cf. another 3% who feel that schools are too pressured)	
Poor discipline	14
(cf. another 1% who felt there was too much discipline)	
Poor member(s) of staff	12
Poor communication between school and parents	10
Lack of facilities	9
Lack of individual guidance	7
Lack of polish or poor speech amongst own sons or boys in general	6
Restricted range of extra-curricular activities	6
(cf. a further 2% who said there was too much sport)	

* These do not total 100% as some parents gave no criticisms and others gave several.

sionally the headmaster); poor communication between the school and the parents; poor facilities and extra-curricular activities. . .and so the list goes on, confirming what the parents believe to be the salient features of a private education.

Criticism of the school is not the same as regret at having made the decision to use the private sector. That the majority of parents appear to be satisfied with their investment is confirmed by the responses to the suggestion that this education and the expenditure that it incurs might be considered to be a waste if the boy fails to achieve the occupational success that is associated with a private education. Thirteen per cent of the parents did agree with this suggestion but the remainder confirmed their belief that the boys will still have benefited from it either by doing better academically than if they had gone to a state school or by gaining the other, non-academic advantages already discussed. Parents appear to be very committed to their belief in the superiority of this sector and one family who had removed their eldest son to a sixth form college as he had shown few signs of succeeding academically at his private school spoke for many when they expressed their deep regret at making this decision and at their failure to recognise the degree to which the private schools develop all aspects of the boys' potential, even if these are not academic. In confirmation of this regret these parents have kept both their other sons in the private sector and the elder of the two is now at his older 'failed' brother's school.

Despite the constraints upon the parents in their choice of a particular school, constraints which on the surface appear to bear hardest upon those whose own education has been within the private sector, the schools do vary with respect to their social intake. Whilst the individual categories of the schools do not draw exclusively on different factions of the non-manual classes, they can often be characterized by an ideal-typical set of parents who come to characterise a particular category but never to completely dominate it for they never form a majority of the parents within it. The schools at the polar end of the status hierarchy within the HMC are the easiest to characterise. Crudely, the occupational status of the father is in direct proportion to the standing of the school so that the major public schools draw disproportionately from the administrative and profess-ional parents. However, there is only a partial relationship between the education that the fathers have received and the type of public school that they use for their sons, as Table 6.8 show.

The fathers who have been grammar school or minor public school

TABLE 6.8 *Choice of school by father's secondary education*

| Father's Secondary School | Type of school | | | | | |
| | Boarding | | | Day | | |
	Major (%)	Medium (%)	Minor (%)	Major (%)	Medium (%)	Minor (%)
Major boarding	40.4	12.0	11.1	13.0	11.1	0
Other HMC	21.3	20.0	11.1	21.7	14.8	15.4
Other private	6.4	24.0	13.9	13.0	3.7	7.7
Grammar	29.8	28.0	47.2	47.8	51.9	46.2
Other State	2.1	16.0	16.7	4.3	18.5	30.8
Total	100%	100%	100%	100%	100%	100%

educated are well represented in all the categories of school; it is the fathers who have had a non-selective state education who are virtually excluded from the major public schools, whilst those who have been educated at the top boarding schools, despite the compromises that they have been forced to make, have been relatively successful in securing places at these schools for their sons.

The minor day schools are clearly the schools of parents who have been state educated and upwardly mobile into their class, mainly the proprietors of large and small businesses or self-employed professionals. The university educated fathers are under-represented in these schools such that the professional fathers using them are likely to have gained their qualifications through part-time study and articles. These are the parents who expect the most from a private education, giving the largest number of reasons for choosing it and placing the greatest reliance upon the power of the schools to help their sons to get on in life, not only through the academic results and the development of the associated discipline but also by making useful social contacts and developing desirable personality traits. These parents possess many of the characteristics described by Bechhofer and Elliott[8] in their study of Edinburgh shopkeepers, in particular the marginality generated by the threat that they feel from both capital and organised labour. When asked who they feel get a raw deal in life, these parents were more likely than the rest of the sample to mention the low paid and those without work but they see both the trade unionists and those with high incomes as doing rather too well in Britain today. Like the other parents in the sample, they are predominantly Tory voters but they are less fully committed than some of the other parents, expressing their doubts about the party and their desire for a realistic alternative with greater frequency. But, unlike some of the other doubters, these parents never vote for the Labour party and rarely for the Liberals.

If the minor day schools harbour the *petit bourgeoisie* in the classical sense of the term, their boarding equivalents are the schools of the farmers. Scattered strategically around rural Britain, they serve to provide conveniently located education for Britain's farming community. They are used by the farmers who have been largely grammar school educated, the working farmers who derive their profit from their own labour rather than from tenanting their land. These schools also educate boys whose fathers have been educated at Britain's major public schools but who have failed to live up to their parents' earlier hopes, the sons of the self-employed professionals and the senior administrators who have been forced to compromise in their selection of a school. One mother, married to a partner in a large firm of stockbrokers, described her bitter disappointment at her son's failure to get into his father's famous boarding school but went on to say how pleased she now is with the school recommended to them by the boy's prep. school headmaster.

The medium and major day schools share in common the facts that their single largest group of parents are those who have passed through the grammar schools and that each has a roughly equal proportion, (12 per cent), of fathers from the major public schools. But, they differ in the social composition and political complexion of the balance of their parents. The major schools rarely attract the fathers educated in the non-selective state sector and draw correspondingly from those who have been to the minor public schools, producing a preponderance of self-employed professionals and senior administrators; the medium day schools are used by fathers from all the educational backgrounds represented in the sample and are correspondingly difficult to characterise. Both categories of school recruit heavily from Class I but vary in the degree to which they are able to attract the third generation members of this class. The major schools are the only day schools to which those who no longer wish or are able to use the boarding schools are prepared to turn in any great number and as such 37 per cent of their intake as opposed to only 17 per cent of those in the medium day schools are long established members of Class I. These major day schools are the meeting ground of the established and the new members of the upper middle class, those at the apex of the service class, for the balance of their intake is predominantly the sons of the successes of the scholarship system, those who have been upwardly mobile into upper service class occupations via the grammar schools. Yet these major day schools are rarely used by the members of the social élite or indeed of the newer occupational élite. However, the two categories of school are primarily distinguished from each other by the political attitudes of their parents. Those in the medium day schools are strictly 'true blue', the loyal Tory voters who name the welfare state scroungers and those who fail to create wealth, such as civil servants and social workers, as the group who are getting an unfair share of Britain's wealth. The major day schools attract the most highly educated and 'liberal' parents. These schools have the same proportion of Oxbridge fathers as the major boarding schools but twice as many who are university educated and also twice the proportion of Oxbridge and university educated mothers. It is here that one has the best chance of finding the few Labour supporters who use the public schools as well as the Liberal and the floating voters. Their parents are more likely than any others to nominate members of the establishment and high earners as candidates for getting the best deal in Britain and those who are prepared to accept responsibility, have no work or work for low pay as the losers.

Like their day counterparts, the medium boarding schools are difficult to characterise for they draw upon parents from the many different educational and occupational backgrounds represented in this sample. It is here that those who are making their way up the occupational hierarchy are the most likely to encounter those who are possibly on the way down, for although these schools are not the first choice of the third generation members of Class I, these parents constitute the largest single group within them. As such they share many of the characteristics of their contemporaries in the schools which form the pinnacle of Britain's public school system, the major boarding schools. These are the schools which conceal within them, but are not constituted of, Britain's social élite as well as certain factions of the financial upper class. Although they are large schools and account for a quarter of all the parents in the sample, they are used by more than two-thirds of the members of the social élite who are clearly distinguishable by their ideology, education and mode of recruitment, a memorial to the life-style and values of the landed class of yesterday.

The proportion of mothers and of fathers in the sample who have an unearned income in excess of £5000 a year is large when compared to the general population but is nevertheless a small minority within this sample, fewer than 10 per cent of all the parents are possessed of an unearned income of this size but two-thirds of them are to be found within these top boarding schools. Whilst this income is tied exclusively to the ownership of capital in excess of £50 000, as discussed in Chapter 2, such large amounts of capital do not always yield unearned income. In the other schools the parents who own this magnitude of wealth are unlikely to hold it in forms which yield unearned income and it is more likely to represent the assets and goodwill of their professional practices, farms or companies. Thus it would appear that the parents who use the major boarding schools are the most likely of all the parents to be linked to the business class[9] either as the result of their consolidation of capital into a form which enables them to exert power not only over their immediate employees but in a far wider sense as the shareholders of large companies, or as the beneficiaries of family wealth. A further indication that these schools can be characterised by their use by a distinct faction of the non-manual class is provided by the concentration within them of fathers who have received their own education in similar or even the same schools. Fifty-nine per cent of the fathers who have been educated at the major boarding schools have succeeded in continuing to educate their sons in a like manner, despite the extent to which they claim to have been constrained to modify their original choice of school. Their presence emphasises the continued existence of a status group which seeks to express its shared identity in common cultural forms, of which the type of educational setting chosen for their sons is but a further example. Whether they seek to do so to the exclusion of the *arrivistes,* searching out subcultural enclaves, is becoming increasingly academic for although the parents who are third generation members of Class I are both the single largest group of parents in these schools and more likely to use them than any of the other public schools, over a quarter of their parents are upwardly mobile members of Class I, mainly those who have benefited from a grammar school education. Typical is this father, the son of a clerical officer in the civil service:

If he is going to one [a public school] he is going to one of the best.

The parents who are still under-represented in these major boarding schools are the owners of industrial and commercial capital, the members of the occupational élite – the men of tomorrow. These parents are more likely to use the medium and even the minor public schools for the education of their sons.

Whilst parents may seek to preserve their social identity by educating their sons alongside those with whom they can identify both culturally and demographically, such that each of the different types of public school can still be characterised by the different factions of the non-manual class who use them, they display a striking convergence in their view of the world which awaits their sons and in what they expect from the schools. Despite their semblance of sharing a common class position, these parents are possessed of a wide array of social origins and a variety of different experiences has brought them to the point where they are able to afford to educate their sons privately. As such, they might legitimately be expected to have a corresponding variety of perceptions of the world in which they live and work yet they share to a remarkable degree a perception of a class structure which is seen as increasingly open and in which social position is believed to be less dependent upon birth and more dependent upon individual merit and ambition. The positions that the parents value and seek for their sons are rarely those with which a public school education has come to be associated, membership of the 'élite' or of a largely hereditary upper class, but positions within the *haute bourgeoisie* or the upper echelons of the service class – the professionals, the senior managers, the successful entrepreneurs. These are their realistic aspirations as parents and in this it is impossible to distinguish between those who originated in the service class and those who are part of upwardly mobile post-war Britain, for the schools are coming to act as melting-pots in which the financial, social and occupational élites are joined by factions of the service class and of the *petit bourgeoisie* to defend the bourgeois values which they believe to be under threat. These values are not the monopoly of any single group of parents represented in the schools today; those who were themselves grammar school educated may have been physically and therefore relationally segregated from their privately educated peers, but either the culture to which each was exposed was remarkably similar or/and bourgeois values have been very successful in challenging those of the established upper class to dictate the basis of social exclusion. Thus the era when land and inherited class position dominated Britain's culture and where a public school education was explicitly concerned with preparation for clearly defined leadership roles has undeniably given way to a new social order. Today the concept of leadership is more diffuse and is hidden in a myriad of organisational roles whose only clear criterion of incumbency is the possession of the necessary academic qualifications.

Parents whose families have traditionally used the public schools, but who are now seeking different qualities from them, have been joined by others who might have entrusted a selective maintained system with the education of their sons, confident in the capacity of their own cultural capital to reproduce their own educational experiences, but who have lost faith in today's secondary schools. Rightly or wrongly, the majority of today's parents believe these schools to have been sacrificed to new educational and moral standards where co-operation and levelling down to a notional average rather than competition and individual achievement are seen as the order of the day. Some of the parents interviewed see these values as beginning to threaten the wider social order and expressed this in their description of the social and financial inequalities generated by over-powerful trade unions and the over-protective welfare state. Whether the parents would now see the educational standards that they value as secure in the hands of the Thatcher government remains a matter of speculation for the interviews were completed within a year of its initial election to office.

The majority of parents interviewed recognise that social inequality is inevitable; what is important to them is the equality of opportunity to become unequal. In this lies the ultimate paradox of their desire for a private education. Few of the parents, in describing the opportunities that they believe exist for both upward and downward mobility, explicitly acknowledged the extent to which those with service class origins have been successful in maintaining this class position without yielding to those who have been upwardly mobile but have accommodated them in an ever-enlarging service class. Their perceptions of a very real danger of downward mobility would appear to be based upon the belief that such mobility results from personal failure or inadequacy rather than from structural factors. In stressing the value of a private education in enhancing their sons' ability to 'get on in the world' by facilitating the attainment of the necessary academic results and/or the requisite attitudes, whilst simultaneously welcoming the introduction of the Assisted Places scheme, the parents are exhibiting their faith in the power of education to stimulate economic growth which can in turn accommodate all those with high academic qualifications. With hindsight, it is to be regretted that the interviews failed to probe the parents' views on the use of educational vouchers, for whilst some versions of such a scheme would undoubtedly relieve at least part of the financial burden of school fees, all versions would ensure a more open competition in the race to be unequal. A discussion of the use of educational vouchers would have confirmed whether, as it appears, the parents do fail to recognise (or possibly to acknowledge) the part that they are playing in preventing the very openness that they claim characterises Britain today, for in purchasing an education which they believe has distinct advantages they are seeking to ensure that their sons are given the opportunity to become the winners of the race to success.

It has been clearly established, through the use of inflow analysis, that the incumbency of élite positions is virtually monopolised by those who have been public school educated and in turn it has been shown that the schools continue to be distinguished by the already privileged boys whom they educate; but what evidence is there to support the belief that it is the public school education *per se* which confers advantage in the sense of securing access either to élite positions as defined by the élite studies or to the occupational positions valued by the parents themselves? Are the majority of parents who believe that a private education does facilitate occupational success correct in this belief or does the truth lie with the minority who see it as more concerned with improving the quality of life? To this question there can be no absolute answer, for if the content of a private education is viewed by some parents as an item strictly for consumption rather than as an investment, this is a social fact which cannot be disputed. Certainly the evidence which links the social origins, type of secondary education and current class position of the fathers in this sample as well as of the men who were the subject of the Oxford Mobility Studies does suggest that a public school education had little to offer over and above that provided by the grammar school when it came to securing occupational success. The importance of the family as the main source of aid and of social contacts to all the groups of parents in this research serves to further reinforce its significance in the perpetuation of privilege.

The information that has been both published and leaked about the effects of comprehensive schooling is at best confused and the collation and interpretation of the relevant statistics too subjected to political bias to be of value in enabling more recent comparisons to be made between the results of private and maintained secondary education. The parents, in believing that private schooling has the power to secure position in the fluid class structure of contemporary

Britain may be merging their experiences and perceptions of the past with a recognition of the changing political and economic conditions which have come to characterise Britain more recently, but *to date* the major significance of the public schools must be seen to lie with their capacity to act as a focus of critique of the provisions of the maintained sector. These schools are only one among a number of forces which retard change in the experience of schooling in the maintained sector and their use as scapegoats for the deep-rooted inequalities which are to be found in all capitalist societies and the clamour to abolish them have served to deflect from the failure to grasp the nettle of inequality.

As the implications of the changing political and technological complexion of Britain become fully evident, the true significance of the private and the public schools may not lie in their past but in their immediate future. The educational policy of the Thatcher government remains somewhat unclear but it exhibits many signs of yielding to the demands of the privateers within it such that there is a very real threat of a return to what Pring[10] has termed 'the elementary school tradition'. By this he means that the maintained schools are 'run by a relatively privileged group of people for others' but not their own children' and 'they [the schools] have a narrow curriculum that stresses the socially useful and the practical and denies the "tools" of critical reflection'. Thus far from impoverishing the maintained sector by forcing it to compete on the terms that it lays down, the private sector, through the support that it is drawing from a privatising government, is increasingly threatening the maintained sector by attracting superior financial and human resources, and this in turn will ensure that the already privileged will come to depend upon it to perpetuate this privilege within their own families.

Appendix: The Methodology

The information contained in this book is based upon interviews that I conducted with a sample of 190 sets of parents, resident in Great Britain, with sons attending the traditionally independent Headmasters' Conference (Public) Schools. I chose the parents at random from a stratified sample of the 122 English schools which fell into this category in 1978. I selected the schools from which the parents were ultimately chosen by stratifying them according to the following variables which I believed to be likely to influence the type of parents who wish to use the schools and therefore the information obtained:

1. whether they are predominantly day or boarding schools
2. their regional location
3. the proportion of boys within them whose parents were receiving some official source of assistance with paying the fees.

I then proceeded to select twenty schools at random from this stratified sample with probability according to the size of the resulting categories.

Two hundred and seventeen parents were selected in this manner and were written to by their headmasters who explained the nature and the purpose of the research and asked them for their co-operation. This proved to be a highly successful method of obtaining a representative sample, for when I telephoned the parents to arrange a mutually convenient time for the interview to take place only fourteen of them declined to be interviewed and were therefore classed as non-respondents, and a further thirteen were non-contactable in the sense of not being available at any of the suggested times, yielding a response rate of nearly 88 per cent. In the event, in thirty-five cases out of the total sample of 190, only one parent was actually interviewed: six are widowed; twenty-one are divorced or separated and the interview was held with the parent who has custody, normally the mother; and in eight families one of the parents was unavailable when I arrived for the interview.

The interviews took place in the parents' homes and I used a semi-structured interview schedule; in all but seven cases where the parents withheld consent I tape-recorded the interviews. In this way it was possible for me to obtain systematically the information that I required whilst simultaneously encouraging uninterrupted discussion. As a consequence of the use of the semi-structured interview schedule, the parents frequently took the initiative and spontaneously introduced relevant topics prior to them being asked to do so. This proved advantageous in promoting a frank discussion, but very occasionally resulted in part of the interview being omitted when I failed to return to topics contained in an earlier part of the schedule, with the consequence that the amount of missing information is higher than necessary. The presence of both parents during the interview similarly had disadvantages which were nevertheless outweighed by the advantages that this produced. It was sometimes difficult to distinguish between the views of the fathers and those of the mothers, particularly when it came to a consideration of the advantages of a private education. The views which have been presented in the text are normally the combined views of both parents, which may well be the most accurate when considering the education of their children. However, the volume and depth of the information that I obtained was far greater than if I had conducted the interviews with each parent separately, for the parents frequently interviewed each other and were more forceful than I could have been in making the other partner explore and explain his/her feelings. Overall, the parents were exceedingly generous with the information that they gave me with the result that the quality of the interviews was very high. I am confident that the data that I have presented are valid and representative of the population of parents using the schools at the time and that this book will stand as a useful benchmark against which future studies can be compared.

Notes and References

1. THE SOCIAL CONTEXT

1. T. Bottomore, *Elites and Society* (London: Watts, 1964).
2. D. Rubenstein, *'The Public Schools'*, in D. Rubenstein and C. Stoneman (eds), *Education for Democracy* (Harmondsworth: Penguin, 1970).
3. Q. Hoare, 'Education: Programmes v. Men', New *Left Review,* Vol. 32, (1965) pp. 40–52.
4. The Education of Elites – Unit 29 of Educational Studies Course: Schooling and Society prepared by M. MacDonald, Walton Hall, Milton Keynes, 1977. This is discussed more fully by J. Wakeford, *The Cloistured Elite* (London: Macmillan, 1969). R. Wilkinson, *The Prefects* (Oxford: Oxford University Press, 1964).
5. J. McConnell, *Eton: How it Works* (London: Faber & Faber, 1967).
6. R. Lambert, *The Chance of a Lifetime: A Study of Boarding Education* (London: Weidenfeld & Nicolson, 1975).
7. C. Barnett, *The Collapse of British Power* (London: Eyre & Methuen, 1972).
8. W. Taylor, *The Secondary Modern School* (London: Faber & Faber, 1963).
9. MacDonald, 'The Education of Elites'.
10. J. Rae, *The Public School Revolution* (London: Faber & Faber, 1981).
11. B. Salter and T. Tapper, *Education, Politics and the State,* ch. 8 'Redefining the Ideology of Public School Education' (London: Grant McIntyre, 1982).
12. A. Giddens, 'The Anatomy of the British Ruling Class'. *New Society,* vol. 50 (1979), no. 88, pp. 8–10.
13. Bottomore, *Elites and Society*
14. P. Stanworth, 'Property, Class and the Corporate Elite', in I. Crewe (ed.), *Elites in Western Democracy, Volume 1* (London: Croom Helm, 1974).
15. V. Pareto, *The Mind and Society, Volume III* (London: Jonathan Cape, 1935).
16. D. Boyd, *Elites and their Education.* NFER, Slough, 1973 provides the most comprehensive summary of available statistics on this subject.
17. Figures taken from W.L. Guttsman, 'The British Political Elite and the Class Structure', in P. Stanworth and A. Giddens (eds): *Elites and Power in British Society* (Cambridge: Cambridge University Press, 1974).
18. D. C. Coleman, 'Gentlemen and Players' in the *Journal of Economic History,* Vol. XXVI, (1972), no. 1, pp. 92–116.

19. Salter and Tapper, *Education, Politics and the State.*
20. R. V. Clements, *Managers: a Study of their Careers in Industry* (London: George Allen & Unwin, 1958).
21. See for example H. Glennerster and R. Pryke, 'The Contribution of the Public Schools: Born to Rule', in J. Urry and J. Wakeford, *Power in Britain* (London: Heinemann Educational Books, 1973).
22. G. Kalton, *The Public Schools: A Factual Survey* (London: Longmans, 1966).
23. G. Mosca, *The Ruling Class* (New York: McGraw-Hill, 1939).
24. J.H. Goldthorpe and C. Llewellyn, 'Class Mobility in Britain: Three Theses Examined', in J.H. Goldthorpe, *Social Mobility and Class Structure in Modern Britain* (Oxford: Clarendon Press, 1980).
25. Translation of the relevant passage of Renner's work is to be found in: T. Bottomore and P. Goode (eds); *Austro-Marxism* (Oxford: Oxford University Press, 1978).
26. Goldthorpe and Llewellyn, 'Class Mobility in Britain: Three Theses Examined'.
27. A.H. Halsey, A.F. Heath and J.M. Ridge, *Origins and Destinations: Family, Class and Education in Modern Britain* (Oxford: Clarendon Press, 1980).
28. A. Heath, *Social Mobility* (Fontana Paperback, 1981).
29. I am grateful to the Oxford Social Mobility Group for making their raw data available to me, all the responsibility for the calculations based on them is my own.
30. R. Miliband, *The State in Capitalist Society* (London: Weidenfeld, 1973).
31. R. Lambert, *The Public School Ethos,* reprinted as Appendix C in 'The Education of Elites'.
32. Quoted in Giddens, 'The Anatomy of the British Ruling Class'.
33. Letter to the *Guardian,* 16th July 1981.
34. Halsey *et al., Origins and Destinations.*
35. A full discussion of this is contained in Chapter 5.
36. Private Schools, *A Labour Party Discussion Document* (London, 1980).
37. Reported by Wendy Berliner, *Guardian,* 26th April 1982.
38. J. Lawson and H. Silver, *A Social History of Education in England* (London: Methuen, 1973).
39. Rae, *The Public School Revolution.*
40. It is difficult to state the exact number of private secondary school places as the DES Statistics of Education give the number of pupils in private schools classified by their age and not by type of school. In 1982 there were 183 500 pupils aged twelve and over in the private sector.
41. R. H. Tawney, *Equality* (London: Allen & Unwin, 1964). First published in 1931 with several subsequent revisions.
42. Board of Education (Public Schools Committee): *The Public Schools and the General Education System.* (London: HMSO, 1944).
43. Public Schools Commission, *First Report* (London: HMSO, 1963).
44. Public Schools Commission, *Second Report* (London: HMSO, 1970).
45. The figures are taken from A *Labour Party Discussion Document* (p.56). John Rae claims that the Secretary of State approved 80 per cent of such applications in 1977/8.

46. Labour Party, *A Plan for Private Schools*. London. TUC-Labour Party Liaison Committee (1981).
47. *Independent Schools and the European Convention of Human Rights* (London: The Independent Schools Information Service, 1982).
48. T. Szamuely, 'Russia and Britain Comprehensive Inequality', in C. B. Cox and A. Dyson (eds.) *The Black Papers on Education 1–3* (London: Davis-Poynter, 1969).
49. Related by Anthony Howard in conversation with the author.
50. R. Hart-Davis (ed.), *Lyttleton Hart-Davis Letters: Correspondence of G. Lyttleton and R. Hart-Davis, Vol. 1, 1955–6* (London: John Murray, 1978).
51. This is documented in detail in Rae, *The Public School Revolution*.

2. WHO ARE THE PARENTS?

1. D. Boyd, *Elites and Their Education* (Slough: NFER, 1973).
2. J. Gathorne-Hardy, *The Public School Phenomenon* (London: Hodder & Stoughton, 1977).
3. T. Bamford, 'Public Schools and Social Class 1801-1850', *British Journal of Sociology,* vol. 12 (1962), pp. 224-35.
4. T. Bamford, *The Rise of the Public Schools* (London: Nelson, 1967).
5. G. Kalton, *The Public Schools: a Factual Survey.* (London: Longmans, 1966).
6. A.H. Halsey, A.F. Heath and J.M. Ridge, *Origins and Destinations: Family, Class and Education in Modern Britain* (Oxford: Clarendon Press, 1980). These classes differ slightly from the top two classes in the Registrar-General's Classification. The occupational titles in these classes and the differences are discussed in I. Reid, *Social Class Differences in Britain* (London: Grant McIntyre, 1981).
7. See the Appendix for details of the selection and composition of the sample.
8. Halsey *et al.* distinguish agricultural workers and smallholders as a separate class. The one smallholder in this sample has been included in Class IV with the farmers.
9. Boyd, *Elites and Their Education.*
10. G. Ingham, 'Divisions within the dominant class and British "exceptionalism"', in A. Giddens and G. Mackenzie (eds) *Social Class and the Division of Labour* (Cambridge: Cambridge University Press, 1982).
11. J. Scott, *The Upper Classes Property and Privilege in Britain* (London: Macmillan, 1982).
12. A. Giddens, *The Class Structure of the Advanced Societies,* 2nd ed. (London: Hutchinson, 1981).
13. F. Parkin, *Class Inequality and Political Order* (London: Paladin, 1972).
14. This was the subject of a SSRC Survey Methods Seminar on 5 November 1981. The paper by John Fox, 'Social Class and Mortality' dealt with this in considerable detail.
15. B. Jackson and D. Marsden, *Education and the Working Class* (London: Routledge & Kegan Paul, 1963).

16. J. Goldthorpe and C. Llewellyn, 'Class Mobility in Britain: Three Theses Examined', in J.H. Goldthorpe *Social Mobility and Class Structure in Modern Britain* (Oxford: Clarendon Press, 1980).
17. Boyd, *Elites and Their Education.*
18. Landowners have been included in Class I for this purpose although technically many of them belong to Class IV by virtue of the fact that they are also farmers with a small number of employees.
19. J. Okley, 'Privileged, schooled and finished: Boarding Education for Girls', in S. Ardener (ed.), *Defining Females* (London: Croom Helm, 1978).
20. Bamford, *The Rise of the Public Schools.*
21. A.H. Halsey, 'Class Ridden Property', in *The Listener,* 19 Jan. 1978.
22. Table 2.7, *Royal Commission on the Distribution of Income and Wealth Report No. 7,* (London: HMSO, 1976).
23. Table 2.2, *Royal Commission on the Distribution of Income and Wealth Report No. 4,* (London: HMSO, 1976).
24. The distributions in Table 2.7 are not strictly comparable to the ones in the Diamond Report (ibid.) both because they relate to a different year and, more significantly, because those in the Diamond Report show the distribution of wealth between wealth holders only, whereas the statistics in this research include all respondents but exclude 'property for use'.
25. For example, J. Fidler, *The British Business Elite* (London: Routledge & Kegan Paul, 1981). This study of the business élite failed to find a single woman director amongst the directors of the largest 188 wholly British owned firms.
26. Scott, *The Upper Classes Property and Privilege in Britain.*
27. H. Newby, *et al.* Property, Paternalism and Power (London: Hutchinson, 1978).
28. Notably T. Nichols, *Ownership, Control and Ideology* (London: Allen & Unwin, 1969).
29. C.D. Harbury and D.M. Hitchens, *Inheritance and Wealth Inequality in Britain* (London: Allen & Unwin, 1979).
30. Newby *et al.,* Property Paternalism and Power.
31. A. Sutherland, 'The Taxation of Agricultural Wealth: Northfield and After', in F. Field (ed.), *The Wealth Report* (London: Routledge & Kegan Paul, 1983).
32. See Chapter 1.
33. R. Lambert, *The Chance of a Lifetime? A Study of Boarding Education* (London: Weidenfeld & Nicolson, 1975).
34. G. Snow, *The Public School in the New Age* (London: Geoffrey Bles, 1959).
35. Okley, 'Privileged, schooled and finished'.
36. D. Smith, 'Codes, Paradigms and Folk Norms: An Approach to Educational Change with Particular Reference to the Work of Basil Bernstein', *British Journal of Sociology,* vol. 10 (1976) pp.1-19.
37. A. Heath, 'What Difference does the Old School Tie Make Now?', *New Society,* vol. 56 (1981).
38. A.H. Halsey *et al., Origins and Destinations: Family, Class and Education in Modern Britain* (Oxford: Clarendon Press, 1980).
39. Unpublished data from Oxford Social Mobility Group.

3 THE PARENTS' SOCIAL NETWORKS

1. J. Clyde Mitchell (ed.), *Social Networks in Urban Situations* (Manchester: Manchester University Press, 1969).
2. P. M. Blau, *Exchange, Power and Social Life* (New York: John Wiley, 1964).
3. R. Titmuss, *Income Distribution and Social Change* (London: Allen & Unwin, 1962).
4. T. Lupton and C. Shirley Wilson, 'The Social Background and Connections of Top Decision Makers', reprinted in J. Urry and J. Wakeford (eds), *Power in Britain* (London: Heinemann, 1975).
5. M. Young and P. Willmott *Family and Kinship in East London* (London: Routledge & Kegan Paul, 1957).
6. C. Bell, *Middle Class Families* (London: Routledge & Kegan Paul, 1971).
7. J. Goldthorpe and C. Llewellyn, 'Class Mobility and Kinship', in J. Goldthorpe, *Social Mobility and Class Structure in Modern Britain* (Oxford: Clarendon Press, 1980).
8. P. Stanworth and A. Giddens, *Elites and Power in British Society* (Cambridge: Cambridge University Press, 1974).
9. J. Scott, *The Upper Classes Property and Privilege in Britain* (London: Macmillan, 1982).
10. M. O'Donnell, *A New Introduction to Sociology,* (London: Harrap, 1981).
11. F. Bechhofer, *et al.,* 'Structure, Consciousness and Action: a Sociological Portrait of the Middle Class', in *British Journal of Sociology,* vol. 29 (1979), no. 4 pp. 410–36.
12. Stanworth and Giddens, *Elites and Power in British Society.*
13. Bell, *Middle Class Families.*
14. J. M. and R. E. Pahl, *Managers and their Wives: a Study of Career and Family Relationships in the Middle Class* (London: Allen Lane The Penguin Press, 1971).
15. Young and Willmott, *Family and Kinship in East London.*
16. For example, F. Musgrove, *The Migratory Elite* (London: Heinemann, 1963).
17. For example, M. Janowitz, 'Some Consequences of Social Mobility in the United States', *Transactions of the Third World Congress of Sociology* (London: International Sociological Association, 1956).
18. J. Goldthorpe and C. Llewellyn, 'Class Mobility and Social Involvement', in J. Goldthorpe, *Social Mobility and Class Structure in Modern Britain.*
19. Bell, *Middle Class Families.*
20. F. Parkin, *Marxism and Class Theory: a Bourgeois Critique* (London: Tavistock, 1979).
21. D.C. Coleman, 'Gentlemen and Players', in *Journal of Economic History,* vol. 26 (1972), no. 1, pp. 92–116.
22. E. Hobsbawm, *The Age of Capital 1848–75* (London: Weidenfeld & Nicolson, 1975).
23. Goldthorpe and Llewellyn, 'Class Mobility and Social Involvement'.

24. Public Schools Commission: *First Report* (The Newsom Report) (London: HMSO, 1968).
25. R. Lambert, *The Chance of a Lifetime? A Study of Boarding Education* (London: Weidenfeld & Nicolson, 1975).
26. R. Lambert, *ibid.*
27. D.S. Morris and K.N. Newton, 'Profile of a Local Political Elite: Businessmen as Community Decision Makers in Birmingham 1838–1966', *in New Atlantis*, vol. 2 (1970), pp. 111–23.
28. A. H. Birch, *Small Town Politics* (Oxford: Oxford University Press, 1959).
29. F. Bechhofer and B. Elliot, 'The Voice of Small Business and the Politics of Survival', in *Sociological Review*, vol. 26 (1978), pp. 57–88.
30. M. Stacey, *Tradition and Change: A Study of Banbury* (Oxford: Oxford University Press, 1960).
31. R. Whitley, 'Commonalities and Connections Among Directors of Large Financial Institutions', *Sociological Review*, vol. 21 (1974).

4 THE LONG TERM GOALS

1. E. Bott, *Family and Social Network*. Second Edition (London: Tavistock, 1971).
2. F. Parkin, *Class Inequality and the Political Order* (London: Paladin, 1971).
3. D. Lockwood, 'Sources of Variation in Working-Class Images of Society', reprinted in M. Bulmer (ed.), *Working-Class Images of Society* (London: Routledge & Kegan Paul, 1975).
4. M. Mann, 'The Ideologies of Non-Skilled Industrial Workers'. Paper presented to the SSRC Conference on The Occupational Community and the Traditional Worker (Durham, 1972).
5. R. Miliband, *The State in Capitalist Society* (London: Quartet Books, 1973).
6. B. Bernstein, *Class, Codes and Control Volume 3*, 2nd ed. (London: Routledge & Kegan Paul, 1977).
7. N. Poulantzas, *Classes in Capitalist Society* (London: New Left Books, 1975).
8. Quoted in H.H. Davis, *Beyond Class Images* (London: Croom Helm, 1979).
9. Bott, *Family and Social Network*.
10. J. Goldthorpe and D. Lockwood, 'Affluence and the British Class Structure', in *Sociological Review*, vol. 11 (1963).
11. See M. Bulmer (ed.), *Working-Class Images of Society*.
 also H. Newby, *The Deferential Worker* (Harmondsworth: Penguin, 1979).
12. P. Townsend, *Poverty in the United Kingdom* (Harmondsworth: Penguin, 1979).
13. K. Roberts *et al., The Fragmentary Class Structure* (London: Heinemann, 1977).
14. J. Fidler, *The British Business Elite* (London: Routledge & Kegan Paul, 1981).
15. Lockwood, 'Sources of Variation in Working-Class Images of Society'.

16. Parkin, *Class Inequality and the Political Order.*
17. Roberts *et al., The Fragmentary Class Structure.*
18. Townsend, *Poverty in the United Kingdom.*
19. Fidler, *The British Business Elite.*
20. D. Cooper, *Psychiatry and Anti-Psychiatry.* (London: Tavistock, 1967).
21. Question Time on BBC 1, 11 December 1980.
22. Peter Jay, ibid.
23. For a fuller discussion of the strands of Thatcherism see R. Dale, 'Thatcherism and Education', in J. Ahier and M. Flude (eds), *Contemporary Education Policy* (London: Croom Helm, 1983).
24. F. Bechhofer and B. Elliott, 'The Voice of Small Business and the Politics of Survival', in *Sociological Review* vol. 26 (1978), pp. 57–88. H. Newby, *et al., Property, Paternalism and Power* (London: Hutchinson, 1978).
25. Ibid.
26. P. Worsthorne, 'Why aristocracy is back in fashion', in *the Sunday Telegraph,* 12 June 1983.
27. Townsend, *Poverty in the United Kingdom.*
28. R. Dahrendorf, *On Britain* (London: BBC Publications, 1982).

5 WHY A PRIVATE EDUCATION?

1. See G. Psacharapoulos, *Returns to Education* (Amsterdam: Elsevier Scientific Publishing Company, 1973) for a fuller discussion of the relationship between education and private rates of return.
2. D. Marsden, *Politics, Equality and Comprehensives* (London: Fabian Tract 411, 1971).
3. J. Ford, *Social Class and the Comprehensive School* (London: Routledge & Kegan Paul, 1969).
4. C. B. Cox and A. Dyson (eds), *The Black Papers on Education 1–3* (London: Davis-Poynter, 1971). C. B. Cox and A. Dyson (eds) *Black Paper No. 4* (London: Dent, 1974). C. B. Cox and R. Boyson (eds) *The Fight for Education* (London: Dent, 1975). *Black Paper 1977* (London: Temple Smith, 1977).
5. A. Bell, Quoted in *Black Paper No. 3*
6. R. Baldwin, 'The Dissolution of the Grammar School', in *Black Paper 1977.*
7. J. Steedman, *Examination Results in Selective and Non-Selective Schools* (London: National Childrens Bureau, 1983).
8. N. Bennett, *Teaching Styles and Pupil Progress* (London: Open Books, 1976).
9. N. Keddie, 'Classroom Knowledge', in M. F. D. Young (ed.), *Knowledge and Control New Directions for The Sociology of Education* (London: Collier-Macmillan, 1971).
10. M. F. D. Young, Introduction to *Knowledge and Control,* ibid.
11. B. Bernstein, 'On the Classification and Framing of Educational Knowledge', in *Knowledge and Control,* ibid.
12. M. F. D. Young, *Sociologists and the Politics of Comprehensive Schooling* (London: Forum, 1975).

13. B. Bernstein, *Class, Codes and Control Vol. 3* (London: Routledge & Kegan Paul, 1975).
14. Bernstein, 'On the Classification and Framing of Educational Knowledge'.
15. S. Bowles and H. Gintis, *Schooling in Capitalist America: Educational Reform and the Contradictions of Economic Life* (London: Routledge & Kegan Paul, 1976).
16. P. Bourdieu, 'Cultural Reproduction and Social Reproduction', in R. Brown (ed.) *Knowledge, Education and Cultural Change* (London: Tavistock, 1973).
17. A. Giddens, *The Class Structure of The Advanced Societies* (London: Hutchinson, 1980).
18. Announced by Sir Keith Joseph in the House of Commons, 14 March 1983.
19. DES, *Teaching Quality* (London: HMSO Cmnd 8836 1983).
20. Bennett, *Teaching Styles and Pupil Progress*.
21. See report on the work of Dr. L. Lowenstein in *Daily Mail* (24 October 1975).
22. L C Comber and R C Whitfield, *Action on Indiscipline* (Birmingham: University of Aston, 1979).
23. DES, *Education in Schools: a Consultative Document.* (London: HMSO Cmnd 6869, 1977).
24. J. Eggleston, *The Sociology of the School Curriculum* (London: Routledge & Kegan Paul, 1977).
25. J. Demaine, *Contemporary Theories in the Sociology of Education* (London: Macmillan, 1981).
26. Centre for Contemporary Studies, *Unpopular Education: Schooling and Social Democracy in England since 1944* (London: Hutchinson, 1981).
27. Normally the interviews were carried out with both parents and the views stated are those of both parents. However in thirty-five families only one parent was interviewed: six are widowed; twenty-one are divorced or separated and the interview was held with the parent who has custody, normally the mother. In eight families only one partner was available for interview.
28. *Public Schools Commission 1st Report* (London: HMSO, 1968).
29. J. Scott, *The Upper Classes: Property and Privilege in Britain* (London: Macmillan, 1982).
30. D. Smith, 'Codes, Paradigms and Folk Norms: An Approach to Educational Change with Particular Reference to the Work of Basil Bernstein', *British Journal of Sociology,* vol. 10 (1976), pp. 1–19.
31. G. Kalton, *The Public Schools: a Factual Survey* (London: Longmans, 1966).
32. A. H. Halsey, *et al. Origins and Destinations: Family, Class and Education in Modern Britain* (Oxford: Clarendon Press, 1980).
33. C. Jencks *et al: Who Gets Ahead? The Determinants of Economic Success* (New York: Basic Books, 1979).
34. R. Collins, 'Functional and Conflict Theories of Educational Stratification', reprinted in J. Karabel and A.H. Halsey (eds): *Power and Ideology in Education* (Oxford: Oxford University Press, 1977).

35. F. Parkin, *Marxism and Class Theory: A Bourgeois Critique* (London: Tavistock, 1979).
36. Ibid.
37. C.R. Soderberg, 'The American Engineer', in K.S. Lynn, *The Professions in America* (Boston: Beacon Press, 1963).
38. J.H. Goldthorpe and C. Llewellyn, 'Class Mobility in Modern Britain: Three Theses Examined', in J.H. Goldthorpe, *Social Mobility and Class Structure in Modern Britain* (Oxford: Clarendon Press, 1980).
39. M. Blaug, *An Introduction to the Economics of Education* (Harmondsworth: Penguin, 1970).
40. Bourdieu, 'Cultural Reproduction and Social Reproduction'.
41. P. Anderson, 'Origins of the Present Crisis', in P. Anderson and R. Blackburn (eds), *Towards Socialism* (London: Cornell University Press, 1966).
42. R. Lambert, *The Chance of a Lifetime? A Study of Boarding Education* (London: Weidenfeld & Nicolson, 1975).
43. R. Dale, 'Thatcherism and Education', in J. Ahier and M. Flude, *Contemporary Education Policy* (Beckenham: Croom Helm, 1983).
44. Lambert, *The Chance of a Lifetime?*
45. Anderson, 'Origins of the Present Crisis'.
46. J. Vaizey, 'The Public Schools', in H. Thomas, *The Establishment* (London: Blond, 1959).
47. Bowles and Gintis, *Schooling in Capitalist America.*
48. G. Salaman and K. Thompson, 'Class Culture and the Persistence of an Elite: the Case of Army Officer Selection', *Sociological Review* (1978), pp. 283–304.
49. D.C. Coleman, 'Gentlemen and Players', *Journal of Economic History*, vol. 126 (1972), pp. 92–116.
50. Quoted by J.R. de Honey, 'Tom Brown's Universe', in B. Simon and I. Bradley, *The Victorian Public School* (London: Gill and Macmillan, 1975).
51. Scott, *The Upper Classes.*
52. D. Marsden, 'Why Do Parents Pay Fees?'', *Where*, vol. 10, (1962), pp. 19–21.
53. Collins, 'Functional and Conflict Theories of Educational Stratification'.
54. R. Hattersley reviewing J.H. Goldthorpe, Social Mobility and Class Structure in Modern Britain, *Sunday Times, February, 1980.*

6 CHOOSING A PUBLIC SCHOOL

1. D. Marsden, 'Why Do Parents Pay Fees', *Where*, vol. 10 (1962), pp. 19–21.
2. See R. Lambert, *The Chance of a Lifetime? A Study of Boarding Education* (London: Weidenfeld & Nicolson, 1975).
3. See Chapter 5
4. For example, R.D. Laing and D. Cooper, *Reason and Violence* (London: Tavistock, 1964). A full account of their work is given in D.H.J.

Morgan, *Social Theory and The Family* (London: Routledge & Kegan Paul, 1975).

5. The figures contained in Table II of the 1979 *Statistical Survey of Independent Schools,* published by the Independent Schools' Information Service, show that 6424 of the pupils of the HMC schools were British nationals with parents living abroad. These account for 13.5 per cent of the pupils in the schools and is closer to my own estimate than I would have expected and suggests that parents who originally boarded their sons for this reason have continued to do so despite their return to this country.

6. The Clarendon Nine are the schools (Charterhouse, Eton, Harrow, Rugby, Shrewsbury, Westminster, Winchester, Merchant Taylors' and St Paul's) which were the subject of study into their affairs in 1861 by the Royal Commission headed by Lord Clarendon.

7. Lambert, *The Chance of a Lifetime?*

8. F. Bechhofer and B. Elliott, 'The Voice of Small Business and the Politics of Survival', in *Sociological Review,* vol. 26 (1978), pp. 57–88.

9. *J. Scott, The Upper Classes: Property and Privilege in Britain* (London: Macmillan, 1982).

10. R. Pring, 'Privatisation of Education', Mimeo (University of Exeter, 1982).

Index of Authors, Politicians, etc.

Index of Subjects

Thatcher government indicating
assisted place scheme putting
more money into private education